If you would like to package Peachtree Complete Accounting 2006 (Educational Version) with this textbook, please contact your Prentice Hall sales representative.

GETTING STARTED WITH PEACHTREE® COMPLETE ACCOUNTING 2006 AND QUICKBOOKS® PRO 2006

Elaine Heldstab, C.P.A.

METROPOLITAN COMMUNITY COLLEGE
Kansas City, Missouri

PEARSON
Prentice
Hall

UPPER SADDLE RIVER, NJ 07458

Cataloging data for this publication can be obtained from the Library of Congress.

AVP/Executive Editor: Wendy Craven
VP/Editorial Director: Jeff Shelstad
Product Development Manager: Pamela Hersperger
Project Manager: Kerri Tomasso
AVP/Executive Marketing Manager: John Wannemacher
Associate Director, Production Editorial: Judy Leale
Senior Managing Editor, Production: Cynthia Regan
Production Editor: Denise Culhane
Permissions Coordinator: Charles Morris
Associate Director, Manufacturing: Vinnie Scelta
Manufacturing Buyer: Diane Peirano
Design/Composition Manager: Christy Mahon
Cover Design: Nancy Thompson
Cover Illustration/Photo: Photodisc
Printer/Binder: Bind-Rite

Pearson Education LTD.
Pearson Education Singapore, Pte. Ltd
Pearson Education, Canada, Ltd
Pearson Education–Japan

Pearson Education Australia PTY, Limited
Pearson Education North Asia Ltd
Pearson Educación de Mexico, S.A. de C.V.
Pearson Education Malaysia, Pte. Ltd.

10 9 8 7 6 5 4 3 2
ISBN: 0-13-175618-4

In memory of my father, William (Bill) T. Edwards.

TABLE OF CONTENTS

CONTENTS

PREFACE

Welcome, Students and Instructors!

Getting Started with Peachtree Complete Accounting 2006 and QuickBooks Pro 2006 was written to provide the accounting student with an overview of how the manual concepts taught in introductory accounting classes can be applied to a computerized accounting environment. The textbook is written as a supplement to introductory accounting classes. The instructor is able to select workshops for the student to complete as homework or projects as necessary. While the book is written using instructions for Peachtree Complete Accounting 2006 and QuickBooks Pro 2006, the concepts learned can be applied to learning many of the other computerized accounting programs available for businesses.

Prerequisites: It is presumed that the user is currently learning the basic accounting skills taught in the first and/or second accounting course(s) and has a basic understanding of Windows.

Software Programs and Data Files: The workshops require the use of the company data files that can be downloaded from the Prentice Hall textbook Web site, www.prenhall.com/compaccounting. If you would like to package Peachtree Complete Accounting 2006 (Educational Version) with this textbook, please contract your Prentice Hall sales representative. The software program for QuickBook Pro 2006 is available as a trial version on the QuickBooks Web site, http://quickbooks.intuit.com. Chapter 11 covers the details of ordering the QuickBooks trial version software. It is recommended that you allow <u>at least two weeks</u> for the software to be delivered. This allows the student to take home a full, working copy of the programs as well as the data files.

Educational Site Licenses: Both QuickBooks and Peachtree have site licenses available for on-campus use.

➢ Intuit has the **QuickBooks: Pro Education Site Licenses** in 10-, 25- and 50-user packs. The QuickBooks Pro 2006 version is available after March 2006. To order a site license, call 888-729-1996.

➢ Sage has the **Peachtree Educational Site License** available for educational institutions. You will need to complete an application and fax it to Sage. You can find all the required information at the Sage Web site, at www.peachtree.com/training/educational_partnerships.cfm.

Coverage: The book contains 20 chapters of computer workshops. Chapters 1–10 use Peachtree Complete Accounting 2006, and Chapters 11–20 use QuickBook Pro 2006. They both use the same company data files.

Instructor Solutions: Excel solutions are provided for all the reports printed in the workshops. There are also active and backup solution files in Peachtree Complete Accounting 2006 and QuickBook Pro 2006 format. The solution files can be downloaded from www.prenhall.com/compaccounting, in the Faculty Resources area. You will need the access codes provided by your Prentice Hall sales representative.

Your comments are welcome. Please e-mail me at eheldstab@earthlink.net with any comments or questions regarding this textbook.

Elaine Heldstab, C.P.A.

CHAPTER 1

System Requirements, Installation, Opening, Backing Up, and Restoring a Company Data File

THIS WORKSHOP COVERS SYSTEM REQUIREMENTS, INSTALLATION, OPENING A COMPANY DATA FILE, BACKING UP A COMPANY DATA FILE, AND RESTORING A COMPANY DATA FILE.

System Requirements

The recommended minimum software and hardware requirements for your computer system to run both Windows and Peachtree Complete Accounting 2006 are as follows:

♦ IBM compatible 300 MHz Pentium II computer minimum; IBM Compatible 450 MHz Pentium II or higher recommended

♦ Windows XP (Service Pack 2)/2000 (Service Pack 3)/ME/98 SE. Product will not operate in a Windows Terminal Server environment using Windows Terminal Services.

♦ 128 MB RAM minimum; 256 MB RAM recommended

♦ 110 MB –250 MB free hard disk space

♦ Internet Explorer 6.0 required. Microsoft Internet Explorer 6.0 is included on the Peachtree CD. Requires 70 MB (or higher) for installation.

♦ Display settings of at least high color (16 bit), SVGA video, and 800X600 resolution with small fonts.

♦ Printers supported by Windows XP/2000/ME/98 SE

♦ Internet access for online features. Minimum connection speed depends on service.

♦ Macromedia Flash Player for in-product demos.

♦ Mouse or compatible pointing device

♦ CD-ROM drive

♦ An additional 60 MB –70 MB free hard disk space to install the audio tutorial and online documentation.

♦ Excel 2000, Excel 2002, or Excel 2003 to use Microsoft Office Excel.

♦ Word 2000, Word 2002, or Word 2003 to use Microsoft Office Word.

Installing Peachtree Complete Accounting 2006

To install Peachtree Complete Accounting 2006 on your hard disk (c: drive):

1. Start Windows.

2. Make sure no other programs are running on your system.

3. Insert the CD that accompanies this textbook in your CD-ROM drive.

4. The *Welcome to Peachtree Accounting* dialog box should display, as shown in Figure 1.1.

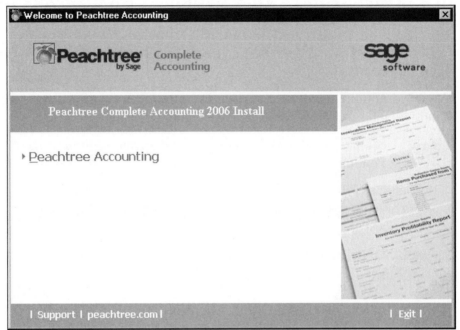

Figure 1.1

> **NOTE:** If Windows does not automatically display Figure 1.1, you need to click the **Start** button and then click **Run**. Then click the **Browse** button to locate your CD—Rom drive. Double –click the **autorun** icon as shown in Figure 1.2.

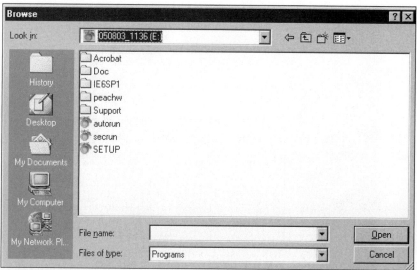

Figure 1.2

5. Click **Peachtree Accounting**

6. Click the **Next** button in the ***Peachtree Accounting Setup*** dialog box, as shown in Figure 1.3.

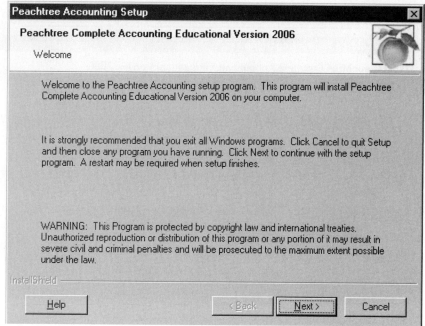

Figure 1-3

7. Click **Yes** to accept the license agreement, as shown in Figure 1.4.

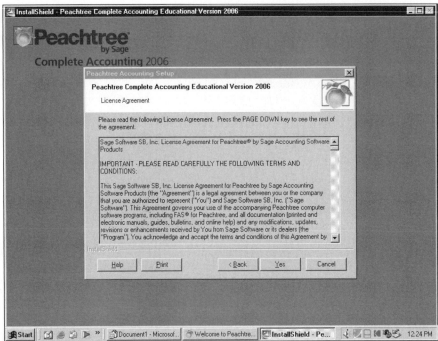

Figure 1.4

8. Click the circular button to select **Standard Setup**, as shown in Figure 1.5.

9. Click the **Next** button.

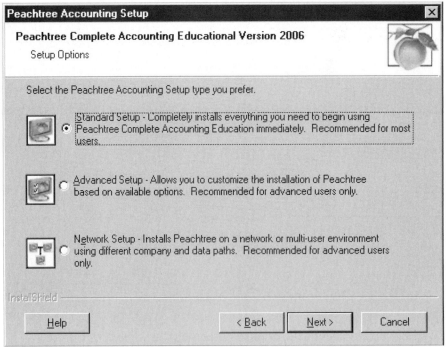

Figure 1.5

10. Select the check box **Add the Peachtree shortcuts to my desktop** (see Figure 1.6). An icon is added to your desktop for easy entry into the program.

11. Click the **Next** button to continue.

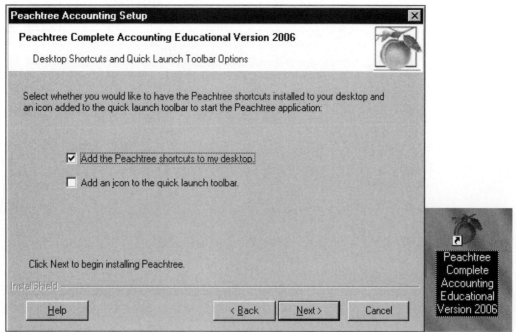

Figure 1.6

12. You will see the screens shown in Figures 1.7 and 1.8 as the software installs.

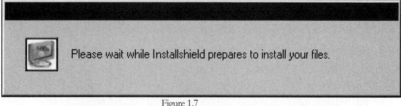

Figure 1.7

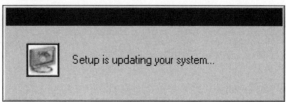

Figure 1.8

13. You are presented with the ***Peachtree Accounting Setup*** dialog box, as shown in Figure 1.9.

14. Click the check box next to **Yes, I would like to start Peachtree Complete Accounting Education,** if it is not already checked.

15. Click the **Finish** button.

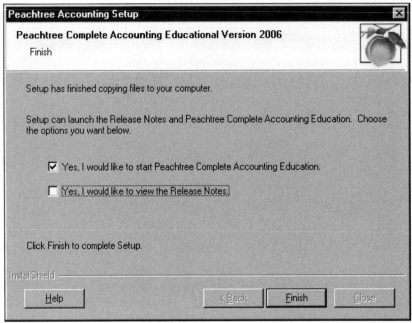

Figure 1.9

16. The program installs in the default folder **C:\Program Files\Sage Software\Peachtree** and automatically installs the demonstration companies in the **Company** directory, as shown in Figure 1.10.

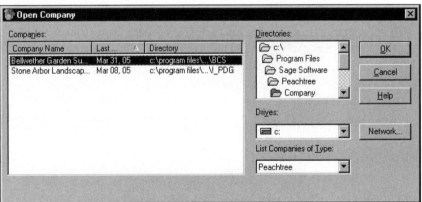

Figure 1.10

17. Your screen should look as shown in Figure 1.11.

18. Click the **Close** button or the icon in the upper-right corner of the *Peachtree Accounting – Start* dialog box.

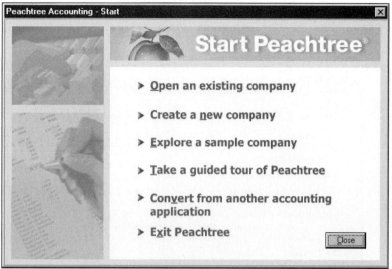

Figure 1.11

19. Your screen should look like Figure 1.12.

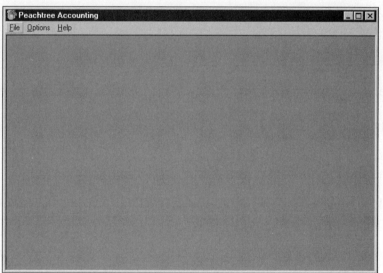

Figure 1.12

Changing the Installation Default Settings to Match the Text Figures

Peachtree installs one set of settings on a computer that has a previous version of Peachtree and a different set of setting on a computer to which you are installing Peachtree for the first time. In order to ensure that your screens will be the same as those in this book, make or confirm the following selections from the **Options** menu:

1. Select **Global** from the **Options** menu on the *Peachtree Accounting* screen.

2. Select the **Accounting** tab, as shown in Figure 1.13.

3. In the section titled **Hide General Ledger Accounts**, remove any checkmarks from the three boxes by clicking on the checkmarks so the boxes are empty, as shown in Figure 1.13.

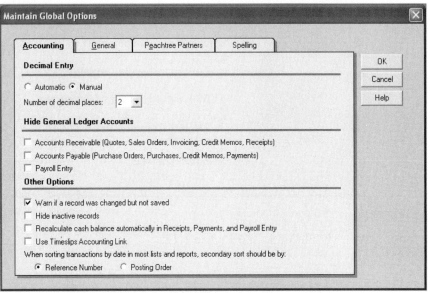

Figure 1.13

4. Click **OK** to save and close the ***Maintain Global Options*** dialog box.

5. Select **Exit** from the **File** menu to exit Peachtree and make the changes permanent.

Installing Student Data Files

After the Peachtree Complete software is loaded, you need to install the company data files that are located on the textbook Web site:

1. Open your browser and go to the www.prenhall.com/compaccounting Web site.

2. Double-click the **Peachtree** link.

3. Double-click the **Getting Started with Peachtree Accounting 2006** student resources.

4. Download the zipped data files to **C:\Program Files\Sage Software\Peachtree\Company**.

5. Close your browser to return to your desktop.

6. Double-Click the **My Computer** icon on your desktop.

7. Locate the zipped files in the **C:\Program Files\Sage Software\Peachtree\Company** directory.

8. Right-Click the zipped data file(s) and select **Extract**. Extract them to the same directory that you downloaded them to.

Using Peachtree Complete Accounting 2006 on a Network

Peachtree Complete Accounting 2006 can be used in a network environment, as long as each student uses a separate student data file source to store his or her data files. Students should consult with their instructor and/or network administrator for specific procedures regarding program installation and any special printing procedures required for proper network operation.

Peachtree will run most efficiently if the student data files are installed on a hard drive. This can occur on the local hard drive or in a unique student folder on a network drive. Because it is possible that student files may be tampered with between class sessions, it is recommended that students backup and restore their files with a floppy disk (or jump drive) each class day. Peachtree's backup and restore functions are quick and easy to follow.

Opening a Company Data File

To open Peachtree software and a company data file, follow these steps:

1. Double-click the **Peachtree** icon on your desktop, and you see the *Peachtree Accounting – Start* screen, as shown in Figure 1.14.

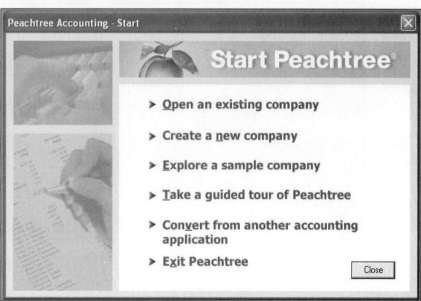

Figure 1.14

2. Select **Open an existing company**. Peachtree then brings up the *Open Company* dialog box, where you can direct Peachtree to the location of the company data files. The files that have been supplied with this text should reside in the same directory as

the Peachtree program files (unless directed otherwise by your instructor). Each company will have its own folder that can be read by the ***Open Company*** dialog box. If you do not see these files when you first open the dialog box, you may need to change the directory or drive to the one your instructor has provided. If you followed the instructions above for installation the directory you will find the data files in **C:\Program Files\Sage Software\Peachtree\Company**. The directory should contain the company data files as shown in Figure 1.15.

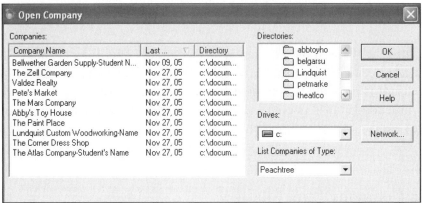

Figure 1.15

3. Select (highlight) the file **The Atlas Company** from the ***Open Company*** dialog box.

4. Click the **OK** button. Your screen should look as shown in Figure 1.16.

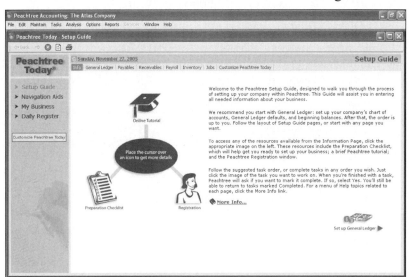

Figure 1.16

Backing Up a Company Data File

Before you start any assignment, it is suggested that you create a backup of the company data file in the event that you need to restore the original file (start the assignment over).

Peachtree has the capability to quickly and easily backup your data to protect against accidental loss. To backup the file The Atlas Company, follow these steps:

1. Select **Back Up** from the **File** menu. This brings up the ***Back Up Company*** dialog box, as shown in Figure 1.17.

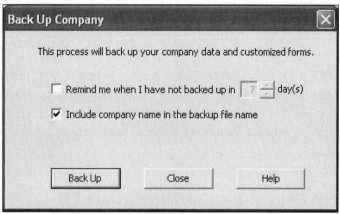

Figure 1.17

2. Select the check box next to **Include company name in the backup file name,** as shown in Figure 1.17. The company name and the date of the backup will be included in the backup file name so you can easily locate the backup.

    ➢ **NOTE:** You could also use this dialog box to have Peachtree provide a reminder at periodic intervals that it is time for a backup.

3. Click the **Back Up** button to continue. You are now presented with a ***Save Backup for The Atlas Company as*** dialog box as shown in Figure 1.18.

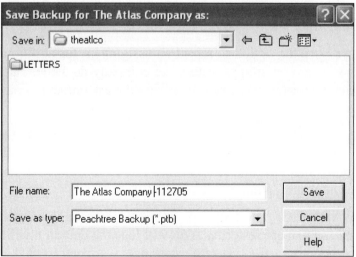

Figure 1.18

Peachtree saves your data files into one compressed .ptb (Peachtree backup) file to any drive or path you specify, including a floppy drive.

4. Use the **Save in** lookup box to save the files to a location specified by your instructor. This could be a network drive, a student floppy disk (or other media), or the local hard drive.

5. Click the **Save** button.

6. Click the **OK** button to complete the process.

> **NOTE:** You should consider saving every day you work on the file to protect yourself against possible loss. Peachtree will use the date as part of the backup name so you could have a separate backup for each day. You do not have to accept the name Peachtree assigns and can use a name with more meaning to you.

Using the Backup Copy of the Company's Data File

At certain times in the assignments, you are asked to make a backup copy of a company's data files. There are several reasons you might want to access the backup copy of a company's data files. For example, you may not have printed a required report in an assignment before advancing the period to a new month or before adding additional transactions. Or, you may have several errors and simply want to start an assignment over or at a specific point prior to the errors rather than correcting the mistakes.

If you backup your data using a different file name each day, you will have the option of restoring from any of these files. It would be wise to indicate in the file name the point in the text (e.g., p125) at which you created each backup so you will know what transactions have been entered.

Restoring a Backup File

You always have the option to repeat an assignment for additional practice or to start an assignment over. You simply restore the company data files back to their original state, using a backup created at the start or during the assignment. You complete the following procedure to restore a file:

1. Open the company data file you wish to restore. Assume that you want to restore The Atlas Company backup. You open that company file by using the *Open Company* dialog box (refer to Figure 1.15) and following the previous instructions to open The Atlas Company file.

> **WARNING:** The company file that you open in Step 1 will be overwritten by the file you are restoring. You will lose the data in this file. If you want to return to the current file (prior to restoring), you need to back it up first. Because you are restoring a file that you just backed up, go ahead and continue with the restore process.

2. Select Restore from the File menu. This brings up the Restore Wizard – Select Backup File dialog box as shown in Figure 1.19. Peachtree defaults to the folder where the regular company files are kept.

   ➢ **NOTE:** If you are keeping your backups on a floppy or on a drive/path other than the one Peachtree is defaulting to, use the **Browse** option to change the drive and select the correct path. You may have several backups made at different points in time, so be sure to select the correct one. At this point you should have only one backup file (the one from earlier in this assignment) to select. So select The Atlas Company-(*date you saved the backup*).

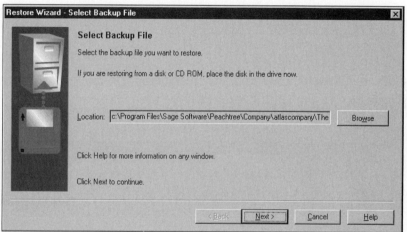

Figure 1.19

3. Click the **Next** button. You now see the *Restore Wizard – Select Company* dialog box, as shown in Figure 1.20.

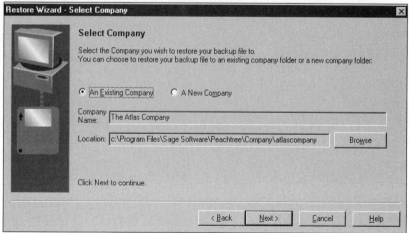

Figure 1.20

4. Click the **Next** button. You now see the *Restore Wizard – Restore Options* dialog box, as shown in Figure 1.21.

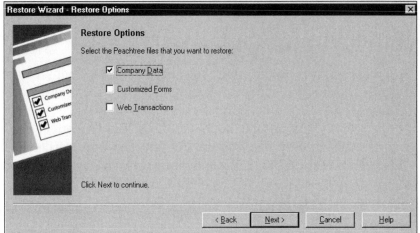

Figure 1.21

5. Click the **Next** button. You are presented with the *Restore Wizard – Confirmation* dialog box, as shown in Figure 1.22.

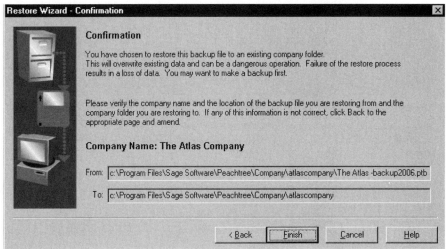

Figure 1.22

6. Click the **Finish** button to close the *Restore Wizard – Confirmation* dialog box.

You are now ready to continue with the workshop in Chapter 2.

CHAPTER 2

Journalizing, Posting, and Printing Reports—The Atlas Company

THIS WORKSHOP COVERS JOURNALIZING, POSTING, AND PRINTING THE GENERAL LEDGER, TRIAL BALANCE, AND CHART OF ACCOUNTS FOR THE ATLAS COMPANY.

Opening the Company Data Files

1. Double-click the **Peachtree** icon on your desktop.

2. Select **Open an existing company file** from the **Peachtree Accounting – Start** dialog box, as shown in Figure 2.1.

Figure 2.1

3. Browse to locate **The Atlas Company**. If you followed the data file installation instructions in Chapter 1, you will find the data files in **C:\Program Files\Sage Software\Peachtree\Company**.

4. In the *Open Company,* dialog box highlight (click) **The Atlas Company** and then click the **Open** button. When the company data file opens, it has the *Peachtree Today – Navigation Aids Sales* dialog box showing (see Figure 2.2). The navigation

aids are an alternative to using the menu bar at the top of your screen. This option is explored in Chapter 3.

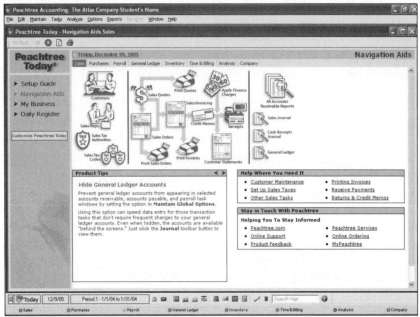

Figure 2.2

5. Close the *Peachtree Today* dialog box, and your screen should look like Figure 2.3.

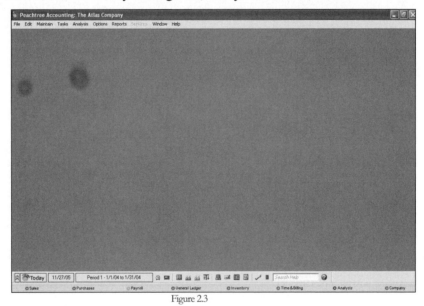

Figure 2.3

6. If you are missing the navigation aids at the bottom of the screen (as shown in Figure 2.4), you can activate them by selecting **View Navigation Aid** from the **Options** menu. It remains on until you turn it off.

Figure 2.4

Adding Your Name to the Company Name

It is important for you to be able to identify the reports you print for each assignment as your own, particularly if you are using a computer that shares a printer with other computers. Peachtree Complete Accounting 2006 prints the company name at the top of each report. To personalize your printed reports so that you can identify both the company and your reports, you need to modify the company name to include your name:

1. Click **Maintain** on the menu bar and select **Company Information** as shown in Figure 2.5.

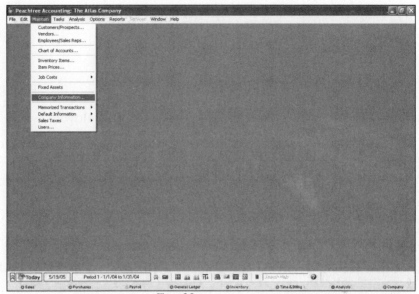

Figure 2.5

The program responds by bringing up the ***Maintain Company Information*** dialog box as shown in Figure 2.6, which allows the user to edit/add information about the company.

2. Click in the **Company Name** field and place your cursor at the end of **The Atlas Company**. If it is already highlighted, you can press the right-arrow key to get to the end of the field.

3. Add a dash and your name (***-Student's Name***) or initials to the end of the company name. Your screen will look similar to Figure 2.6, except that it will have your name or initials instead of *Student's Name*.

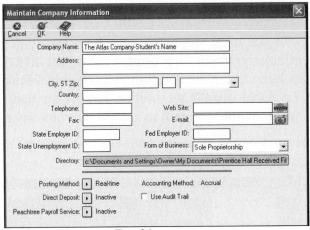

Figure 2.6

4. Click the **OK**  button to return to the main window.

    You can now exit the software program and reopen it to see the changes in the title bar.

5. Click the **Close** button to close the Peachtree Software program.

6. Double-click the **Peachtree** icon on your desktop to open the software program.

7. Click **Open an Existing Company** and select The Atlas Company.

8. Click **OK** to open the company data file. Your title bar should look as shown in Figure 2.7.

Peachtree Accounting: The Atlas Company-Student's Name

Figure 2.7

Recording a Journal Entry

> **TRANSACTION: On 1/1/04 the owner of The Atlas Company invested $10,000 in the business.**
>
> **ANALYSIS: You will want to debit (increase) the cash account (1110) for $10,000 and credit (increase) the owner's capital account (3110) for $10,000.**

The following steps will walk you through entering a general journal entry.

1. Select **General Journal Entry** from the **Tasks** menu to open the *General Journal Entry* dialog box, shown in Figure 2.8.

2. In the **Date** field enter **1/1/04**. Tab to the **Reference** field.

3. In the **Reference** field enter "Memo 1". TAB twice.

    ➢ **NOTE:** Pressing the **Enter** key also moves you from field to field.

4. In the **GL Account** (general ledger account) column, click the lookup button (magnifying glass icon) and click **1110 Cash**. The program enters the account number into the **GL Account** field and automatically moves you to the **Description** field.

5. In the **Description** field enter **Initial investment of cash by owner** and then press **Tab** to move to the **Debit** field.

6. In the **Debit** field enter **10000.00**. Press the **Tab** key three times to move through the **Credit** and **Job** fields. You end up in the **GL Account** column on the second row.

7. In the **Account No** field, click the lookup button and select **3110 Owner's Capital**. Use the scrollbar if the account is not visible in the lookup list.

8. In the **Description** field press the **Tab** key to move to the **debit** field. The program automatically enters the same description as in the first line. Tab to the **Credit** field.

9. In the **Credit** field enter **10000**.

10. Press the **Tab** key twice to move the cursor back to the **GL Account No** field.

This completes the data you need to enter into the *General Journal Entry* dialog box for the journal entry. Your screen should look as shown in Figure 2.8.

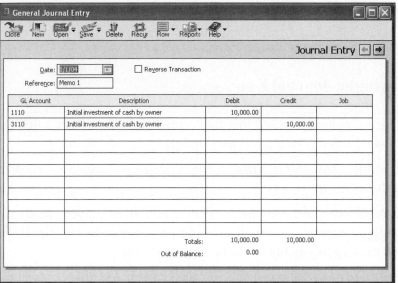

Figure 2.8

Before posting this transaction, you should verify that the information is correct by reviewing the journal entry. If you have made an error, use the following editing techniques to correct any error(s).

Editing a Journal Entry

♦   Using your mouse, click in the field that contains the error. This highlights the selected text box information so that you can change it.

♦   Type the correct information; then press the **Tab** key to enter it. You can then either tab to other fields needing corrections or again use the mouse to click in the proper field.

◆ If you have selected an incorrect account, use the pull-down menu to select the correct account. This replaces the incorrect account with the correct account.

◆ To discard an entry and start over, click the **Delete** Delete icon. You are not given the opportunity to verify this step, so make sure you want to delete the transaction before selecting this option.

➤ **NOTE:** Even though the **Save** icon is available if the entry is out of balance (total debits must equal total credits), the program does not allow you to post the transaction until the entry is in balance. You see the information box shown in Figure 2.9 if your entry is not in balance.

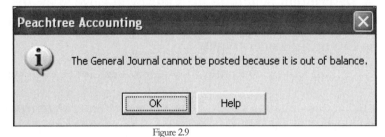

Figure 2.9

◆ Review the journal entry for accuracy after making any corrections.

Posting (Saving) a Journal Entry

1. Once you have verified that the journal entry is correct, click the **Save** Save icon to post a transaction to the general ledger.

2. Keep the *General Journal Entry* dialog box open to record the additional journal entries below.

A blank *General Journal Entry* dialog box is displayed, ready for additional journal entries to be recorded. The software automatically increases the **Reference** field by 1 and does so as long as you remain in this input screen.

➤ **TIP:** To move between the journal entries, use the arrow buttons on the *General Journal Entry* screen (see Figure 2.10). To look at the entry you just entered, click the back arrow. If you do that, you will need to click the **Save** Save icon again to bring up a blank *General Journal Entry* dialog box. This does not post the transaction twice; it just saves the entry with the corrected information.

Figure 2.10

Entering Additional Journal Entries

1. Enter the **date** listed for each transaction. You may can the + key to advance the date or click the calendar icon next to the field to select the date from a calendar.

2. Accept Peachtree's additional number added to Memo 1 if it is showing in the **Reference** field by pressing the Tab key. You may also type the entry number in the Reference field. (e.g., Memo, Memo 1, Memo 2).

Here are the transactions for January:

2004
Jan.

	1	Paid rent for two months in advance, $400.
	3	Purchased office supplies on account, $100.
	9	Billed a customer for fees earned, $1,500.
	13	Paid telephone bill, $180.
	20	Owner withdrew $500 from the business.
	27	Received $450 for fees earned (cash sale)
	31	Paid salaries expense, $700.

3. After you have entered the additional journal entries, click the **Close** button ☒ or icon ▣Close to close the *General Journal Entry* dialog box.

Displaying and Printing a General Journal

1. Select **General Ledger** from the **Reports** menu to bring up the *Select a Report* dialog box (see Figure 2.11).

2. Click **General Ledger** in the **Report Area** section of the screen.

3. The section titled **Report List** shows the reports available for the general ledger.

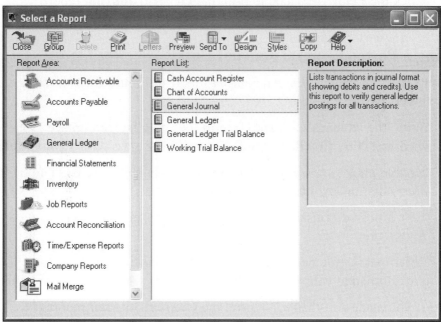

Figure 2.11

4. Double-click **General Journal** from the **Report List** section. The report displays, as shown in Figure 2.12. The scrollbars can be used to advance the display to view other portions of the report.

➢ **NOTE:** You can display the entire **General Journal** window by clicking the **maximize** ▣ button.

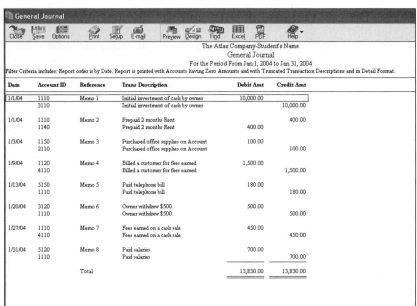

Figure 2.12

5. Click the **Print** [Print] icon to print the **General Journal** report.

Correcting a Posted General Journal Entry

Compare your printed General Journal report to Figure 2.12. If you note an error at this point, you can fix it easily:

1. With the **General Journal** report on your screen, place your cursor over the incorrect entry (it will resemble a magnifying glass with a z in the center).

2. Double-click the entry you want to correct, and you are taken to the *General Journal Entry* dialog box that contains the entry.

3. Edit a posted transaction by using the same procedures as for editing an unposted transaction.

4. After making the necessary changes, click the **Save** icon to save your changes. You are returned to your **General Journal** report, where you can view the changes made.

5. If you made any changes, reprint the **General Journal** report.

6. Click the **Close** [Close] icon or button [X] to close the **General Journal** report.

Displaying and Printing the General Ledger Report

1. Double-click the **General Ledger** report in the **Report List** section of the *Select a Report* dialog box. Your screen should look like Figure 2.13.

The Atlas Company-Student's Name
General Ledger
For the Period From Jan 1, 2004 to Jan 31, 2004
Filter Criteria includes: Report order is by ID. Report is printed with Truncated Transaction Descriptions and in Detail Format.

Account ID Account Description	Date	Reference	Jrnl	Trans Description	Debit Amt	Credit Amt	Balance
1110	1/1/04			Beginning Balance			
Cash	1/1/04	Memo 1	GENJ	Initial investment of c	10,000.00		
	1/1/04	Memo 2	GENJ	Prepaid 2 months Rent		400.00	
	1/13/04	Memo 5	GENJ	Paid telephone bill		180.00	
	1/20/04	Memo 6	GENJ	Owner withdrew $500.		500.00	
	1/27/04	Memo 7	GENJ	Fees earned on a cash s	450.00		
	1/31/04	Memo 8	GENJ	Paid salaries		700.00	
				Current Period Change	10,450.00	1,780.00	8,670.00
	1/31/04			Ending Balance			8,670.00
1120	1/1/04			Beginning Balance			
Accounts Receivable	1/9/04	Memo 4	GENJ	Billed a customer for f	1,500.00		
				Current Period Change	1,500.00		1,500.00
	1/31/04			Ending Balance			1,500.00
1140	1/1/04			Beginning Balance			
Prepaid Rent	1/1/04	Memo 2	GENJ	Prepaid 2 months Rent	400.00		
				Current Period Change	400.00		400.00
	1/31/04			Ending Balance			400.00
1150	1/1/04			Beginning Balance			
Office Supplies	1/3/04	Memo 3	GENJ	Purchased office suppli	100.00		
				Current Period Change	100.00		100.00
	1/31/04			Ending Balance			100.00
2110	1/1/04			Beginning Balance			
Accounts Payable	1/3/04	Memo 3	GENJ	Purchased office suppli		100.00	
				Current Period Change		100.00	-100.00
	1/31/04			Ending Balance			-100.00

Figure 2.13

You do not see the entire report on the screen (or in Figure 2.13). You can use the scrollbars to advance the display to view other portions of the report. You can also double-click any transaction to bring up the entry window for that transaction if you need to make corrections.

2. Click the **Print** [Print] icon to print the **General Ledger** report.

3. Click **OK** on the *Print* dialog box.

4. Click the **Close** button or icon to exit the **General Ledger** report.

Displaying and Printing the General Ledger Trial Balance

1. In the *Select a Report* dialog box, double-click the **General Ledger Trial Balance** report in the **Report List** section. Your screen will look like Figure 2.14. You can use the scroll bar to advance the display to view other portions of the report.

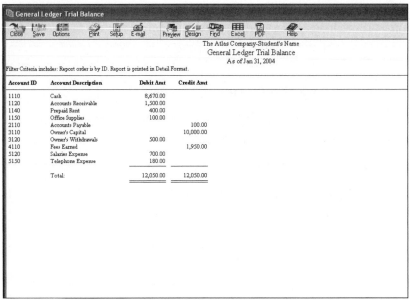

Figure 2.14

2. Click the **Print** icon to print the **Trial Balance** Report.

3. Click **OK** on the *Print* dialog box.

4. Click the **Close** button to exit the Trial Balance report.

Displaying and Printing the Chart of Accounts Report

1. Select **General Ledger** and then **Chart of Accounts** in the *Select a Report* window. Your screen will look like Figure 2.15.

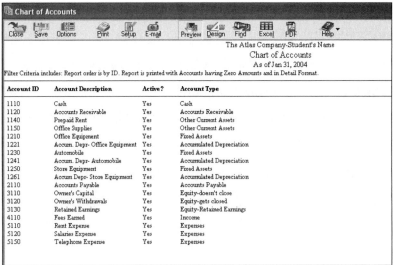

Figure 2.15

2. Click the **Print** icon to print the **Chart of Accounts** report.

3. Click **OK** on the *Print* dialog box.

4. Click the **Close** button to exit the Chart of Accounts report.

5. Click the **Close** button to exit the *Select a Report* dialog box.

Backing Up Your Company Data File

1. Select **Backup** from the **File** menu.

2. Click the check box to include the company name in the file name.

3. Add **Final** to the file name.

4. Select the **Save in** lookup box to find the location your instructor has identified for you to keep your backup file(s).

5. Click **Save**.

6. Click **OK**.

   ➢ **NOTE:** Refer to Chapter 1 for more detailed instructions on backing up files.

Exiting the Peachtree Complete Accounting 2006 Program

1. Select on **Exit** from the **File** menu to end the current work session and return to your Windows desktop.

2. If you are asked if you wish to save any unposted work, click the **Yes** button.

CHAPTER 3

Compound Journal Entries, Adjusting Entries, and Printing Financial Reports—The Zell Company

THIS WORKSHOP COVERS MAKING COMPOUND JOURNAL ENTRIES, ADJUSTING ENTRIES, AND PRINTING FINANCIAL REPORTS FOR THE ZELL COMPANY.

Opening The Zell Company

1. Double-click the **Peachtree**  icon on your desktop to open the software program.

2. Click **Open existing company** and then locate and select the **The Zell Company**.

3. Click **Open.**

   ➢ **NOTE:** Refer to Chapter 1 for more detailed instructions on opening a company file.

Backing Up Your Company Data File

1. Select **Backup** from the **File** menu.

2. Click the check box to include the company name in the file name.

3. Add **Start** to the file name.

4. Select the **Save in** lookup box to find the location your instructor has identified for your backup file(s).

5. Click **Save.**

6. Click **OK.**

   ➢ **NOTE:** Refer to Chapter 1 for more detailed instructions on backing up files.

Adding your Name to the Company Name

> ➢ **NOTE:** Refer to Chapter 2 for detailed instructions on adding your name to the company name.

1. Click the **Maintain** menu option and select **Company Information**. The program responds by bringing up the *Maintain Company Information* dialog box, which allows you to edit/add information about the company.

2. Click in the **Company Name** field and make sure your cursor is at the end of **The Zell Company**.

3. Add a dash and your name (**-Student's Name**).

4. Click the **OK** button.

5. Exit the software program and reopen it to see your name in the title bar.

6. If you see the *Peachtree Today – Setup Guide* dialog box, as shown in Figure 3.1 click **Navigation Aids** on the left side of the screen.

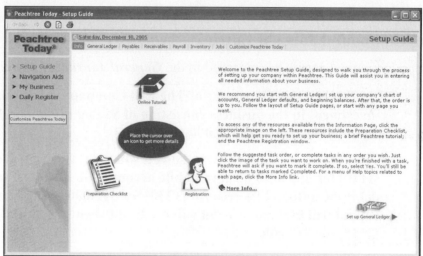

Figure 3.1

7. If you get the information window shown in Figure 3.2, click the **Yes** button to make the Navigation Aids window your default page.

Figure 3.2

8. Click the **General Ledger** tab (highlighted in Figure 3.3) on the *Peachtree Today – Navigation Aids General Ledger* dialog box. Your screen will look like Figure 3.3.

Figure 3.3

Recording Compound Journal Entries

Compound journal entries are recorded in the *General Journal Entry* dialog box.

> **TRANSACTION: The owner of The Zell Company made an investment in the business consisting of $5,000 in cash and an automobile valued at $12,000 on 1/1/04.**
>
> **ANALYSIS: Cash will increase, so you will debit the cash account (1110) for $5,000. The automobile account will increase, so you will debit the automobile account (1230) for $12,000. The owner's capital will increase, so you will credit the owner's capital account (3110) for $17,000.**

1. Click the **General Journal Entry** icon on the *Peachtree Today -Navigation Aids General Ledger* dialog box.

2. You see a blank *General Journal Entry* dialog box like the one shown in Figure 3.4.

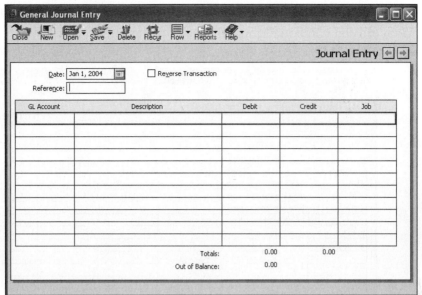

Figure 3.4

3. In the **Date** field enter **1/1/04** (the transaction date) and then press the **Tab** key.

4. In the **Reference** field enter **Memo** and then press the **Tab** key twice.

5. In the **GL Account** field, Click the lookup button (magnifying glass icon) and then click **1110 Cash**. The insertion point automatically moves to the **Description** field.

6. In the **Description** field enter **Initial investment by owner** and then press the **Tab** key.

7. In the **Debit** field enter **5000** and then press **Tab** three times to move back to the **GL Account** field.

8. On the second row of the **GL Account** column, Click the lookup button (magnifying glass icon) and double-click **1230 Automobile**. The cursor automatically moves to the **Description** field.

9. The **Description** field should repeat the description from the first line by default. Press the **Tab** key again to move to the **Debit** field.

10. In the **Debit** field enter **12000**. Click the **Tab** key three times to move the cursor back to the **GL Account** field. You should now have two debit entries.

11. On the third row, in the **GL Account** column, click the lookup button and click **3110 Owner's Capital**. Press **Tab** to move to the **Description** field.

12. The **Description** field should repeat the description from the first two entries by default. Press the **Tab** key again twice to move to the **Credit** field.

13. In the **Credit** field enter **17000**. Click the **Tab** key twice to move the cursor back to the **GL Account** field.

This completes the data you need to enter in the **_General Journal Entry_** dialog box to record the compound journal entry for the initial investment by the owner. Your screen should look like Figure 3.5.

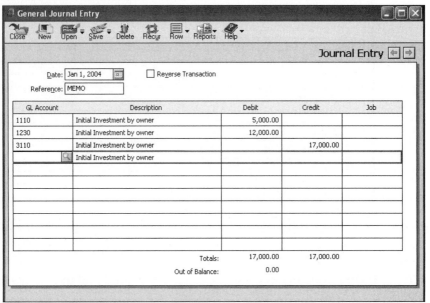

Figure 3.5

14. Review the compound journal entry for accuracy, making any corrections required by following the instructions in Chapter 2 for correcting journal entries.

15. Click the **Save** icon to post this transaction.

16. Keep the **_General Journal Entry_** dialog box open to record the following additional journal entries.

Recording Additional Journal Entries

Analyze and record the following additional journal entries:

1. In the **Date** field enter the date listed for each transaction. You can use the + key to advance the date or click the calendar icon next to the field to select the date from a calendar.

2. In the **Reference** field enter **Memo** for each transaction or accept Peachtree's additional number added to **Memo** by pressing the **Tab** key:

> 2004
> Jan.   1   Paid rent for two months in advance, $500.
>   3   Purchased office supplies ($200) and office equipment ($1,100), both on account (a compound journal entry). Be sure to use the asset accounts.
>   9   Billed a customer for fees earned, $2,000.

  13 Paid telephone bill, $150.
  20 Owner withdrew $475 from the business for personal use.
  27 Received $600 for fees earned.
  31 Paid salaries expense, $800.

3. Click the **Close** button or icon to exit the ***General Journal Entry*** dialog box after you have entered all the transactions. You should now be looking at the ***Peachtree Today - Navigation Aids General Ledger*** dialog box.

Displaying and Printing the General Journal

1. Click the **General Journal** icon from the reports section of the ***Peachtree Today - Navigation Aids General Ledger*** dialog box. You are presented with the ***General Journal*** dialog box, shown in Figure 3.6, which lets you change the options for the report.

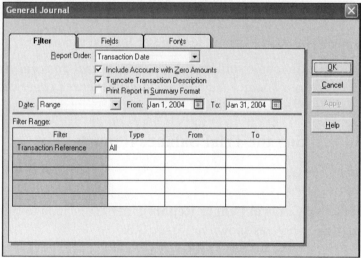

Figure 3.6

2. Click **OK** to accept all the default report settings.

3. Your screen looks like Figure 3.7.

The Zell Company
General Journal
For the Period From Jan 1, 2004 to Jan 31, 2004
Filter Criteria includes: Report order is by Date. Report is printed with Accounts having Zero Amounts and with Truncated Transaction Descriptions and in Detail Format.

Date	Account ID	Reference	Trans Description	Debit Amt	Credit Amt
1/1/04	1110	MEMO	Initial Investment by owner	5,000.00	
	1230		Initial Investment by owner	12,000.00	
	3110		Initial Investment by owner		17,000.00
1/1/04	1140	MEMO 1	Paid rent for two months in advance	500.00	
	1110		Paid rent for two months in advance		500.00
1/3/04	1150	MEMO 2	Purchased office supplies and office equipm	200.00	
	1210		Purchased office supplies and office equipm	1,100.00	
	2110		Purchased office supplies and office equipm		1,300.00
1/9/04	1120	MEMO 3	Billed a customer for fees earned	2,000.00	
	4110		Billed a customer for fees earned		2,000.00
1/13/04	5150	MEMO 4	Paid telephone bill	150.00	
	1110		Paid telephone bill		150.00
1/20/04	3120	MEMO 5	Owner withdraw	475.00	
	1110		Owner withdraw		475.00
1/27/04	1110	MEMO 6	Received money for fees earned	600.00	
	4110		Received money for fees earned		600.00
1/31/04	5120	MEMO 7	Paid salaries	800.00	
	1110		Paid salaries		800.00
		Total		22,825.00	22,825.00

Figure 3.7

4. Compare the transactions on your screen to these in Figure 3.7. If a posted transaction needs to be changed, you can zoom in on the transaction to make the correction, as you did in Chapter 2.

5. Click the **Print** icon to print the General Journal report.

6. Click the **Close** icon or button to exit the *General Journal Report* screen and return to the *Peachtree Today – Navigation Aids General Ledger* dialog box.

Displaying and Printing the Trial Balance Reports

1. Click the **All General Ledger Report** icon to bring up the *Select a Report* dialog box, as shown in Figure 3.8.

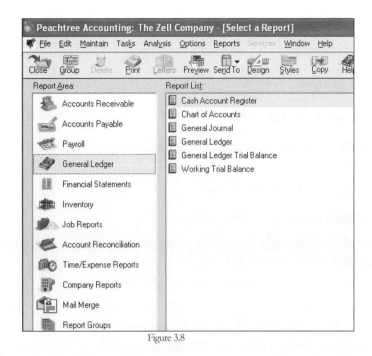

Figure 3.8

2. Double-click the **General Ledger Trial Balance** [General Ledger Trial Balance] button in the **Report List** section.

3. Your screen looks like Figure 3.9.

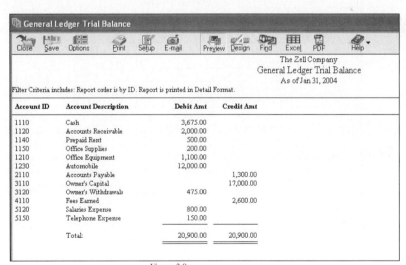

Figure 3.9

4. Compare your screen to Figure 3.9. If your figures do not match the ones in Figure 3.9, make corrections to your journal entries. See Chapter 2 for instructions on correcting a journal entry.

5. Click the **Print** icon to print the **General Ledger Trial Balance** report.

6. Click the **Close** button to exit the *General Ledger Trial Balance* screen.

7. Click the **Close** button to close the *Select a Report* dialog box. You should once again be looking at the *Peachtree Today – Navigation Aids General Ledger* dialog box.

Adjusting Journal Entries

1. Click the **General Journal Entry** icon on the *Peachtree Today – Navigation Aids General Ledger* dialog box.

2. In the **Date** field enter **1/31/04**.

3. In the **Reference** field enter **ADJ**.

4. Enter all the adjustments on the same page before posting (saving). See the *General Journal Entry* window in Figure 3.10.

    a. One month's rent has expired.
    b. An inventory shows $25 of office supplies remaining.
    c. Depreciation on office equipment, $50.
    d. Depreciation on automobile, $150.

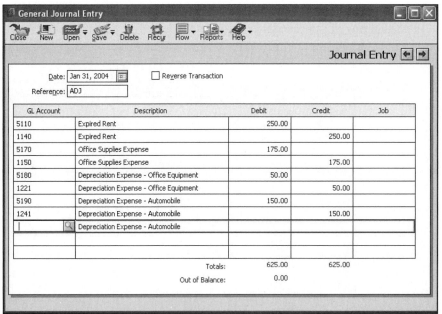

Figure 3.10

5. Click the **Save** button.

6. Click the **Close** button to exit the *General Journal Entry* screen.

Displaying and Printing the General Journal, General Ledger and Trial Balance Reports

1. Display and print the reports shown in Figure 3.11, 3.12, and 3.13 from the **General Ledger** option of the *Select a Report* dialog box.

The Zell Company
General Journal
For the Period From Jan 1, 2004 to Jan 31, 2004
Filter Criteria includes: Report order is by Date. Report is printed with Accounts having Zero Amounts and with Truncated Transaction Descriptions and in Detail Form

Date	Account ID	Reference	Trans Description	Debit Amt	Credit Amt
	1230		Initial Investment by owner	12,000.00	
	3110		Initial Investment by owner		17,000.00
1/1/04	1140	MEMO 1	Paid rent for two months in advance	500.00	
	1110		Paid rent for two months in advance		500.00
1/3/04	1150	MEMO 2	Purchased office supplies and office equipm	200.00	
	1210		Purchased office supplies and office equipm	1,100.00	
	2110		Purchased office supplies and office equipm		1,300.00
1/9/04	1120	MEMO 3	Billed a customer for fees earned	2,000.00	
	4110		Billed a customer for fees earned		2,000.00
1/13/04	5150	MEMO 4	Paid telephone bill	150.00	
	1110		Paid telephone bill		150.00
1/20/04	3120	MEMO 5	Owner withdraw	475.00	
	1110		Owner withdraw		475.00
1/27/04	1110	MEMO 6	Received money for fees earned	600.00	
	4110		Received money for fees earned		600.00
1/31/04	5110	ADJ	Expired Rent	250.00	
	1140		Expired Rent		250.00
	5170		Office Supplies Expense	175.00	
	1150		Office Supplies Expense		175.00
	5180		Depreciation Expense - Office Equipment	50.00	
	1221		Depreciation Expense - Office Equipment		50.00
	5190		Depreciation Expense - Automobile	150.00	
	1241		Depreciation Expense - Automobile		150.00

Figure 3.11

The Zell Company
General Ledger
For the Period From Jan 1, 2004 to Jan 31, 2004
Filter Criteria includes: Report order is by ID. Report is printed with Truncated Transaction Descriptions and in Detail Format.

Account ID Account Description	Date	Reference	Jrnl	Trans Description	Debit Amt	Credit Amt	Balance
1110	1/1/04			Beginning Balance			
Cash	1/1/04	MEMO	GENJ	Initial Investment by	5,000.00		
	1/1/04	MEMO 1	GENJ	Paid rent for two mon		500.00	
	1/13/04	MEMO 4	GENJ	Paid telephone bill		150.00	
	1/20/04	MEMO 5	GENJ	Owner withdraw		475.00	
	1/27/04	MEMO 6	GENJ	Received money for fe	600.00		
	1/31/04	MEMO 7	GENJ	Paid salaries		800.00	
				Current Period Change	5,600.00	1,925.00	3,675.00
	1/31/04			Ending Balance			3,675.00
1120	1/1/04			Beginning Balance			
Accounts Receivable	1/9/04	MEMO 3	GENJ	Billed a customer for f	2,000.00		
				Current Period Change	2,000.00		2,000.00
	1/31/04			Ending Balance			2,000.00
1140	1/1/04			Beginning Balance			
Prepaid Rent	1/1/04	MEMO 1	GENJ	Paid rent for two mon	500.00		
	1/31/04	ADJ	GENJ	Expired Rent		250.00	
				Current Period Change	500.00	250.00	250.00
	1/31/04			Ending Balance			250.00
1150	1/1/04			Beginning Balance			
Office Supplies	1/3/04	MEMO 2	GENJ	Purchased office suppli	200.00		
	1/31/04	ADJ	GENJ	Office Supplies Expens		175.00	
				Current Period Change	200.00	175.00	25.00
	1/31/04			Ending Balance			25.00

Figure 3.12

		The Zell Company General Ledger Trial Balance As of Jan 31, 2004	

Filter Criteria includes: Report order is by ID. Report is printed in Detail Format.

Account ID	Account Description	Debit Amt	Credit Amt
1110	Cash	3,675.00	
1120	Accounts Receivable	2,000.00	
1140	Prepaid Rent	250.00	
1150	Office Supplies	25.00	
1210	Office Equipment	1,100.00	
1221	Accum. Depr- Office Equipment		50.00
1230	Automobile	12,000.00	
1241	Accum. Depr- Automobile		150.00
2110	Accounts Payable		1,300.00
3110	Owner's Capital		17,000.00
3120	Owner's Withdrawals	475.00	
4110	Fees Earned		2,600.00
5110	Rent Expense	250.00	
5120	Salaries Expense	800.00	
5150	Telephone Expense	150.00	
5170	Supplies Expense	175.00	
5180	Depr Expense- Office Equipmen	50.00	
5190	Depr Expense- Automobile	150.00	
	Total:	21,100.00	21,100.00

Figure 3.13

2. Review your printed reports. If you have made an error in a posted journal entry, make the necessary changes and reprint the reports, as needed.

Displaying and Printing the Income Statement

1. Select the **Financial Statements** option in the **Report Area** section of the *Select a Report* dialog box.

2. Double-click **<Standard> Income Stmnt** in the *Select a Report* dialog box.

3. Click the **OK** button to accept the defaults and display the report on your screen. Your screen looks like Figure 3.14.

The Zell Company
Income Statement
For the One Month Ending January 31, 2004

	Current Month			Year to Date	
Revenues					
Fees Earned	$ 2,600.00	100.00	$	2,600.00	100.00
Total Revenues	2,600.00	100.00		2,600.00	100.00
Cost of Sales					
Total Cost of Sales	0.00	0.00		0.00	0.00
Gross Profit	2,600.00	100.00		2,600.00	100.00
Expenses					
Rent Expense	250.00	9.62		250.00	9.62
Salaries Expense	800.00	30.77		800.00	30.77
Telephone Expense	150.00	5.77		150.00	5.77
Supplies Expense	175.00	6.73		175.00	6.73
Depr Expense- Office Equipment	50.00	1.92		50.00	1.92
Depr Expense- Automobile	150.00	5.77		150.00	5.77
Total Expenses	1,575.00	60.58		1,575.00	60.58
Net Income	$ 1,025.00	39.42	$	1,025.00	39.42

Figure 3.4

4. Click the **Print** icon to print the **Income Statement** report.

5. Click the **Close** button or icon to return to the *Select a Report* dialog box.

Displaying and Printing the Balance Sheet

1. Double-click **<Standard> Balance Sheet** in the *Select a Report* dialog box.

2. Click the **OK** button to accept the defaults and display the report on your screen. (see Figures 3.15 and 3.16).

The Zell Company
Balance Sheet
January 31, 2004

ASSETS

Current Assets		
Cash	$ 3,675.00	
Accounts Receivable	2,000.00	
Prepaid Rent	250.00	
Office Supplies	25.00	
Total Current Assets		5,950.00
Property and Equipment		
Office Equipment	1,100.00	
Accum. Depr- Office Equipment	(50.00)	
Automobile	12,000.00	
Accum. Depr- Automobile	(150.00)	
Total Property and Equipment		12,900.00
Other Assets		
Total Other Assets		0.00
Total Assets		$ 18,850.00

Figure 3.15

	LIABILITIES AND CAPITAL	
Current Liabilities		
Accounts Payable	$ 1,300.00	
Total Current Liabilities		1,300.00
Long-Term Liabilities		
Total Long-Term Liabilities		0.00
Total Liabilities		1,300.00
Capital		
Owner's Capital	17,000.00	
Owner's Withdrawals	(475.00)	
Net Income	1,025.00	
Total Capital		17,550.00
Total Liabilities & Capital	$ 18,850.00	

Figure 3.16

> **NOTE:** You can use the scrollbars to advance the display to the **Owner's Equity** section of the **Balance Sheet** report. The Statement of Owner's Equity appears on the **Balance Sheet** when you select the **<Standard>** Balance Sheet report.

3. Click the **Print** button to print the **Balance Sheet** report.

4. Click the **Close** button to close the **Balance Sheet** report.

5. Click the **Close** button to exit the *Select a Report* window.

Backing Up Your Company Data File

1. Select **Backup** from the **File** menu.

2. **Click** the check box to include the company name in the file name.

3. Select the **Save in** lookup box to find the location your instructor has identified for you to keep your backup file(s).

4. Click **Save.**

5. Click **OK.**

> **NOTE:** Refer to Chapter 1 for more detailed instructions on backing up files.

Exiting the Peachtree Complete Accounting 2006 Program

1. Click on **Exit** on the File menu to end the current work session and return to your Windows desktop.

2. If you are asked if you wish to save any unposted work, click the **Yes** button.

CHAPTER 4

The Closing Process -- Valdez Realty

THIS WORKSHOP COVERS THE ACCOUNTING CYCLE FOR VALDEZ REALTY FOR TWO MONTHS, USING GENERAL JOURNAL ENTRIES, AND ADJUSTING JOURNAL ENTRIES.

On June 1, Juan Valdez opened a real estate office called Valdez Realty.

Opening the Valdez Realty Company

1. Double-click the **Peachtree** icon on your desktop to open the software program.

2. Click **Open existing company** and locate and select **Valdez Realty**.

3. Click **Open**.

   ➢ **NOTE:** Refer to Chapter 1 for more detailed instructions on opening a company file.

Backing Up Your Company Data File

1. Select **Backup** from the **File** menu.

2. Click the check box to include the company name in the file name.

3. Select the **Save in** lookup box to find the location your instructor has identified for you to keep your backup file(s).

4. Click **Save**.

5. Click **OK**.

   ➢ **NOTE:** Refer to Chapter 1 for more detailed instructions on backing up files.

Adding Your Name to the Company Name

1. Click the **Maintain** menu option and select **Company Information**. The program responds by bringing up the *Maintain Company Information* dialog box, which allows you to edit/add information about the company.

2. Click in the **Company Name** field and make sure your cursor is at the end of **Valdez Realty**.

3. Add a dash and your name (**-Student's Name**).

4. Click the **OK** button.

> ➤ **NOTE:** Refer to Chapter 2 for more detailed instructions on adding your name to a file name.

Valdez Realty—The June Accounting Cycle

Recording the June General Journal Entries

1. Click the **Task** menu and select **General Journal Entry**. This opens the *General Journal Entry* window.

2. In the **Date** field enter the date listed for each transaction.

3. In the **Reference** field enter **Memo** for each transaction or accept Peachtree's additional number added to **Memo** by pressing the **Tab** key:

   2004
   Jun. 1 Juan Valdez invested $7,000 cash in the real estate agency along with $3,000 in office equipment.
   1 Rented office space and paid three months' rent in advance, $2,100.
   1 Bought an automobile on account, $12,000.
   4 Purchased office supplies for cash, $300.
   5 Purchased additional office supplies on account, $150.
   6 Sold a house and collected a $6,000 commission.
   8 Paid gas bill, $22.
   15 Paid the salary of the office secretary, $350.
   17 Sold a building lot and earned a commission, $6,500. Expected receipt 7/8/04.
   20 Withdrew $1,000 from the business to pay personal expenses.
   21 Sold a house and collected a $3,500 commission.
   22 Paid gas bill, $25.
   24 Paid $600 to repair automobile.
   30 Paid the salary of the office secretary, $350.
   30 Paid the June telephone bill, $510.
   30 Received advertising bill for June, $1,200. The bill is to be paid on 7/2/04.

4. Review the journal entries and make any corrections, following the instructions in Chapter 2 for editing a journal entry.

5. Click the **Close** button to exit the *General Journal Entry* window.

Displaying and Printing the Working Reports for June

1. Click the **Reports** menu and select **General Ledger**. This brings up the *Select a Report* window.

   ➢ **NOTE:** Refer to Chapter 2 for more detailed instructions regarding printing reports.

2. Double-click the **General Journal** report to display the report on your screen. (see Figure 4.1).

Valdez Realty
General Journal
For the Period From Jun 1, 2004 to Jun 30, 2004
Filter Criteria includes: Report order is by Date. Report is printed with Accounts having Zero Amounts and with Truncated Transaction Descriptions and in Detail Format.

Date	Account ID	Reference	Trans Description	Debit Amt	Credit Amt
6/1/04	1110	MEMO	Owner Investment	7,000.00	
	1210		Owner Investment	3,000.00	
	3110		Owner Investment		10,000.00
6/1/04	1140	MEMO1	Prepaid 3 months rent	2,100.00	
	1110		Prepaid 3 months rent		2,100.00
6/1/04	1230	MEMO2	Purchased Automobile on account	12,000.00	
	2110		Purchased Automobile on account		12,000.00
6/4/04	1150	MEMO3	Purchased Office Supplies with cash	300.00	
	1110		Purchased Office Supplies with cash		300.00
6/5/04	1150	MEMO4	Purchased office supplies on account	150.00	
	2110		Purchased office supplies on account		150.00
6/6/04	1110	MEMO5	Collected Commission on sale of house	6,000.00	
	4110		Collected Commission on sale of house		6,000.00
6/8/04	5130	MEMO6	Paid gas bill	22.00	
	1110		Paid gas bill		22.00
6/15/04	5120	MEMO7	Paid salary of the office secretary	350.00	
	1110		Paid salary of the office secretary		350.00
6/17/04	1120	MEMO8	Earned commission on account	6,500.00	
	4110		Earned commission on account		6,500.00

Figure 4.1

3. Click the **Print** icon.

4. Click the **Close** button to return to the *Select a Report* window.

5. Double-click the **Trial Balance** report in the *Select a Report* window. The window shown in Figure 4.2 appears.

Valdez Realty
General Ledger Trial Balance
As of Jun 30, 2004
Filter Criteria includes: Report order is by ID. Report is printed in Detail Format.

Account ID	Account Description	Debit Amt	Credit Amt
1110	Cash	11,243.00	
1120	Accounts Receivable	6,500.00	
1140	Prepaid Rent	2,100.00	
1150	Office Supplies	450.00	
1210	Office Equipment	3,000.00	
1230	Automobile	12,000.00	
2110	Accounts Payable		13,350.00
3110	Juan Valdez, Capital		10,000.00
3120	Juan Valdez Withdrawals	1,000.00	
4110	Commissions Earned		16,000.00
5120	Salaries Expense	700.00	
5130	Gas Expense	47.00	
5140	Repairs Expense	600.00	
5150	Telephone Expense	510.00	
5160	Advertising Expense	1,200.00	
	Total:	39,350.00	39,350.00

Figure 4.2

6. Click the **Print** icon.

7. Click the **Close** button or icon to close the **Trial Balance** report.

8. Review your printed reports. If you have made an error in a posted journal entry, correct the error and reprint the reports before proceeding.

9. Click the **Close** button or icon on the *Select a Report* window.

Adjusting Journal Entries for June

Use the Trial Balance report you just printed to adjust the following journal entries:

1. Click the **Task** menu and select **General Journal Entry** to open the *General Journal Entry* dialog box.

2. In the **Date** field enter **June 30, 2004**.

3. In the **Reference** field enter **ADJ JUNE**.

4. Enter all these adjustments as a single journal entry

    a. One month's rent has expired.

    b. An inventory shows $50 of office supplies remaining.

    c. Depreciation on office equipment, $100.

    d. Depreciation on automobile, $200.

5. Review your journal entry and make any necessary corrections. The total of the general journal entry for the adjustments should be $1,400.00.

6. Click the **Save** icon.

7. Click the **Close** button to exit the *General Journal Entry* dialog box.

Printing the Final Reports for June

1. Print the **General Journal**, **Trial Balance**, **General Ledger**, **Income Statement** and **Balance Sheet** reports accepting all defaults. (see Figures 4.3 –4.8).

    ➤ **Note:** See the detailed instructions in Chapter 2 for printing reports.

Valdez Realty
General Journal
For the Period From Jun 1, 2004 to Jun 30, 2004

Filter Criteria includes: Report order is by Date. Report is printed with Accounts having Zero Amounts and with Truncated Transaction Descriptions a

Date	Account ID	Reference	Trans Description	Debit Amt	Credit Amt
6/1/04	1110	MEMO	Owner Investment	7,000.00	
	1210		Owner Investment	3,000.00	
	3110		Owner Investment		10,000.00
6/1/04	1140	MEMO1	Prepaid 3 months rent	2,100.00	
	1110		Prepaid 3 months rent		2,100.00
6/1/04	1230	MEMO2	Purchased Automobile on account	12,000.00	
	2110		Purchased Automobile on account		12,000.00
6/4/04	1150	MEMO3	Purchased Office Supplies with cash	300.00	
	1110		Purchased Office Supplies with cash		300.00
6/5/04	1150	MEMO4	Purchased office supplies on account	150.00	
	2110		Purchased office supplies on account		150.00
6/6/04	1110	MEMO5	Collected Commission on sale of house	6,000.00	
	4110		Collected Commission on sale of house		6,000.00
6/8/04	5130	MEMO6	Paid gas bill	22.00	
	1110		Paid gas bill		22.00
6/15/04	5120	MEMO7	Paid salary of the office secretary	350.00	
	1110		Paid salary of the office secretary		350.00
6/17/04	1120	MEMO8	Earned commission on account	6,500.00	
	4110		Earned commission on account		6,500.00

Figure 4.3

Valdez Realty
General Ledger Trial Balance
As of Jun 30, 2004

Filter Criteria includes: Report order is by ID. Report is printed in Detail Format.

Account ID	Account Description	Debit Amt	Credit Amt
1110	Cash	11,243.00	
1120	Accounts Receivable	6,500.00	
1140	Prepaid Rent	1,400.00	
1150	Office Supplies	50.00	
1210	Office Equipment	3,000.00	
1221	Accum. Depr- Office Equipment		100.00
1230	Automobile	12,000.00	
1241	Accum. Depr- Automobile		200.00
2110	Accounts Payable		13,350.00
3110	Juan Valdez, Capital		10,000.00
3120	Juan Valdez Withdrawals	1,000.00	
4110	Commissions Earned		16,000.00
5110	Rent Expense	700.00	
5120	Salaries Expense	700.00	
5130	Gas Expense	47.00	
5140	Repairs Expense	600.00	
5150	Telephone Expense	510.00	
5160	Advertising Expense	1,200.00	
5170	Office Supplies Expense	400.00	
5180	Depr Expense- Office Equipmen	100.00	
5190	Depr Expense- Automobile	200.00	
	Total:	39,650.00	39,650.00

Figure 4.4

Valdez Realty
General Ledger
For the Period From Jun 1, 2004 to Jun 30, 2004
Filter Criteria includes: Report order is by ID. Report is printed with Truncated Transaction Descriptions and in Detail Format.

Account ID Account Description	Date	Reference	Jrnl	Trans Description	Debit Amt	Credit Amt	Balance
1110	6/1/04			Beginning Balance			
Cash	6/1/04	MEMO	GENJ	Owner Investment	7,000.00		
	6/1/04	MEMO1	GENJ	Prepaid 3 months rent		2,100.00	
	6/4/04	MEMO3	GENJ	Purchased Office Suppl		300.00	
	6/6/04	MEMO5	GENJ	Collected Commission	6,000.00		
	6/8/04	MEMO6	GENJ	Paid gas bill		22.00	
	6/15/04	MEMO7	GENJ	Paid salary of the offic		350.00	
	6/20/04	MEMO9	GENJ	Juan Valdez withdrawal		1,000.00	
	6/21/04	MEMO10	GENJ	Earned Commission o	3,500.00		
	6/22/04	MEMO11	GENJ	Paid gas bill		25.00	
	6/24/04	MEMO12	GENJ	Paid automobile repair		600.00	
	6/30/04	MEMO13	GENJ	Paid the salary of the		350.00	
	6/30/04	MEMO14	GENJ	Paid the June telephon		510.00	
				Current Period Change	16,500.00	5,257.00	11,243.00
	6/30/04			Ending Balance			11,243.00
1120	6/1/04			Beginning Balance			
Accounts Receivable	6/17/04	MEMO8	GENJ	Earned commission on	6,500.00		
				Current Period Change	6,500.00		6,500.00
	6/30/04			Ending Balance			6,500.00
1140	6/1/04			Beginning Balance			
Prepaid Rent	6/1/04	MEMO1	GENJ	Prepaid 3 months rent	2,100.00		
	6/30/04	ADJ JUNE	GENJ	Rent expired		700.00	
				Current Period Change	2,100.00	700.00	1,400.00

Figure 4.5

Valdez Realty
Income Statement
For the Six Months Ending June 30, 2004

	Current Month			Year to Date	
Revenues					
Commissions Earned	$ 16,000.00	100.00	$	16,000.00	100.00
Total Revenues	16,000.00	100.00		16,000.00	100.00
Cost of Sales					
Total Cost of Sales	0.00	0.00		0.00	0.00
Gross Profit	16,000.00	100.00		16,000.00	100.00
Expenses					
Rent Expense	700.00	4.38		700.00	4.38
Salaries Expense	700.00	4.38		700.00	4.38
Gas Expense	47.00	0.29		47.00	0.29
Repairs Expense	600.00	3.75		600.00	3.75
Telephone Expense	510.00	3.19		510.00	3.19
Advertising Expense	1,200.00	7.50		1,200.00	7.50
Office Supplies Expense	400.00	2.50		400.00	2.50
Depr Expense- Office Equipment	100.00	0.63		100.00	0.63
Depr Expense- Automobile	200.00	1.25		200.00	1.25
Miscellaneous Expense	0.00	0.00		0.00	0.00
Total Expenses	4,457.00	27.86		4,457.00	27.86
Net Income	$ 11,543.00	72.14	$	11,543.00	72.14

Figure 4.6

```
                                            Valdez Realty
                                            Balance Sheet
                                            June 30, 2004

                                                  ASSETS

Current Assets
Cash                              $        11,243.00
Accounts Receivable                         6,500.00
Prepaid Rent                                1,400.00
Office Supplies                                50.00
                                      _____

Total Current Assets                                        19,193.00

Property and Equipment
Office Equipment                            3,000.00
Accum. Depr- Office Equipment                (100.00)
Automobile                                 12,000.00
Accum. Depr- Automobile                      (200.00)
                                      _____

Total Property and Equipment                               14,700.00

Other Assets
                                      _____

Total Other Assets                                              0.00
                                                         _____

Total Assets                      $                         33,893.00
                                                         ==============



                                          LIABILITIES AND CAPITAL
```

Figure 4.7

```
Current Liabilities
Accounts Payable                  $        13,350.00

Total Current Liabilities                                  13,350.00

Long-Term Liabilities
                                      _____

Total Long-Term Liabilities                                    0.00
                                                         _____

Total Liabilities                                          13,350.00

Capital
Juan Valdez, Capital                       10,000.00
Juan Valdez Withdrawals                    (1,000.00)
Net Income                                 11,543.00
                                      _____

Total Capital                                              20,543.00
                                                         _____

Total Liabilities & Capital       $                        33,893.00
                                                         ==============
```

Figure 4.8

2. Review your printed reports.

3. If you made an error in a posted journal entry, make any necessary corrections.

4. Reprint all reports in which you made corrections.

Preparing to Close the Books for June

Computerized accounting systems maintain all their input in compartments called *periods*. Some systems identify these periods with the name of the month or with a simple numeric designation, such as 1, 2, 3, and so on. Valdez Realty is currently in Period 6, the June period. (You can see this in the status bar at the bottom of the screen.) Valdez has elected to use a calendar year.

You need to change the current period to the July period prior to inputting the July transactions in Part B of this workshop. You must always tell Peachtree to move to the next accounting period before starting on the transactions for a new month. This process is the equivalent of closing in a manual accounting system, although the temporary accounts are not really closed until the end of the year. You advance the period after you back up your June accounting records.

Backing Up the Company Data File

It is always wise to back up accounting data at the end of each month, saving it into a file that you keep until the end of the year:

1. Select **Backup** from the **File** menu.

2. Click the check box to include the company name in the file name.

3. Add **EndJun** to the name of the file. Most companies save the monthly backup files until the year is over and taxes have been filed.

4. Select the **Save in** lookup box to find the location your instructor has identified for you to keep your backup file(s).

5. Click **Save.**

6. Click **OK.**

   ➢ **NOTE:** Refer to Chapter 1 for more detailed instructions on backing up files.

Advancing the Accounting Period to July

You now need to advance the period to prepare Peachtree for the July transactions:

1. Click **System** from the **Tasks** menu.

2. Select **Change Accounting Periods**. Your screen should look like Figure 4.9.

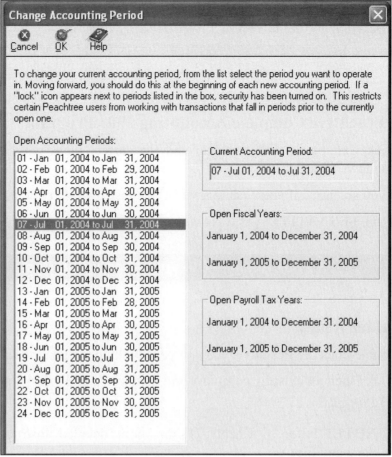

Figure 4.9

3. Using the **Open Accounting Periods** list on the left, select **07- Jul 1, 2004 to Jul 31, 2004.**

4. Click the **OK** icon at the top of the screen.

5. You are asked whether you want to print reports before continuing. Because you have already printed the reports, click the **No** button.

6. If you are presented with the window shown in Figure 4.10, check the box next to **Do not display this message again** and Click the **No** button.

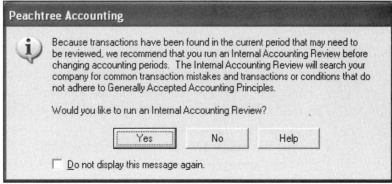

Figure 4.10

> **NOTE:** As shown in Figure 4.11, the status bar at the bottom of the screen now reflects that you are in **Period 7 - 7/1/04 to 7/31/04**.

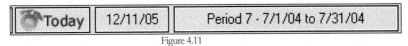

Figure 4.11

Exiting the Peachtree Complete Accounting 2006 Program

1. Click **Exit** on the **File** menu to end the current work session and return to your Windows desktop.

2. If you are asked if you wish to save any unposted work, click the **Yes** button.

   > **ALTERNATIVE:** Continue with the July Accounting Cycle.

Valdez Realty—The July Accounting Cycle

Opening Valdez Realty

1. Double-click the **Peachtree** icon on your desktop to open the software program.

2. Click **Open an existing company** and then locate and select **Valdez Realty.**

3. Click **Open.**

   > **NOTE:** Refer to Chapter 1 for more detailed instructions about opening company files.

Recording the July General Journal Entries

1. From the **Tasks** menu select **General Journal Entry**. You should now be looking at the *General Journal Entry* dialog box.

2. In the **Date** field enter the date listed for each transaction.

3. In the **Reference** field enter **Memo** or accept Peachtree's additional number added to **Memo** by pressing **Tab:**

   2004
   Jul.
   - 1 Purchased additional office supplies on account, $700.
   - 2 Paid advertising bill for June, $1,200.
   - 3 Sold a house and collected a commission, $6,600.
   - 6 Paid for gas expense, $29.
   - 8 Collected the $6,500 commission from sale of building lot on 6/17/04 (collected the accounts receivable).
   - 12 Paid $300 to send employees to realtors' workshop (miscellaneous expense).
   - 15 Paid the salary of the office secretary, $350.
   - 17 Sold a house and earned a commission of $2,400. Expect receipt on 8/10/04.

18   Sold a building lot and collected a commission of $7,000.

22   Sent a check for $40 to help sponsor a local road race to aid the public (miscellaneous expense).

24   Paid for repairs to automobile, $590.

28   Withdrew $1,800 from the business to pay personal expenses.

30   Paid the salary of the office secretary, $350.

30   Paid the July telephone bill, $590.

30   Advertising bill for July, $1,400. The bill is to be paid on 8/2/04.

4.   After you have posted (saved) all the journal entries, click the **Close** button or icon to exit the *General Journal Entry* dialog box.

Printing the Working Reports for July

1.   Print the General Journal report (see Figure 4.12) and Trial Balance report (see Figure 4.13), accepting all defaults.

Valdez Realty
General Journal
For the Period From Jul 1, 2004 to Jul 31, 2004
Filter Criteria includes: Report order is by Date. Report is printed with Accounts having Zero Amounts and with Truncated Transaction Descripti

Date	Account ID	Reference	Trans Description	Debit Amt	Credit Amt
7/1/04	1150	Memo	Purchased office supplies on account	700.00	
	2110		Purchased office supplies on account		700.00
7/2/04	2110	Memo1	Paid advertising Bill for June	1,200.00	
	1110		Paid advertising Bill for June		1,200.00
7/3/04	1110	Memo2	Received commission on sale of house	6,600.00	
	4110		Received commission on sale of house		6,600.00
7/6/04	5130	Memo3	Paid gas expense	29.00	
	1110		Paid gas expense		29.00
7/8/04	1110	Memo4	Collected accounts receivable	6,500.00	
	1120		Collected accounts receivable		6,500.00
7/12/04	5200	Memo5	Workshop for Employees	300.00	
	1110		Workshop for Employees		300.00
7/15/04	5120	Memo6	Paid the salary of the office secretary	350.00	
	1110		Paid the salary of the office secretary		350.00
7/17/04	1120	Memo7	Earned commission on sale of house	2,400.00	
	4110		Earned commission on sale of house		2,400.00
7/18/04	1110	Memo8	Received a commission on the sale of buildi	7,000.00	
	4110		Received a commission on the sale of buildi		7,000.00

Figure 4.12

```
                                          Valdez Realty
                                   General Ledger Trial Balance
                                        As of Jul 31, 2004
Filter Criteria includes: Report order is by ID. Report is printed in Detail Format.

Account ID   Account Description          Debit Amt     Credit Amt

1110         Cash                         26,094.00
1120         Accounts Receivable           2,400.00
1140         Prepaid Rent                  1,400.00
1150         Office Supplies                 750.00
1210         Office Equipment              3,000.00
1221         Accum. Depr- Office Equipment               100.00
1230         Automobile                   12,000.00
1241         Accum. Depr- Automobile                     200.00
2110         Accounts Payable                         14,250.00
3110         Juan Valdez, Capital                     10,000.00
3120         Juan Valdez Withdrawals       2,800.00
4110         Commissions Earned                       32,000.00
5110         Rent Expense                    700.00
5120         Salaries Expense              1,400.00
5130         Gas Expense                      76.00
5140         Repairs Expense               1,190.00
5150         Telephone Expense             1,100.00
5160         Advertising Expense           2,600.00
5170         Office Supplies Expense         400.00
5180         Depr Expense- Office Equipmen   100.00
5190         Depr Expense- Automobile        200.00
5200         Miscellaneous Expense           340.00

             Total:                       56,550.00     56,550.00
```

Figure 4.13

2. Review your printed reports. If you made an error in a posted journal entry, correct the error before proceeding. Reprint the reports, if necessary.

Adjusting Journal Entries for July

Using the Trial Balance report you just printed for July, analyze and enter the following journal entries for the end of July:

1. Open the *General Journal Entry* dialog box from the **Task** menu.

2. In the **Date** field enter **7/31/04**.

3. In the **Reference** field enter **ADJ JULY**.

4. Enter the following adjustments as one general journal entry:

   a. One month's rent has expired.

   b. An inventory shows $90 of office supplies remaining.

   c. Depreciation on office equipment, $100.

   d. Depreciation on automobile, $200.

5. Click the **Save** button.

6. Click the **Close** button to exit the *General Journal Entry* window.

Printing the Final Reports for July

1. Print the General Journal, Trial Balance, General Ledger, Income Statement, and Balance Sheet reports, accepting all defaults (see Figures 4/14 – 4.19).

- 50 -

> **NOTE:** Refer to Chapter 2 for more detailed instructions regarding printing reports.

				Valdez Realty	
				General Journal	
				For the Period From Jul 1, 2004 to Jul 31, 2004	
Filter Criteria includes: Report order is by Date. Report is printed with Accounts having Zero Amounts and with Truncated Transaction Descriptions					
Date	**Account ID**	**Reference**	**Trans Description**	**Debit Amt**	**Credit Amt**
7/22/04	5200	Memo9	Sponsored a local road race	40.00	
	1110		Sponsored a local road race		40.00
7/24/04	5140	Memo10	Automobile repairs	590.00	
	1110		Automobile repairs		590.00
7/28/04	3120	Memo11	Juan Valdez withdrew funds	1,800.00	
	1110		Juan Valdez withdrew funds		1,800.00
7/30/04	5120	Memo12	Paid the salary of the office secretary	350.00	
	1110		Paid the salary of the office secretary		350.00
7/30/04	5150	Memo13	Paid telephone bill	590.00	
	1110		Paid telephone bill		590.00
7/30/04	5160	Memo14	Received advertising bill to pay in August	1,400.00	
	2110		Received advertising bill to pay in August		1,400.00
7/31/04	5110	ADJ JULY	One months rent expired	700.00	
	1140		One months rent expired		700.00
	5170		Supplies expense	660.00	
	1150		Supplies expense		660.00
	5180		Depreciation on office equipment	100.00	
	1221		Depreciation on office equipment		100.00
	5190		Depreciation on automobile	200.00	
	1241		Depreciation on automobile		200.00
		Total		31,509.00	31,509.00

Figure 4.14

Valdez Realty
General Ledger Trial Balance
As of Jul 31, 2004

Filter Criteria includes: Report order is by ID. Report is printed in Detail Format.

Account ID	Account Description	Debit Amt	Credit Amt
1110	Cash	26,094.00	
1120	Accounts Receivable	2,400.00	
1140	Prepaid Rent	700.00	
1150	Office Supplies	90.00	
1210	Office Equipment	3,000.00	
1221	Accum. Depr- Office Equipment		200.00
1230	Automobile	12,000.00	
1241	Accum. Depr- Automobile		400.00
2110	Accounts Payable		14,250.00
3110	Juan Valdez, Capital		10,000.00
3120	Juan Valdez Withdrawals	2,800.00	
4110	Commissions Earned		32,000.00
5110	Rent Expense	1,400.00	
5120	Salaries Expense	1,400.00	
5130	Gas Expense	76.00	
5140	Repairs Expense	1,190.00	
5150	Telephone Expense	1,100.00	
5160	Advertising Expense	2,600.00	
5170	Office Supplies Expense	1,060.00	
5180	Depr Expense- Office Equipmen	200.00	
5190	Depr Expense- Automobile	400.00	
5200	Miscellaneous Expense	340.00	
	Total:	56,850.00	56,850.00

Figure 4.15

Valdez Realty
General Ledger
For the Period From Jul 1, 2004 to Jul 31, 2004

Filter Criteria includes: Report order is by ID. Report is printed with Truncated Transaction Descriptions and in Detail Format.

Account ID Account Description	Date	Reference	Jrnl	Trans Description	Debit Amt	Credit Amt	Balance
1110	7/1/04			Beginning Balance			11,243.00
Cash	7/2/04	Memo1	GENJ	Paid advertising Bill fo		1,200.00	
	7/3/04	Memo2	GENJ	Received commission	6,600.00		
	7/6/04	Memo3	GENJ	Paid gas expense		29.00	
	7/8/04	Memo4	GENJ	Collected accounts rec	6,500.00		
	7/12/04	Memo5	GENJ	Workshop for Employ		300.00	
	7/15/04	Memo6	GENJ	Paid the salary of the		350.00	
	7/18/04	Memo8	GENJ	Received a commissio	7,000.00		
	7/22/04	Memo9	GENJ	Sponsored a local road		40.00	
	7/24/04	Memo10	GENJ	Automobile repairs		590.00	
	7/28/04	Memo11	GENJ	Juan Valdez withdrew f		1,800.00	
	7/30/04	Memo12	GENJ	Paid the salary of the		350.00	
	7/30/04	Memo13	GENJ	Paid telephone bill		590.00	
				Current Period Change	20,100.00	5,249.00	14,851.00
	7/31/04			Ending Balance			26,094.00
1120	7/1/04			Beginning Balance			6,500.00
Accounts Receivable	7/8/04	Memo4	GENJ	Collected accounts rec		6,500.00	
	7/17/04	Memo7	GENJ	Earned commission on	2,400.00		
				Current Period Change	2,400.00	6,500.00	-4,100.00
	7/31/04			Ending Balance			2,400.00

Figure 4.16

	Valdez Realty
	Income Statement
	For the Seven Months Ending July 31, 2004

	Current Month		Year to Date	
Revenues				
Commissions Earned	$ 16,000.00	100.00	$ 32,000.00	100.00
Total Revenues	16,000.00	100.00	32,000.00	100.00
Cost of Sales				
Total Cost of Sales	0.00	0.00	0.00	0.00
Gross Profit	16,000.00	100.00	32,000.00	100.00
Expenses				
Rent Expense	700.00	4.38	1,400.00	4.38
Salaries Expense	700.00	4.38	1,400.00	4.38
Gas Expense	29.00	0.18	76.00	0.24
Repairs Expense	590.00	3.69	1,190.00	3.72
Telephone Expense	590.00	3.69	1,100.00	3.44
Advertising Expense	1,400.00	8.75	2,600.00	8.13
Office Supplies Expense	660.00	4.13	1,060.00	3.31
Depr Expense- Office Equipment	100.00	0.63	200.00	0.63
Depr Expense- Automobile	200.00	1.25	400.00	1.25
Miscellaneous Expense	340.00	2.13	340.00	1.06
Total Expenses	5,309.00	33.18	9,766.00	30.52
Net Income	$ 10,691.00	66.82	$ 22,234.00	69.48

Figure 4.17

	Valdez Realty
	Balance Sheet
	July 31, 2004
	ASSETS

Current Assets		
Cash	$ 26,094.00	
Accounts Receivable	2,400.00	
Prepaid Rent	700.00	
Office Supplies	90.00	
Total Current Assets		29,284.00
Property and Equipment		
Office Equipment	3,000.00	
Accum. Depr- Office Equipment	(200.00)	
Automobile	12,000.00	
Accum. Depr- Automobile	(400.00)	
Total Property and Equipment		14,400.00
Other Assets		
Total Other Assets		0.00
Total Assets		$ 43,684.00

Figure 4.18

		LIABILITIES AND CAPITAL
Current Liabilities		
Accounts Payable	$ 14,250.00	
Total Current Liabilities		14,250.00
Long-Term Liabilities		
Total Long-Term Liabilities		0.00
Total Liabilities		14,250.00
Capital		
Juan Valdez, Capital	10,000.00	
Juan Valdez Withdrawals	(2,800.00)	
Net Income	22,234.00	
Total Capital		29,434.00
Total Liabilities & Capital	$	43,684.00

Figure 4.19

2. Review your printed reports. If you have made an error in a posted journal entry, use the procedures detailed in Chapter 2 to make any necessary corrections. Reprint all reports in which corrections are made.

Backing Up Your Company Data File

1. Select **Backup** from the **File** menu.

2. Click the check box to include the company name in the file name.

3. Add **End July** to the file name to make sure you can recognize what the backup represents.

4. Select the **Save in** lookup box to find the location your instructor has identified for you to keep your backup file(s).

5. Click **Save.**

6. Click **OK**.

   ➢ **NOTE:** Refer to Chapter 1 for more detailed instructions on backing up files.

Advancing the Accounting Period to August

You now need to advance the period to prepare Peachtree for the August transactions:

1. Using your mouse, click on **System** from the **Tasks** menu and select **Change Accounting Periods**.

2. Using the pulldown menu, select **period 8 - Aug 1, 2004 to Aug 31, 2004** and click the **OK** button.

3. You are asked whether you wish to print reports before continuing. Because you have already printed the reports, click **No.**

4. As shown in Figure 4.20, the status bar at the bottom of your screen now reflects that you are in **Period 8 - 8/1/04 to 8/31/04**.

| Today | 12/11/05 | Period 8 - 8/1/04 to 8/31/04 |

Figure 4.20

Backing Up Your Company Data File

1. Select **Backup** from the **File** menu.

2. Click the check box to include the company name in the file name.

3. Add **Final** to the file name to make sure you can recognize what the backup represents.

4. Select the **Save in** lookup box to find the location your instructor has identified for you to keep your backup file(s).

5. Click **Save.**

6. Click **OK**.

> **NOTE:** Refer to Chapter 1 for more detailed instructions on backing up files.

Exiting the Peachtree Complete Accounting 2006 Program

1. Click **Exit** from the **File** Menu to end the current work session and return to your Windows desktop.

2. If you are asked if you wish to save any unposted work, click the **Yes** button.

CHAPTER 5

Payroll Requirements for the First Quarter—Pete's Market

THIS WORKSHOP COVERS PAYROLL: THE CALCULATION OF EMPLOYEE PAYCHECKS AND PAYMENT OF THE PAYROLL TAX LIABILITIES FOR THE FIRST QUARTER OF 2004 (JANUARY, FEBRUARY, AND MARCH).

Company Information

Pete's Market, owned by Pete Real, is located at 4 Sun Avenue, Swampscott, Massachusetts 01970. His employer identification number is 42-4583312.

Peachtree automatically calculates federal income tax (FIT), state income tax (SIT), Social Security, Medicare, federal unemployment tax (FUTA), and state unemployment tax (SUTA). The calculations in the Education version are examples and should not be used for a live payroll.

Employees are paid monthly. The payroll is recorded and paid on the last day of each month. The company uses a payroll checking account, and the net pay must be transferred to that account as part of the payroll process.

The Payroll module in Peachtree Complete Accounting 2006 is designed to work with the General Ledger module in an integrated fashion. When transactions are recorded in the Payroll Journal, the program automatically updates the employee records, records the journal entry, and posts to all the accounts affected in the general ledger.

The following are the employees of Pete's Market and the monthly wages they will earn for the first payroll quarter:

	January	February	March
Fred Flynn	$2,500	$2,590	$2,500
Mary Jones	3,000	3,000	3,000
Lilly Vron	3,000	3,400	3,000

The trial balance for Pete's Market at 1/1/04 appears in Figure 5.1.

You can print the Trial Balance report for yourself; to do so, in the *Select a Report* dialog box, under the **General Ledger** report section, select the **General Ledger Trial Balance** report.

```
                                                        Pete's Market
                                              General Ledger Trial Balance
                                                   As of Jan 31, 2004
Filter Criteria includes: Report order is by ID. Report is printed in Detail Format.

Account ID    Account Description        Debit Amt     Credit Amt

1010          Cash                       84,964.04
2310          FIT Payable                               1,415.94
2320          SIT Payable                                 535.50
2330          Social Security Tax Payable               1,116.00
2335          Medicare Tax Payable                        261.00
2340          FUTA Payable                                 48.00
2350          SUTA Payable                              1,587.60
3569          Pete Reel, Capital                       80,000.00

              Total:                     84,964.04     84,964.04
```

Figure 5.1

Opening the Pete's Market File

1. Double-click the **Peachtree** icon on your desktop to open the software program.

2. Click **Open an existing company**, and then locate and select **Pete's Market**.

3. Click **Open**.

   ➢ **NOTE:** Refer to Chapter 1 for more detailed instructions on opening company files.

Backing Up Your Company Data File

1. Select **Back up** from the **File** menu.

2. Click the check box to include the company name in the file name.

3. Add **Start** to the company name.

4. Select the **Save in** lookup box to find the location your instructor has identified for you to keep your backup file(s).

5. Click **Save.**

6. Click **OK**.

   ➢ **NOTE:** Refer to Chapter 1 for more detailed instructions on backing up files.

Adding your name to the company name

1. Click the **Maintain** menu, and then select **Company Information**. The program responds by bringing up the *Maintain Company Information* dialog box, which allows you to edit/add information about the company.

2. Click in the **Company Name** field and make sure your cursor is at the end of **Pete's Market**.

3. Add a dash and your name (**-Student's Name**).

4. Click the **OK** button.

   ➤ **NOTE:** Refer to Chapter 2 for more detailed instructions on adding your name to the company name.

Pete's Market—January Payroll Transactions

Recording the Payment of December's Payroll Liabilities and Taxes

Record the payment of December's payroll liabilities, using the *General Journal Entry* window:

1. Using the Trial Balance report for January 1, 2004, you can find the payroll liability amounts to make the tax payments.

2. Click **General Journal Entry** from the **Task** menu to open the *General Journal Entry* window.

3. In the **Date** field enter the date for each transaction.

4. Enter **Memo** in the **Reference** text box for each transaction or accept Peachtree's number added to **Memo** by pressing Tab.

5. Use the Cash account (number 1010) to pay these liabilities:

   2004
   Jan. 15 Record the compound journal entry for the payment of federal taxes including Social Security, Medicare, and FIT from last month's payroll. In the description field enter **941 Payment**. Total payment, $2,792.94.
   15 Record the payment of the SIT. Total, $535.50
   31 Record the payment of SUTA from last quarter. Total, $1,587.60.
   31 Record the payment of FUTA owed. In the description field enter **940 Payment** Total, $48.00

6. Close the *General Journal Entry* window.

7. Select **General Ledger** from the **Reports** menu. Select **General Ledger Trial Balance** from the **Report List** area of the *Select a Report* dialog box to verify that you have properly paid all the liabilities. Your screen should look like Figure 5.2.

Pete's Market-Student Name
General Ledger Trial Balance
As of Jan 31, 2004

Filter Criteria includes: Report order is by ID. Report is printed in Detail Format.

Account ID	Account Description	Debit Amt	Credit Amt
1010	Cash	80,000.00	
3569	Pete Reel, Capital		80,000.00
	Total:	80,000.00	80,000.00

Figure 5.2

8. Click the **Print** button to print the **General Ledger Trial Balance** report, accepting all defaults.

9. After you have verified the payment of the liabilities, close the General Ledger Trial Balance report and the *Select a Report* dialog box.

Recording the January Payroll

Peachtree has two options for paying employees. Both are available using the **Payroll navigation aid** at the bottom of your screen.

➢ **NOTE:** If the Navigation Aid toolbar is not showing, go to the **Options** menu and select **View Navigation Aids**.

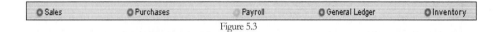

Figure 5.3

1. Click the **Payroll** Payroll icon on the Navigation Aids toolbar. This brings up the *Peachtree Today – Navigation Aids Payroll* dialog box, shown in Figure 5.4

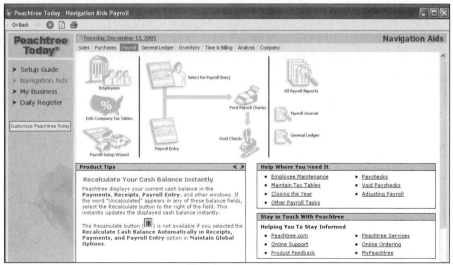

Figure 5.4

There are two options in the center section of the ***Peachtree Today - Navigation Aids Payroll*** dialog box:

- **Select for Payroll Entry** selects all employees who meet specific criteria

- **Payroll Entry** allows you to select the employees one by one.

2. Because the company is paying all the salaried employees, select the **Select for Payroll Entry** 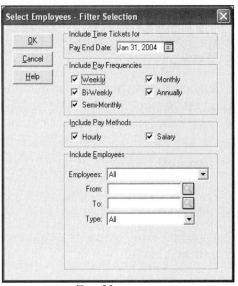 icon. This brings up the ***Select Employees – Filter Selection*** dialog box, as shown in Figure 5.5.

Figure 5.5

3. Because the company pays its employees monthly, on the last day of the month, change **Pay End Date** to **January 31, 2004**.

➢ **NOTE:** You can use the small calendar to the right of the field to select the date, or you can type the date in the field.

The other filters allow you to specify a certain pay frequency, pay method (hourly and/or salary), type of employee, or range of employees by employee number. You can explore these options, but be sure to return the dialog box to the values shown in Figure 5.5.

4. Click the **OK** button to continue. This brings up the ***Select Employees to Pay*** dialog box, shown in Figure 5.6.

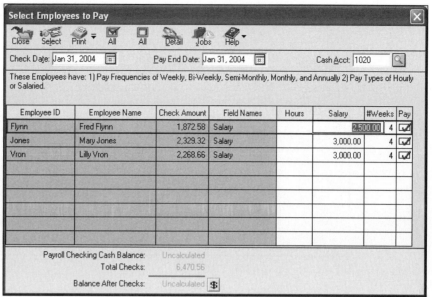

Figure 5.62

Notice that Peachtree has selected all three of the employees by flagging each for payment with a red checkmark in the Pay column. It has also calculated all the required withholdings and payroll taxes for each employee.

5. Because the employees are paid on the last day of the month, make sure the **Check Date** reflects **January 31, 2004**.

6. In the **Cash Acct** field, enter **1020** for the Payroll checking account.

CHECK IT OUT: If you want to see the detail on any of the employees, simply double-click that employee's entry to open the *Select Employees to Pay – Detail* dialog box, as shown in Figure 5.7.

Double-click the **Fred Flynn** entry. You can change any of the numbers presented in the white fields of this dialog box by double-clicking the number you want to change. Be sure that you do not change any of the information presented at this time.

Click the **Cancel** icon or the **Close** button on the *Select Employees to Pay – Detail* dialog box. If you are asked if you want to save the changes, click **No.**

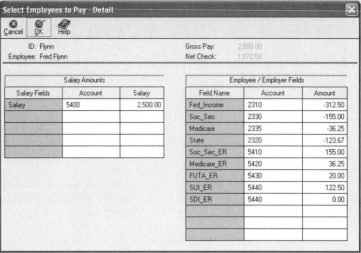

Figure 5.7

Printing Employee Paychecks

1. Click the **Print** ![Print icon] icon to print the checks and post this transaction.

2. The ***Print Forms: Payroll Checks*** dialog box is presented (see Figure 5.8).

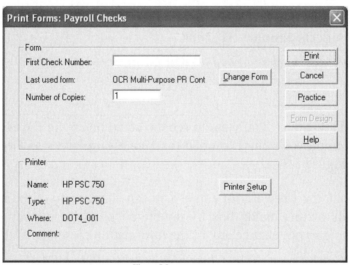

Figure 5.8

3. Click the **Change Form** button, and you are presented with the screen shown in Figure 5.9.

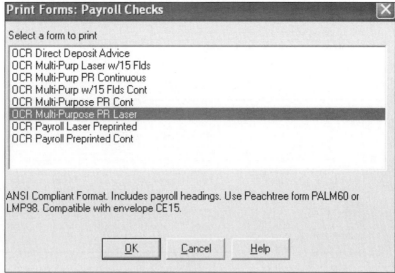

Figure 5.9

4. Select **OCR Multi-Purpose PR Laser**, to print to a blank sheet of paper, when the format does not matter. In a working situation, you would determine the correct form to use.

5. Click the **OK** button to return to the ***Print Forms: Payroll Checks*** dialog box.

6. In the first **Check number** field enter **001** because this is the first set of payroll checks you will issue for this company.

7. Click **OK** to print the checks.

You may need to tell your printer to continue because it will wait for you to insert the check forms. After you tell it to continue, it prints the checks on the blank paper.

When the checks have finished printing, you are asked to confirm the printing process. This feature allows you to print the checks a second time if something interfered with the printing process the first time through.

8. Click the **Yes** button to confirm that the checks printed properly. Peachtree creates and posts all the necessary journal entries internally.

Displaying and Printing a Payroll Register

1. In the ***Peachtree Today – Navigations Aids Payroll*** dialog box select the **All Payroll Reports** option from the right section of the window. This brings up the ***Select a Report*** dialog box, which lists the payroll reports you can display and print.

2. Double-click the **Payroll Register** report to see the details of the checks you just issued (see Figure 5.10).

Pete's Market-Student Name
Payroll Register
For the Period From Jan 1, 2004 to Jan 31, 2004
Filter Criteria includes: Report order is by Check Date. Report is printed in Detail Format.

Employee ID Employee SS No Reference Date	Pay Type	Pay Hrs	Pay Amt	Amount	Gross State SUI_ER	Fed_Income Soc_Sec_ER SDI_ER	Soc_Sec Medicare_ER	Medicare FUTA_ER
Flynn	Salary		2,500.00	1,872.58	2,500.00	-312.50	-155.00	-36.25
Fred Flynn					-123.67	-155.00	-36.25	-20.00
					-122.50			
001								
1/31/04								
Jones	Salary		3,000.00	2,329.32	3,000.00	-310.00	-186.00	-43.50
Mary Jones					-131.18	-186.00	-43.50	-24.00
					-147.00			
002								
1/31/04								
Vron	Salary		3,000.00	2,268.66	3,000.00	-366.25	-186.00	-43.50
Lilly Vron					-135.59	-186.00	-43.50	-24.00
					-147.00			
003								
1/31/04								
Summary Total	Salary		8,500.00	6,470.56	8,500.00	-988.75	-527.00	-123.25
1/1/04 thru 1/31/04					-390.44	-527.00	-123.25	-68.00
					-416.50			

Figure 5.10

3. Click the **Print** icon, accepting all the defaults.

4. Click the **Close** button or icon to exit the report.

5. Click the **Close** button or icon on the *Select a Report* window.

Transferring Funds from One Checking Account to Another

Because the paychecks are drawn on the Payroll Checking account, you need to transfer money from the Regular Cash account to cover the net pay (the amount of the checks) to the Payroll Checking account. Refer to the Payroll Register report you just printed (as shown in Figure 5.10), and you see $6,470.56 in the total row/net pay column at the bottom of the report.

1. Click the **General Ledger** icon on the **Navigation Aids** toolbar or the **General Ledger File** tab in the *Peachtree Today - Navigation Aids* dialog box.

2. Click the **General Journal Entry** icon in the left section of your screen. This brings up the *General Journal Entry* window.

3. In the **Date** field enter **1/31/04**, and press the **Tab** key.

4. In the **Reference** field enter **Memo** and press the **Tab** key.

5. Select **GL Account 1020 Payroll Checking Cash**.

6. Enter **Transfer net payroll** in the **Description** field.

7. Enter **6470.56** in the **Debit** field.

8. On the second line in the **GL Account** select **1010 Cash**.

9. Tab to the **Credit** field and enter **6470.56** again.

10. Click the **Save** icon to post the transaction.

11. Click the **Close** button or icon to exit the *General Journal Entry* window.

Printing the General Journal and the General Ledger Trial Balance

1. Click the **General Journal** [General Journal] icon located in the far right section of the *Peachtree Today – Navigation Aids - General Ledger* dialog box.

2. When the *General Journal* window opens, click **OK** to accept all defaults. The window shown in Figure 5.11 appears.

3. Click the **Print** icon and then **OK**.

			Pete's Market-Student Name		
			General Journal		
			For the Period From Jan 1, 2004 to Jan 31, 2004		
Filter Criteria includes: Report order is by Date. Report is printed with Accounts having Zero Amounts and with Truncated Transaction Descriptio					
Date	**Account ID**	**Reference**	**Trans Description**	**Debit Amt**	**Credit Amt**
1/15/04	2310	MEMO	941 Payment	1,415.94	
	2330		941 Payment	1,116.00	
	2335		941 Payment	261.00	
	1010		941 Payment		2,792.94
1/15/04	2320	MEMO1	SIT Payment	535.50	
	1010		SIT Payment		535.50
1/31/04	2350	MEMO2	SUTA - Tax Payment	1,587.60	
	1010		SUTA - Tax Payment		1,587.60
1/31/04	2340	MEMO3	940 Payment	48.00	
	1010		940 Payment		48.00
1/31/04	1020	MEMO4	Transfer net payroll	6,470.56	
	1010		Transfer net payroll		6,470.56
		Total		11,434.60	11,434.60

Figure 5.11

4. Click the **Close** button on the General Journal report, and you are returned to the *Peachtree Today - General Ledger Navigation Aid* window.

5. Click the **All General Ledger Reports** icon to bring up the *Select a Report* dialog box.

6. Double-click **General Ledger Trial Balance** in the **Report List** section of the *Select a Report* window.

7. Click the **Print** icon and then **OK**. The report shown in Figure 5.12 prints.

```
                                              Pete's Market-Student Name
                                              General Ledger Trial Balance
                                                   As of Jan 31, 2004
Filter Criteria includes: Report order is by ID. Report is printed in Detail Format.

Account ID    Account Description        Debit Amt      Credit Amt

1010          Cash                       73,529.44
2310          FIT Payable                                 988.75
2320          SIT Payable                                 390.44
2330          Social Security Tax  Payable              1,054.00
2335          Medicare Tax  Payable                       246.50
2340          FUTA  Payable                                68.00
2350          SUTA  Payable                               416.50
3569          Pete Reel, Capital                       80,000.00
5400          Wages Expense               8,500.00
5410          Social Security Tax Expense   527.00
5420          Medicare Tax Expense         123.25
5430          FUTA Expense                  68.00
5440          SUTA Expense                 416.50

              Total:                      83,164.19      83,164.19
```

Figure 5.12

8. Review your printed reports. If you have made an error in a posted journal entry, make any corrections, using the detailed instructions in Chapter 2.

9. Reprint the reports if you make changes.

10. Click the **Close** button to exit the report displayed on your screen and return to the *Navigation Aid* window.

Backing Up Your Company Data File

It is always wise to backup accounting data at the end of each month, saving it to a folder that you keep until the end of the year. Follow these steps:

1. Click the **Company** icon in the **Navigation Aid** toolbar. Click the **Backup** icon located in the third section of the *Company Navigation Aid* window.

2. In the *Backup* window make sure to check the box to include the company name.

3. Add **EndJan** to the file name to make sure you can recognize what the backup represents.

4. Click **OK**.

Advancing the Period to February

You now need to advance the period to prepare Peachtree for the February transactions:

1. Double-click the period in the Peachtree status bar at the bottom of your screen, as shown in Figure 5.13.

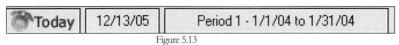

Figure 5.13

2. You now see the *Change Accounting Period* dialog box, shown in Figure 5.14.

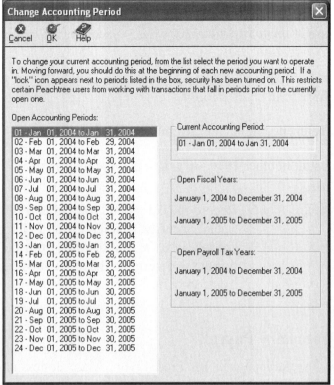

Figure 5.14

3. From the **Open Accounting Periods** list select **2 - Feb 1, 2004 to Feb 29, 2004**.

4. Click the **Ok** icon.

5. You may be asked whether you want to print the reports before continuing. Because you have already printed the reports, select **No**.

6. Note that the status bar at the bottom of the screen now reflects Period 2, ash shown in Figure 5.15.

Figure 5.15

Pete's Market—February Payroll Transactions

Paying the January Payroll Liabilities and Taxes

Record the following general journal entry:

1. Click the **General Ledger** icon in the **Navigation Aids** toolbar at the bottom of your screen.

2. Click on **General Journal Entry** icon in the center section of the *Peachtree Today Navigation Aids – General Ledger* dialog box. This brings up the *General Ledger Entry* dialog box.

3. In the **Date** field enter **2/16/04**.

4. In the **Reference** field enter **Memo**.

5. Use account number **1010 – Cash** to pay the liability:

> 2004
> Feb.   16   Record the compound journal entry for the payment of Social Security, Medicare, and FIT from last month's payroll. Use the trial balance from 1/31/04 that you just printed to determine the amounts owed (liabilities). Total amount, $2,289.25.

Recording the February Payroll

Record the February payroll for Fred Flynn, Mary Jones, and Lilly Vron. Both Fred Flynn and Lilly Vron are making more than their usual amounts this month. Fred will earn $2,590 instead of his usual $2,500, and Lilly will earn $3,400 instead of her usual $3,000. Refer to the beginning of this chapter for the table of wages.

1. Click the **Payroll** icon in the **Navigation Aids** toolbar at the bottom of your screen.

2. With the *Peachtree Today Navigation Aids—Payroll* dialog box on your screen, click the **Select for Payroll Entry** icon. This brings up the *Select Employees – Filter Selection* dialog box.

3. Change the **Date** to reflect February 29, 2004.

4. Click **OK** to accept the defaults.

5. Double-click Fred's ($2,590) and Lilly's ($3,400) **salary** fields to change their salaries to the correct amounts for February.

6. In the **Cash Account** field, be sure to use account **1020**, the payroll account.

7. Print the payroll checks the same way you did in January, except using the date February 29.

8. Peachtree automatically starts with Check 004.

Printing the Payroll Register

Print the Payroll Register report, accepting all defaults, just like January except, using the date February 29 for your report. Your printed report should look like Figure 5.16.

Pete's Market-Student Name
Payroll Register
For the Period From Feb 1, 2004 to Feb 29, 2004
Filter Criteria includes: Report order is by Check Date. Report is printed in Detail Format.

Employee ID Employee SS No Reference Date	Pay Type	Pay Hrs	Pay Amt	Amount	Gross State SUI_ER	Fed_Income Soc_Sec_ER SDI_ER	Soc_Sec Medicare_ER	Medicare FUTA_ER
Flynn Fred Flynn 004 2/29/04	Salary		2,590.00	1,935.09	2,590.00 -128.44 -126.91	-328.33 -160.58	-160.58 -37.56	-37.56 -20.72
Jones Mary Jones 005 2/29/04	Salary		3,000.00	2,329.32	3,000.00 -131.18 -147.00	-310.00 -186.00	-186.00 -43.50	-43.50 -24.00
Vron Lilly Vron 006 2/29/04	Salary		3,400.00	2,516.86	3,400.00 -156.79 -166.60	-466.25 -210.80	-210.80 -49.30	-49.30 -27.20
Summary Total 2/1/04 thru 2/29/04	Salary		8,990.00	6,781.27	8,990.00 -416.41 -440.51	-1,104.58 -557.38	-557.38 -130.36	-130.36 -71.92

Figure 5.16

Transferring Funds from One Checking Account to Another

Because the paychecks are drawn on the Payroll Checking account, you need to transfer money from the Regular Cash account, 1010, to cover the net pay (the amount of the checks) to the Payroll Checking Account, 1020. Refer to the Payroll Register report, shown in Figure 5.16, and you see $6,781.27 in the total row/net pay column at the bottom of the report.

1. Click the **General Ledger** icon on the **Navigation Aids** toolbar at the bottom of your screen.

2. Click the **General Journal Entry** icon in the left section of your screen. This brings up the *General Journal Entry* window.

3. In the **Date** field enter **2/29/04** and then press the **Tab** key.

4. In the **Reference** field enter **Memo** and then press the **Tab** key.

5. In the **GL Account** field select **1020 Payroll Checking Cash**.

6. Enter **Transfer net payroll** in the **Description** field.

7. Enter **6781.27** in the **Debit** field.

8. On the second row in the **GL Account** select **1010 Cash**.

9. Tab to the **Credit** field and enter **6781.27**.

10. Click the **Save** button to post the transaction.

11. Click the **Close** button or icon to exit the *General Journal Entry* window.

Printing the General Journal and Trial Balance Reports

1. Click the **General Journal** icon in the right section of the *Peachtree Today Navigation Aids - General Ledger* window.

2. Click **OK** to accept the default settings. The report shown in Figure 5.17 appears.

Pete's Market-Student Name
General Journal
For the Period From Feb 1, 2004 to Feb 29, 2004

Filter Criteria includes: Report order is by Date. Report is printed with Accounts having Zero Amounts and with Truncated Transaction Descri

Date	Account ID	Reference	Trans Description	Debit Amt	Credit Amt
2/16/04	2310	MEMO	941 Payment	988.75	
	2330		941 Payment	1,054.00	
	2335		941 Payment	246.50	
	1010		941 Payment		2,289.25
2/29/04	1020	MEMO	Transfer Funds	6,781.27	
	1010		Transfer Funds		6,781.27
		Total		9,070.52	9,070.52

Figure 5.17

3. Click **Print**.

4. Click the **Close** button to exit the report.

5. Double-click **General Ledger Trial Balance** in the *Select a Report* dialog box. The report shown in Figure 5.18 appears.

Pete's Market-Student Name
General Ledger Trial Balance
As of Feb 29, 2004

Filter Criteria includes: Report order is by ID. Report is printed in Detail Format.

Account ID	Account Description	Debit Amt	Credit Amt
1010	Cash	64,458.92	
2310	FIT Payable		1,104.58
2320	SIT Payable		806.85
2330	Social Security Tax Payable		1,114.76
2335	Medicare Tax Payable		260.72
2340	FUTA Payable		139.92
2350	SUTA Payable		857.01
3569	Pete Reel, Capital		80,000.00
5400	Wages Expense	17,490.00	
5410	Social Security Tax Expense	1,084.38	
5420	Medicare Tax Expense	253.61	
5430	FUTA Expense	139.92	
5440	SUTA Expense	857.01	
	Total:	84,283.84	84,283.84

Figure 5.18

6. Click **Print** and accept all defaults.

7. Click the **Close** button to exit the report.

8. Click **Close** to exit the *Select a Report* window.

Backing Up Your Company Data File

1. Select **Back up** from the **File** menu.

2. **Click** the check box to include the company name in the file name.

3. Add **EndFeb** to the file name to make sure you can recognize what the backup represents.

4. Select the **Save in** lookup box to find the location your instructor has identified for you to keep your backup file(s).

5. Click **Save**.

6. Click **OK**.

   ➢ **NOTE:** Refer to Chapter 1 for more detailed instructions on backing up files.

Advancing the Period to March

1. Double-click the period in the Peachtree status bar at the bottom of your screen (See Figure 5.19).

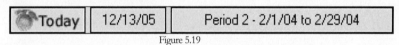

Figure 5.19

2. Using the pull-down menu, select **Period 3 - Mar 1, 2004 to Mar 31, 2004** and Click the **OK** button.

3. You are asked whether you want to print reports before continuing. Because you have already printed the reports, click **No**.

4. Note that the status bar at the bottom of the screen now reflects Period 3 (see Figure 5.20).

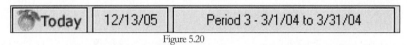

Figure 5.20

Pete's Market—March Payroll Transactions

Recording the Payment of February's Payroll Liabilities and Taxes

Record the following general journal entry, following the detailed instructions for January but using the date below:

2004
Mar.   14   Record the compound journal entry for the deposit of Social
              Security, Medicare, and FIT from last month's payroll.

Recording the March Payroll

Record the March payroll for all three employees, using the detailed instructions for January. Be sure to date both the payroll and the checks March 31, 2004, and use the Payroll Checking account (1020). All three employees will receive their normal salary for this pay period.

Printing the Employee Paychecks

Print the employees' paychecks, following the detailed instructions for January. Date the checks March 31, 2004.

Displaying and Printing the Payroll Register for March

Print the Payroll Register report for March (see Figure 5.21), following the detailed instructions for January.

```
                                        Pete's Market-Student Name
                                          Payroll Register
                                  For the Period From Mar 1, 2004 to Mar 31, 2004
Filter Criteria includes: Report order is by Check Date. Report is printed in Detail Format.
```

Employee ID Employee SS No Reference Date	Pay Type	Pay Hrs	Pay Amt	Amount	Gross State SUI_ER	Fed_Income Soc_Sec_ER SDI_ER	Soc_Sec Medicare_ER	Medicare FUTA_ER
Flynn Fred Flynn 007 3/31/04	Salary		2,500.00	1,872.58	2,500.00 -123.67 -122.50	-312.50 -155.00	-155.00 -36.25	-36.25 -15.28
Jones Mary Jones 008 3/31/04	Salary		3,000.00	2,329.32	3,000.00 -131.18 -147.00	-310.00 -186.00	-186.00 -43.50	-43.50 -8.00
Vron Lilly Vron 009 3/31/04	Salary		3,000.00	2,268.66	3,000.00 -135.59 -147.00	-366.25 -186.00	-186.00 -43.50	-43.50 -4.80
Summary Total 3/1/04 thru 3/31/04	Salary		8,500.00	6,470.56	8,500.00 -390.44 -416.50	-988.75 -527.00	-527.00 -123.25	-123.25 -28.08

Figure 5.21

Transferring Funds from one Checking Account to Another

Enter the journal entry for $6,470.56 to transfer funds into the Payroll Checking account, 1020, from the Cash account, 1010. See the detailed instructions for January, except use the date March 31, 2004.

Printing the General Journal and Trial Balance Reports

1. Print the General Journal and Trial Balance reports accepting all defaults (see Figures 5.22 and 5.23).

Pete's Market-Student Name
General Journal
For the Period From Mar 1, 2004 to Mar 31, 2004

Filter Criteria includes: Report order is by Date. Report is printed with Accounts having Zero Amounts and with Truncated Transaction Descriptions.

Date	Account ID	Reference	Trans Description	Debit Amt	Credit Amt
3/15/04	2310	MEMO	941 Payment	1,104.58	
	2330		941 Payment	1,114.76	
	2335		941 Payment	260.72	
	1010		941 Payment		2,480.06
3/29/04	1020	MEMO	Transfer funds	6,470.56	
	1010		Transfer funds		6,470.56
		Total		8,950.62	8,950.62

Figure 5.22

Pete's Market-Student Name
General Ledger Trial Balance
As of Mar 31, 2004

Filter Criteria includes: Report order is by ID. Report is printed in Detail Format.

Account ID	Account Description	Debit Amt	Credit Amt
1010	Cash	55,508.30	
2310	FIT Payable		988.75
2320	SIT Payable		1,197.29
2330	Social Security Tax Payable		1,054.00
2335	Medicare Tax Payable		246.50
2340	FUTA Payable		168.00
2350	SUTA Payable		1,273.51
3569	Pete Reel, Capital		80,000.00
5400	Wages Expense	25,990.00	
5410	Social Security Tax Expense	1,611.38	
5420	Medicare Tax Expense	376.86	
5430	FUTA Expense	168.00	
5440	SUTA Expense	1,273.51	
	Total:	84,928.05	84,928.05

Figure 5.23

2. Close the *Select a Report* dialog box.

Backing Up March Data

1. From the **File** menu click **Back up**.

2. Click the check box to include the company name in the file name.

3. Add **EndMar** to the file name to make sure you can recognize what the backup represents.

4. Click **OK**.

Advancing the Period to April

1. Double-click the period in the Peachtree status bar at the bottom of your screen.

2. Using the pull-down menu, select **4 – Apr 1, 2004 to Apr 30, 2004**.

3. Click the **OK** button.

4. You are asked whether you wish to print the reports before continuing. Because you have already printed the reports, click **No**.

5. The status bar at the bottom of the screen should now say **Period 4 – 4/1/04 to 4/30/04**.

Pete's Market—April Payroll Transactions

Paying the March Payroll Liabilities and Taxes

Record the following general journal entries, using the dates listed; reference as **Memo**. Pay the liabilities from account **1010 (Cash)**. You can find the payroll liabilities amount on the Trial Balance report you printed for March 31, 2004:

2004
Apr.
15 Record the compound journal entry for the deposit of Social Security, Medicare, and FIT from last month's payroll.
15 Record the payment of SIT from last quarter.
30 Record the payment of SUTA from last quarter.
30 Record the payment of FUTA tax owed.

Printing the Reports for April

Print the General Journal and Trial Balance reports, accepting all defaults (see Figures 5.24 and 5.25).

Pete's Market-Student Name
General Journal
For the Period From Apr 1, 2004 to Apr 30, 2004
Filter Criteria includes: Report order is by Date. Report is printed with Accounts having Zero Amounts and with Truncated Transaction Descriptions and in Detail Fo

Date	Account ID	Reference	Trans Description	Debit Amt	Credit Amt
4/15/04	2310	MEMO	941 Payment	988.75	
	2330		941 Payment	1,054.00	
	2335		941 Payment	246.50	
	1010		941 Payment		2,289.25
4/15/04	2320	MEMO1	SIT payment	1,197.29	
	1010		SIT payment		1,197.29
4/30/04	2350	MEMO2	SUTA payment	1,273.51	
	1010		SUTA payment		1,273.51
4/30/04	2340	MEMO3	FUTA payment	168.00	
	1010		FUTA payment		168.00
		Total		4,928.05	4,928.05

Figure 5.24

Pete's Market-Student Name
General Ledger Trial Balance
As of Apr 30, 2004

Filter Criteria includes: Report order is by ID. Report is printed in Detail Format.

Account ID	Account Description	Debit Amt	Credit Amt
1010	Cash	50,580.25	
3569	Pete Reel, Capital		80,000.00
5400	Wages Expense	25,990.00	
5410	Social Security Tax Expense	1,611.38	
5420	Medicare Tax Expense	376.86	
5430	FUTA Expense	168.00	
5440	SUTA Expense	1,273.51	
	Total:	80,000.00	80,000.00

Figure 5.25

Backing Up Your Company Data File

1. Select **Back up** from the **File** menu.

2. Click the check box to include the company name in the file name.

3. Add **EndApril** to the file name.

4. Select the **Save in** lookup box to find the location your instructor has identified for you to keep your backup file(s).

5. Click **Save**.

6. Click **OK**.

> **NOTE:** Refer to Chapter 1 for more detailed instructions on backing up files.

Exiting the Peachtree Complete Accounting 2006 Program

1. Click **Exit** from the **File** menu to end the current work session and return to your Windows desktop.

2. If you are asked if you wish to save any un-posted work, click the **Yes** button.

CHAPTER 6

Accounts Receivable and Accounts Payable--The Mars Company

THIS WORKSHOP COVERS ACCOUNTS RECEIVABLE AND ACCOUNTS PAYABLE FOR THE MARS COMPANY

Opening the Mars Company File

1. Double-click the **Peachtree** icon on your desktop to open the software program.

2. Click **Open an existing company** and locate and select the **The Mars Company**.

3. Click **Open**.

   ➢ **NOTE:** Refer to Chapter 1 for more detailed instructions on opening files.

Backing Up Your Company Data File

1. Select **Back up** from the **File** menu.

2. **Click** the check box to include the company name in the file name.

3. Add **Start** to the file name.

4. Select the **Save in** lookup box to find the location your instructor has identified for you to keep your backup file(s).

5. Click **Save**.

6. Click **OK**.

   ➢ **NOTE:** Refer to Chapter 1 for more detailed instructions on backing up files.

Adding Your Name to the Company Name

1. Click the **Maintain** menu option and then select **Company Information**. The program responds by bringing up the *Maintain Company Information* dialog box, allowing you to edit/add information about the company.

2. Click in the **Company Name** field and make sure your cursor is at the end of **The Mars Company**.

3. Add a dash and your name (-Student's Name).

4. Click the **OK** button.

   ➢ **NOTE**: Refer to Chapter 2 for more detailed instructions on adding your name to a file name.

The Mars Company: Accounts Receivable

Sales/Invoicing and Cash Receipts Overview

The **Sales/Invoicing** and **Receipts** windows in Peachtree Complete Accounting 2006 are designed to work with the Accounts Receivable and General Ledger modules in an integrated fashion. When transactions are recorded in the *Sales/Invoicing* and *Receipts* windows, the program automatically posts to the customer's account in the Accounts Receivable subsidiary ledger, records the journal entry, and posts to all accounts affected in the general ledger.

However, the type of transactions recorded in the **Sales/Invoicing** and **Receipts** windows in Peachtree Complete Accounting 2006 differ from the types of transactions recorded in the journals in a manual accounting system. An explanation of the differences appears in the following table:

Name of Computerized Entry Window	Types of Transactions Recorded in Computerized Journal
Sales/Invoicing	Sales of merchandise on account Sales returns and allowances
Receipts	Cash sales Payments from credit customers on account

Aged Receivables Report

An Aged Receivables report (the computerized version of a schedule of accounts receivable) for The Mars Company appears in Figure 6.1 (terms of 2/10, n/30 are offered to customers of The Mars Company):

The Mars Company Aged Receivables As of Mar 1, 2004

Filter Criteria includes: Report order is by ID. Report is printed in Detail Format.

Customer ID Customer Contact Telephone 1	Invoice/CM #	0-30	31-60	61-90	Over 90 days	Amount Due
001 John Dunbar John	910	500.00				500.00
001 John Dunbar		500.00				500.00
002 Kevin Tucker Kevin	912	550.00				550.00
002 Kevin Tucker		550.00				550.00
Report Total		1,050.00				1,050.00

Figure 6.1

Recording a Sale on Account

TRANSACTION: On March 1, 2004, the company sold merchandise to Kevin Tucker on account for $800, Invoice 913, terms 2/10, n/30, consisting of the following items:		
Stock #	**Description**	**Quantity**
001	Space Age Lamp	2
002	Solar Clock	5
005	Space Shuttle Model	1

1. Select **Sales/Invoicing** from the **Tasks** menu.

2. Using the magnifying glass next to the **Customer ID** field, select **Kevin Tucker** by double-clicking his name. Press the Tab key until you get to the **Date** field.

3. The **Date** field should already reflect March 1, 2004, but if it does not, type in the date or use the calendar to the right of the field to select the date.

4. In the **Invoice No.** field type **913**. Tab until you reach the **Quantity** field.

5. In the **Quantity** field type **2.00** and then click the Tab key.

6. In the **Item** field use the look up menu and select the first item, **001 Space Age Lamp** by double-clicking it.

7. The **Description** field automatically fills in with information stored in the Inventory module. In fact, Peachtree fills in all the remaining fields as you tab through them until you are back to the **Quantity** field.

8. Enter the remaining items from the preceding table in the same manner as the lamp (see Figure 6.2).

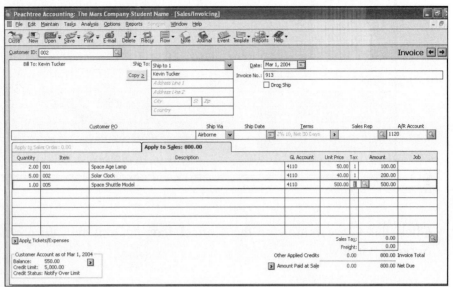

Figure 6.2

Reviewing a Sales Journal

Before posting this transaction, you may wish to see how Peachtree will record the transaction.

1. Click the **Journal** icon on the **Icon** toolbar.

   This brings up the *Accounting Behind the Screens* dialog box (see Figure 6.3), which gives you a look at the workings of the program. It shows you which accounts will be debited and which accounts will be credited.

Peachtree uses a perpetual inventory system and has created the entries to move the goods sold out of the Inventory account and into the Cost of Sales (COGS) account. This shows as: **To be calculated**.

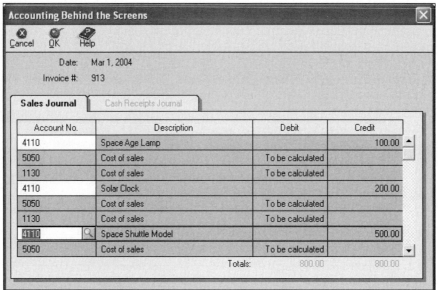

Figure 3

2. Click the **Close** button or the **Cancel** icon to exit the *Accounting Behind the Screens* window.

Editing a Sale Entry Prior to Posting

1. If you have made an error anywhere on the invoice, simply **click** the field that contains the error and correct it.

Printing Invoices

1. Click the **Print** icon. The default form should be **Invoice**.

   ➢ **NOTE:** If **Invoice** is not selected as the default form, click the **Change Form** button and scroll until you reach **Invoice**; select it and click the **OK** button.

   ➢ **ALTERNATIVE:** If you wish to batch print later, you can simply click the **Save** icon to store the invoice for printing. You will find the option to print invoices in the *Select a Report* dialog box under **Accounts Receivable**. In this workshop you should print all your invoices as you create them.

2. You are returned to the *Sales/Invoicing* dialog box.

Entering a Credit Memo

> **TRANSACTION: On March 5, 2004, the company issued Credit Memorandum CM14 to Kevin Tucker for the return of one of the lamps he purchased.**

Peachtree uses the *Sales/Invoicing* entry screen, to record credits issued to customers. There are two primary differences between an invoice and a credit memorandum. One is that quantities will be entered as negative amounts, and the second is that the printing will be accomplished with a Credit form rather than an Invoice form.

1. With the *Sales/Invoicing* window open from the previous transaction, use the magnifying glass next to the **Customer ID** field and select **Kevin Tucker** by clicking his name. Press the Tab key to move the cursor to the **Date** field.

2. In the **Date** field type the date **Mar 5, 2004** or use the calendar to the right of the field to select this date.

3. In the **Invoice No.** field type in **CM14**. Tab until you reach the **Quantity** field.

4. In the **Quantity** field type **-1.00** and click **Tab**.

5. In the **Item** field use the lookup menu to select the first item **001 Space Age Lamp** by double-clicking it.

6. This moves you to the **Description** field, which automatically fills in with information stored in the Inventory module. In fact, Peachtree fills in all the remaining fields as you tab through them until you are back to the **Quantity** field. (See Figure 6.4.)

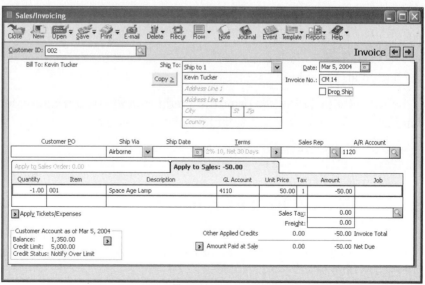

Figure 44

> ➤ **CHECK IT OUT:** You can use the **Journal** icon to see what this entry will look like in the Sales journal. Close the ***Accounting Behind the Screens*** window to return to the ***Sales/Invoicing*** screen.

Printing the Credit Memo

1. Click the **Print** icon to print this transaction.

2. You are taken to the ***Print Forms: Invoices*** dialog box. Because the last form used was the invoice, the system has defaulted to it. You want the **Negative Invoice** as the form on which to print the credit memo.

3. Click the **Change Form** button to open the ***Print Forms: Invoices/Pkg.Slips*** dialog box, shown in Figure 6.5.

4. Select **Negative Invoice**. Click **OK**.

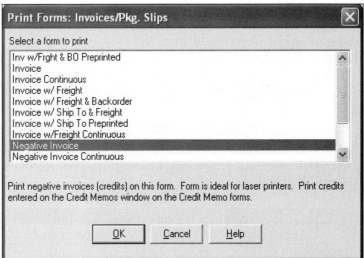

Figure 6.5

5. Click the **Print** button to print the credit memo. If you alternate between invoices and credit memos, you will want to make sure you are printing on the correct form.

6. Close the ***Sales/Invoicing*** dialog box.

Recording a Cash Receipt from a Customer

TRANSACTION: On March 8, 2004, the company received Check 1623 from Kevin Tucker in the amount of $550 in payment of Invoice 912.

1. Select **Receipts** from the **Tasks** menu.

2. Peachtree places the current date in the **Deposit ticket ID** field. Change it to the date of the transaction, **030804**.

3. In the **Customer** field use the magnifying glass to select customer **Kevin Tucker**. This brings up a listing of the invoices and credits currently open in his account.

4. In the **Reference** field enter Kevin's check number **1623**.

5. Leave the **Receipt Number** field blank. Peachtree requires the use of a receipt number for its cash receipts. A receipt number can be assigned in the printing process. Once a numbering sequence has been started, Peachtree automatically assigns the next number.

6. In the **Date** field enter **March 8, 2004**.

7. In the **Pay** column are small boxes that you can check by clicking them. This marks the invoice selected for payment with the check received. Check the box at the end of the line containing Invoice 912.

8. Note that the **Receipt Amount** field automatically reflects the amount of Kevin's payment. See Figure 6.6.

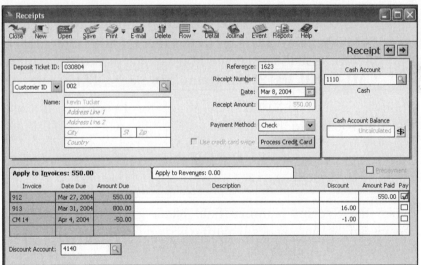

Figure 6.6

> ➢ **NOTE:** If you were receiving cash as the result of a cash sale or for any other reason other than a payment on account, you would use the **Apply to Revenues** tab instead of the **Apply to Invoices** tab. In the **Apply to Revenues** dialog box, you can use any general ledger account you would like to offset the receipt of the cash.

9. Click the **Print** icon.

10. For the **Receipt Number** enter **101**.

11. Accept the default form **Multi-Purpose 2 Stub Receipt**, as shown in Figure 6.7.

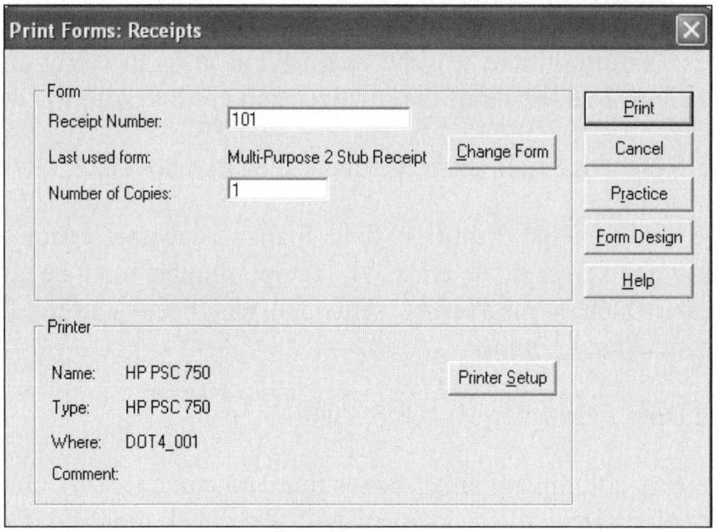

Figure 6.7

12. Click **Print**.

Recording Additional Cash Receipts

> **TRANSACTION: On March 10, 2004, the company received Check 1634 from Kevin Tucker in the amount of $735 in payment of invoice 9130 ($800), dated March 1, less Credit Memorandum CM14 ($50), less 2% discount ($16 – 1 = $15 net sales discount).**

1. Follow the detailed instructions above for **Recording a Cash Receipt from a Customer** to record this receipt.

2. Select both the invoice and the credit memo by clicking in the Pay column for both transactions (see Figure 6.8).

3. Leave the **Receipt Number** field blank (see Figure 6.8). Peachtree assigns the receipt number automatically during printing.

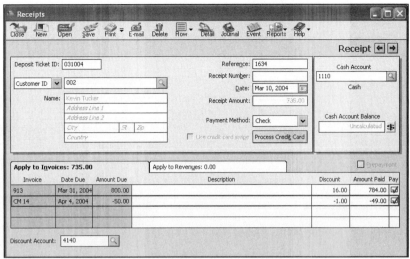

Figure 6.8

4. Click the **Print** icon.

5. Peachtree automatically enters the next number for the receipt number.

6. Click **Print** to print the receipt.

7. Click the **Close** button or icon to exit the *Receipts* window.

Displaying and Printing the Aged Receivables Report

1. From the **Reports** menu, select **Accounts Receivable**. This brings up the *Select a Report* dialog box, containing a list of the accounts receivable reports available in Peachtree (see Figure 6.9).

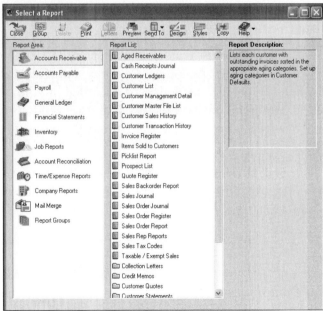

Figure 6.9

2. Select **Aged Receivables** to bring up the schedule of receivables still owed to The Mars Company (see Figure 6.10).

```
                                                    The Mars Company-Student Name
                                                           Aged Receivables
                                                           As of Mar 31, 2004
Filter Criteria includes: Report order is by ID. Report is printed in Detail Format.

Customer ID        Invoice/CM #        0-30      31-60      61-90    Over 90 days    Amount Due
Customer
Contact
Telephone 1

001                910                 500.00                                       500.00
John Dunbar
John

001                                    500.00                                       500.00
John Dunbar

Report Total                           500.00                                       500.00
```

Figure 6.10

3. Click the **Print** icon to print the report.

4. Close the Aged Receivables report and the *Select a Report* window.

The Mars Company: Accounts Payable

Recording Purchases and Cash Payments

The *Purchases* and *Payments* windows in Peachtree Complete Accounting 2006 are designed to work with the Accounts Payable and General Ledger modules in an integrated fashion. When transactions are recorded in the **Purchases** and **Payments** windows, the program automatically posts to the vendor's account in the Accounts Payable subsidiary ledger, records the journal entry, and posts to all accounts affected in the general ledger.

However, the type of transactions recorded in the *Purchases* and *Payments* windows in Peachtree Complete Accounting 2006 differ from the types of transactions recorded in these journals in a manual accounting system. An explanation of the differences appears in the following table:

Name of Computerized Entry Window	Types of Transactions Recorded in Computerized Journal
Purchases	Purchases of merchandise and other

	items on account
	Purchase returns and allowances
Payments	Payments to creditors
	Cash payments to vendors

Aged Payables Report

An Aged Payables report (the computerized version of a schedule of accounts payable) for The Mars Company appears in Figure 6.11.

The Mars Company-Student Name
Aged Payables
As of Mar 1, 2004

Filter Criteria includes: Report order is by ID. Report is printed in Detail Format.

Vendor ID Vendor Contact Telephone 1	Invoice/CM #	0 - 30	31 - 60	61 - 90	Over 90 days	Amount Due
001 Lara's Space Prints Lara	569	435.00				435.00
001 Lara's Space Prints		435.00				435.00
002 Young's Space Simulations Pat	790	112.00				112.00
002 Young's Space Simulations		112.00				112.00
Report Total		547.00				547.00

Figure 6.11

Purchasing and Receiving Inventory

TRANSACTION: On March 15, 2004, the company purchased merchandise from Young's Space Simulations on account for $165.50, Invoice 7960, terms 2/10, n/30, consisting of the following:

Stock #	Description	Quantity
001	Space Age Lamp	5
004	Simulated Moon Rock	9

1. Select **Purchases/Receive Inventory** from the **Tasks** menu, which brings up the *Purchases/Receive Inventory* dialog box.

2. Using the magnifying glass next to the **Vendor ID** field, select **002 Young's Space Simulations** by clicking it.

3. In the **Date** field enter **Mar 15, 2004** or use the calendar to the right of the field to select this date.

4. In the **Invoice No.** field enter **7960**.

5. In the **Quantity** field enter **5.00**.

6. In the **Item** field click the lookup menu and select the first item, **001 Space Age Lamp**, by double-clicking it.

7. The **Description** field automatically fills in with information stored in the Inventory module. In fact, Peachtree fills in all the remaining fields as you tab through them until you are back to the **Quantity** field.

   ➢ **NOTE:** If your unit price is different from the one in the Peachtree Inventory module, you can easily change the amount rather than tabbing through that field.

   ➢ **NOTE:** If the company were purchasing something besides merchandise inventory, you would skip over the Quantity and Item fields and fill in the Description, GL Account, and Amount fields based on what the company purchased and the cost.

8. In the **Quantity** field enter **9**.

9. In the **Item** field select **004 Simulated Moon Rock** (see Figure 6.12).

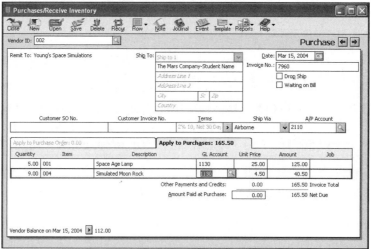

Figure 6.12

> ➢ **CHECK IT OUT:** Before saving this transaction, you may wish to see how Peachtree will record the transaction. Click the **Journal** icon on the toolbar. This takes you to the *Accounting Behind the Screens* window. As shown in Figure 6.13, it shows which accounts that will be debited and which accounts will be credited. Close the *Accounting Behind the Screens* window to continue with the transaction.

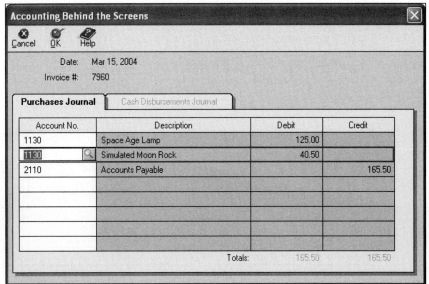

Figure 6.13

10. If you have made an error anywhere on the invoice, simply click in the field that contains the error and correct it.

11. Click the **Save** icon to post this transaction. A blank *Purchases/Receive Inventory* screen is displayed, ready for additional purchase transactions to be recorded.

Recording the Return of Merchandise Purchased (Entering Debit Memo)

> **TRANSACTION: On March 17, 2004, the company returned two of the Space Age Lamps to Young's Space Simulations, with a value of $50, and issued Debit Memo DM27.**

1. Select **Purchases/Receive Inventory** from the **Tasks** menu.

2. In the **Vendor ID** field click the lookup icon and select **002 Young's Space Simulations** by clicking it.

3. In the **Date** field enter **Mar 17, 2004** or use the calendar to the right of the field to select this date.

4. In the **Invoice No.** field enter **DM27**.

5. In the **Quantity** field enter **-2.00** and click **Tab**.

6. In the **Item** field use the lookup menu and select the first item, **001 Space Age Lamp**, by double-clicking it. Peachtree fills in all the remaining fields as you tab through them until you are back to the **Quantity** field (see Figure 6.14).

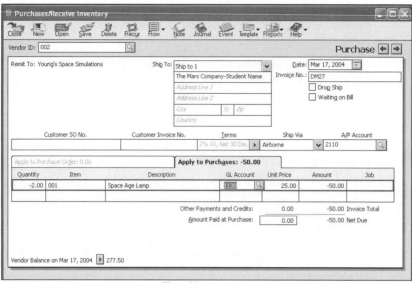

Figure 6.14

> ➢ **CHECK IT OUT:** Before saving this transaction, you may wish to see how Peachtree will record the transaction. Click the **Journal** icon on the toolbar. This brings up the *Accounting Behind the Screens* window and allows you to see which accounts will be debited and which accounts will be credited. Close the *Accounting Behind the Screens* window to continue.

7. If you have made an error anywhere on the invoice, simply click in the field that contains the error and correct it.

8. After verifying that the journal entry is correct, Click the **Save** icon to post this transaction.

9. Close the *Purchases/Receive Inventory* window.

Recording a Payment to a Vendor

> **TRANSACTION: On March 25, 2004, the company issued Check 437 to Young's Space Simulations in the amount of $225.19 in payment of Invoices 790 ($112) and 7960 ($165.50), dated March 15, less Debit Memorandum DM27 ($50), less 2% discount ($5.56 – 1.00 = $4.56 net purchases discount).**

1. Select **Payments** from the **Tasks** menu.

2. Using the magnifying glass, select vendor **Young's Space Simulations**. This brings up a list of the invoices and credits currently open for this account.

3. In the **Date** field type **March 25, 2004** or use the calendar to select this date.

4. In the **Pay** column are small boxes that you can check by clicking them. This marks the invoices selected for payment with the check you are creating. Click the boxes at the ends of the lines containing Invoice 790 and 7960 and Debit Memo DM27,

which is associated with this invoice. You may need to use the scrollbar to mark all three items.

> **NOTE:** If the company needed to make a payment for something that is not already recorded in the Accounts Payable report, you could use the **Apply to Expenses** tab instead of the **Apply to Invoices** tab that is used here. You could write a check for any purpose, including prepaid expenses, using this feature.

5. The field for the amount of the check automatically reflects the amount of this payment ($225.19).

6. Leave the **Check Number** field blank (see Figure 6.15). This field is used only to enter a check that has already been written or printed. You will enter the check number when you print the check.

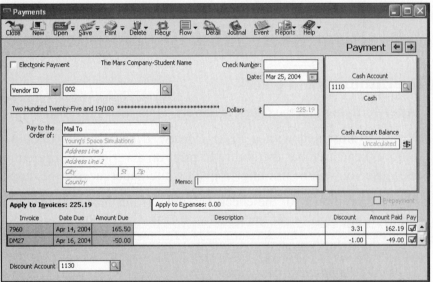

Figure 6.15

> **CHECK IT OUT:** Before printing this check, you may wish to see how Peachtree will record the transaction. Click the **Journal** icon on the toolbar. You can see which accounts will be debited and which accounts credited (see Figure 6.16). Close the *Accounting Behind the Screens* window to continue.

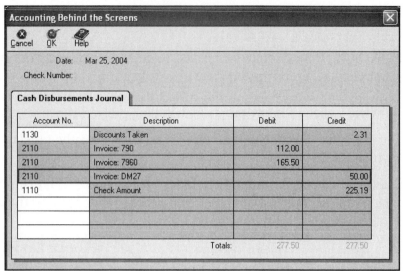

Figure 6.16

Printing the Disbursement Check

1. After verifying that the check is correct, click the **Print** icon to print this check.

2. You are presented with a *Print Forms: Disbursement Checks* selection box. As before, Peachtree has the ability to print on a variety of different blank check forms. Because you will be printing on plain white paper, accept the default form.

3. You are prompted for the check number. If Peachtree automatically fills in a check number, highlight it and enter **437**.

4. Click the **Print** button.

5. Close the *Payments* dialog box.

Displaying and Printing a Vendor Aged Payables Report

1. Select **Accounts Payable** from the **Reports** menu.

2. On the *Select a Report* dialog box select **Aged Payables** from the **Report List** section of your screen to bring up the schedule of payables still owed by The Mars Company (see Figure 6.17).

The Mars Company-Student Name
Aged Payables
As of Mar 31, 2004

Filter Criteria includes: Report order is by ID. Report is printed in Detail Format.

Vendor ID Vendor Contact Telephone 1	Invoice/CM #	0 - 30	31 - 60	61 - 90	Over 90 days	Amount Due
001 Lara's Space Prints Lara	569	435.00				435.00
001 Lara's Space Prints		435.00				435.00
Report Total		435.00				435.00

Figure 6.17

3. Click the **Print** icon to print the report.

4. Close the Aged Payables report window. Leave the *Select a Report* dialog box open.

Displaying and Printing the General Ledger Trial Balance and the General Ledger Reports

1. From the *Select a Report* dialog box, select **General Ledger** from the **Report Area** portion of the window.

2. Print the reports shown in Figures 6.18 and 6.19, accepting all the defaults:

The Mars Company-Student Name
General Ledger Trial Balance
As of Mar 31, 2004

Filter Criteria includes: Report order is by ID. Report is printed in Detail Format.

Account ID	Account Description	Debit Amt	Credit Amt
1110	Cash	11,059.81	
1120	Accounts Receivable	500.00	
1130	Inventory	4,139.19	
2110	Accounts Payable		435.00
3110	Janice Mars, Capital		14,904.00
4110	Sales		750.00
4140	Sales Discounts	15.00	
5050	Cost of Goods Sold	375.00	
	Total:	16,089.00	16,089.00

Figure 6.18

Account ID Account Description	Date	Reference	Jrnl	Trans Description	Debit Amt	Credit Amt	Balance
Accounts Receivable	3/1/04	913	SJ	Kevin Tucker	800.00		
	3/5/04	CM 14	SJ	Kevin Tucker		50.00	
	3/8/04	1623	CRJ	Kevin Tucker - Invoic		550.00	
	3/10/04	1634	CRJ	Kevin Tucker - Invoic	50.00		
	3/10/04	1634	CRJ	Kevin Tucker - Invoic		800.00	
				Current Period Change	850.00	1,400.00	-550.00
	3/31/04			Ending Balance			500.00
1130	3/1/04			Beginning Balance			4,401.00
Inventory	3/1/04	913	COGS	Kevin Tucker - Item:		250.00	
	3/1/04	913	COGS	Kevin Tucker - Item:		50.00	
	3/1/04	913	COGS	Kevin Tucker - Item:		100.00	
	3/5/04	CM 14	COGS	Kevin Tucker - Item:	25.00		
	3/15/04	7960	PJ	Young's Space Simulati	125.00		
	3/15/04	7960	PJ	Young's Space Simulati	40.50		
	3/17/04	DM27	PJ	Young's Space Simulati		50.00	
	3/25/04	437	CDJ	Young's Space Simulati		3.31	
	3/25/04	437	CDJ	Young's Space Simulati	1.00		
				Current Period Change	191.50	453.31	-261.81
	3/31/04			Ending Balance			4,139.19

The Mars Company-Student Name
General Ledger
For the Period From Mar 1, 2004 to Mar 31, 2004
Filter Criteria includes: Report order is by ID. Report is printed with Truncated Transaction Descriptions and in Detail Format.

Figure 6.19

> **CHECK IT OUT:** You may wish to experiment with some of the other reports that are available in the various areas of Peachtree's report area. Some examples you might want to see are sales journal, purchases journal, cash receipts journal, etc.

3. Close the General Ledger report window and the *Select a Report* window.

Backing Up Your Company Data File

1. Select **Backup** from the **File** menu.

2. **Click** the check box to include the company name in the file name.

3. Add **Final** to the file name.

4. Select the **Save in** lookup box to find the location your instructor has identified for you to keep your backup file(s).

5. Click **Save**.

6. Click **OK**.

> **NOTE:** Refer to Chapter 1 for more detailed instructions on backing up files.

Exiting the Peachtree Complete Accounting 2006 Program

1. Click **Exit** on the **File** menu to end the current work session and return to your Windows desktop.

2. If you are asked if you wish to save any unposted work, click the **Yes** button.

PEACHTREE
Workshop

Chapter 7

Abby's Toy House--Mini Practice Set

THIS WORKSHOP IS DESIGNED TO REVIEW THE CONCEPTS IN

➤ CHAPTER 2—GENERAL LEDGER TRANSACTIONS

➤ CHAPTER 6—ACCOUNTS RECEIVABLE AND ACCOUNTS PAYABLE TRANSACTIONS

Opening Abby's Toy House

1. Double-click on **Peachtree** icon on your desktop to open the software program.

2. Click **Open an existing company** and then locate and select **Abby's Toy House**.

3. Click **Open**.

   ➤ NOTE: Refer to Chapter 1 for more detailed instructions on opening files.

Backing Up Your Company Data File

1. Select **Backup** from the **File** menu.

2. **Click** the check box to include the company name in the file name.

3. Add **Start** to the file name.

4. Select the **Save in** lookup box to find the location your instructor has identified for you to keep your backup file(s).

5. Click **Save**.

6. Click **OK**.

   ➤ NOTE: Refer to Chapter 1 for more detailed instructions on backing up files.

Adding Your Name to the Company Name

1. Click the **Maintain** menu option and then select **Company Information**. The program responds by bringing up the *Maintain Company Information* dialog box, which allows you to edit/add information about the company.

2. Click in the **Company Name** field and make sure your cursor is at the end of **Abby's Toy House**.

3. Add a dash and your name (-Student's Name).

4. Click the **OK** button.

> ➢ **NOTE**: Refer to Chapter 2 for more detailed instructions on adding your name to a company name.

Recording Transactions for March

Record the following transactions, using the appropriate entry windows. The entry windows used in this workshop include **General Journal Entry** (G), **Sales/Invoicing** (S), **Receipts** (R), **Purchases/Receive Inventory** (PU), and **Payments** (PA).

Use the forms Invoice, Negative Invoice, Multi-purpose 2 stub Receipt (for receipts) and OCR Multi-Purp AP Continuous (for checks), changing the starting numbers as needed.

Here are the transactions for March:

2004
Mar.   1   Abby Ellen invested $8,000 in the toy store. Use "Memo1" for the Reference Number (G).

1   Paid three months' rent in advance, using an electronic funds transfer (EFT) in the amount of $3,000. Reference Number "Memo 2" (G).

3   Purchased merchandise from Earl Miller Company on account, $4,000, Invoice 410, consisting of the following: 6 Mountain Bikes, 12 Bike Carriers, 8 Deluxe Bike Seats (PU).

3   Sold merchandise to Bill Burton on account, $1,000, Invoice 1, consisting of the following: 1 Mountain Bike, 1 Bike Carrier (S).

6   Sold merchandise to Jim Rex on account for $700, Invoice 2, consisting of the following: 3 Bike Carriers, 1 Deluxe Bike Seat (S).

10   Purchased merchandise from Earl Miller Co. on account, $1,200, Invoice 415, consisting of the following: 2 Mountain Bikes, 4 Bike Carriers (PU).

10   Sold merchandise to Bill Burton on account for $600, Invoice 3, consisting of the following: 3 Bike Carriers (S).

10   Paid cleaning service $300, using an EFT. Reference No. Memo3 (G).

11   Jim Rex returned merchandise for $300 to Abby's Toy House, consisting of the following: 1 Bike Carrier, 1 Deluxe Bike Seat. Abby issued credit memorandum 1 (CM1) to Jim Rex for $300 (S). Remember to use negative quantities and the Negative Invoice Plain form.

11   Purchased merchandise from Minnie Katz on account, $4,000, Invoice 311, consisting of the following: 2 Doll Houses w/ Furniture, 4 Porcelain Face Dolls, 10 Yo Yo's, Designer, 10 Magic Kits (PU).

12   Issued Check 1 to Earl Miller Co. in the amount of $3,920, in payment of Invoice 410 ($4,000), dated March 2, less 2% discount

($80) (PA).

13 Sold $1,300 of toy merchandise for cash, consisting of the following: 1 Doll House w/ Furniture, 1 Magic Kit. (Use the Receipts (R) window, skip the Customer ID field, type CASH in the Name field, in the Reference field enter the date, and use Receipt Number 1. Change Payment Method to Cash. Use the Apply to Revenues tab and list the items sold, accepting all other defaults.)

13 Paid salaries, $600, using an EFT (G).

14 Returned merchandise to Minnie Katz in the amount of $1,000, consisting of the following: 1 Doll House w/ Furniture, 2 Porcelain Face Dolls. Abby's Toy House issued Debit Memorandum 1 (DM1) (PU). Remember to enter quantity as negative.

14 Sold merchandise for $4,000 cash, consisting of the following: 3 Mountain Bikes, 3 Bike Carriers, 2 Magic Kits, 4 Yo Yo's, Designer. Use Receipt Number 2. See transaction from March 13 for procedures (R).

16 Received Check 9823 from Jim Rex in the amount of $392, in payment of Invoice 2 ($700), dated March 6, less Credit Memorandum 1 ($300), less 2% discount ($14 – 6 = $8 net sales discount). Use Receipt Number 3 (R).

16 Received Check 4589 from Bill Burton in the amount of $1,000, in payment of Invoice 1, dated March 2. Use Receipt Number 4 (R). Notice that Peachtree does not factor in the discount because it is past the discount date.

16 Sold merchandise to Amy Rose on account, $4,000, Invoice 4, consisting of the following: 1 Porcelain Face Doll, 3 Mountain Bikes, 4 Bike Carriers, 3 Deluxe Bike Seats. Remember to use the Invoice Plain form (S).

21 Purchased delivery truck on account from Sam Katz Garage, $3,000, Invoice 111 (PU). Because this is not an inventory item, you do not need to fill in the Item field. You must type in the Description. Peachtree defaults the GL code to a delivery truck since this vendor was set up to do so. You need to type in the purchase price in the Amount field.

22 Sold to Bill Burton merchandise on account for $900, Invoice 5, consisting of the following: 3 Magic Kits (S).

23 Issued Check 2 to Minnie Katz in the amount of $2,970, in payment of Invoice 311 ($4,000), dated March 11, less Debit Memorandum 1 ($1,000), less 1% discount ($40 – 10 = $30 net purchases discount) (PA).

24 Sold toy merchandise on account to Amy Rose, $1,100, Invoice 6, consisting of the following: 1 Porcelain Face Doll, 1 Magic Kit, 3 Yo

Yo's, Designer (S). Select Yes when the over-credit-limit message appears.

25 Purchased toy merchandise for cash from Woody Smith while waiting for an account to be approved, $600, Check 3, consisting of the following: 2 Marionettes, Hand Carved. Use the PA window, Apply to Expenses tab, and list the items purchased.

27 Purchased toy merchandise from Woody Smith on account for $4,800, Invoice 211, consisting of the following: 16 Marionettes, Hand Carved (PU).

28 Received Check 4598 from Bill Burton in the amount of $882, in payment of Invoice 5 ($900), dated March 22, less 2% discount ($18). Use Receipt Number 5 (R).

28 Received Check 3217 from Amy Rose in the amount of $1,078, in payment of Invoice 6, dated March 24, less 2% discount ($22). Use Receipt Number 6 (R).

28 Abby invested an additional $5,000 in the business (G).

29 Purchased merchandise on account from Earl Miller Co., $1,400, Invoice 436, consisting of the following: 3 Mountain Bike, 2 Bike Carriers (PU).

30 Issued Check 4 to Earl Miller Co. in the amount of $1,372, in payment of Invoice 436 ($1,400), dated March 29, less 2% discount ($28) (PA).

30 Sold merchandise to Bonnie Flow Company on account for $3,000, Invoice 7, consisting of the following: 5 Marionettes, Hand Carved (S).

Printing the Reports for Abby's Toy House

Print the reports shown in Figures 7.1 through 7.5, accepting all defaults.

Abby's Toy House-Students Name
Aged Receivables
As of Mar 31, 2004

Filter Criteria includes: Report order is by ID. Report is printed in Detail Format.

Customer ID Customer Contact Telephone 1	Invoice/CM #	0-30	31-60	61-90	Over 90 days	Amount Due
001 Amy Rose		4,000.00				4,000.00
002 Bill Burton Bill	3	600.00				600.00
002 Bill Burton		600.00				600.00
003 Bonnie Flow Company Bonnie	7	3,000.00				3,000.00
003 Bonnie Flow Company		3,000.00				3,000.00
Report Total		7,600.00				7,600.00

Figure 7.1

Abby's Toy House-Students Name
Aged Payables
As of Mar 31, 2004

Filter Criteria includes: Report order is by ID. Report is printed in Detail Format.

Vendor ID Vendor Contact Telephone 1	Invoice/CM #	0 - 30	31 - 60	61 - 90	Over 90 days	Amount Due
001 Earl Miller Company		1,200.00				1,200.00
003 Sam Katz Garage Sam	111	3,000.00				3,000.00
003 Sam Katz Garage		3,000.00				3,000.00
004 Woody Smith Woody	211	4,800.00				4,800.00
004 Woody Smith		4,800.00				4,800.00
Report Total		9,000.00				9,000.00

Figure 7.2

Abby's Toy House-Students Name
General Journal
For the Period From Mar 1, 2004 to Mar 31, 2004

Filter Criteria includes: Report order is by Date. Report is printed with Accounts having Zero Amounts and with Truncated Transaction Descriptions

Date	Account ID	Reference	Trans Description	Debit Amt	Credit Amt
3/1/04	1110	Memo1	Owner Investment	8,000.00	
	3110		Owner Investment		8,000.00
3/1/04	1140	Memo2	Prepaid 3 months rent	3,000.00	
	1110		Prepaid 3 months rent		3,000.00
3/10/04	5620	Memo3	Paid cleaning service	300.00	
	1110		Paid cleaning service		300.00
3/10/04	5610	Memo4	Paid salaries	600.00	
	1110		Paid salaries		600.00
3/28/04	1110	Memo5	Owner Investment	5,000.00	
	3110		Owner Investment		5,000.00
		Total		16,900.00	16,900.00

Figure 7.3

Abby's Toy House-Students Name
General Ledger
For the Period From Mar 1, 2004 to Mar 31, 2004

Filter Criteria includes: Report order is by ID. Report is printed with Truncated Transaction Descriptions and in Detail Format.

Account ID Account Description	Date	Reference	Jrnl	Trans Description	Debit Amt	Credit Amt	Balance
1110	3/1/04			Beginning Balance			
Cash	3/1/04	Memo1	GENJ	Owner Investment	8,000.00		
	3/1/04	Memo2	GENJ	Prepaid 3 months rent		3,000.00	
	3/10/04	Memo3	GENJ	Paid cleaning service		300.00	
	3/10/04	Memo4	GENJ	Paid salaries		600.00	
	3/12/04	1	CDJ	Earl Miller Company		3,920.00	
	3/13/04	031304	CRJ	Cash	1,300.00		
	3/14/04	031404	CRJ	Cash	4,000.00		
	3/16/04	9823	CRJ	Jim Rex	392.00		
	3/16/04	4589	CRJ	Bill Burton	1,000.00		
	3/23/04	2	CDJ	Minnie Katz		2,970.00	
	3/25/04	3	CDJ	Woody Smith		600.00	
	3/28/04	4598	CRJ	Bill Burton	882.00		
	3/28/04	3217	CRJ	Amy Rose	1,078.00		
	3/28/04	Memo5	GENJ	Owner Investment	5,000.00		
	3/30/04	4	CDJ	Earl Miller Company		1,372.00	
				Current Period Change	21,652.00	12,762.00	8,890.00
	3/31/04			Ending Balance			8,890.00
1120	3/1/04			Beginning Balance			
Accounts Receivable	3/3/04	1	SJ	Bill Burton	1,000.00		
	3/6/04	2	SJ	Jim Rex	700.00		
	3/10/04	3	SJ	Bill Burton	600.00		
	3/11/04	CM1	SJ	Jim Rex		300.00	
	3/16/04	9823	CRJ	Jim Rex - Invoice: 2		700.00	
	3/16/04	9823	CRJ	Jim Rex - Invoice: CM	300.00		

Figure 7.4

<table>
<tr><td colspan="5" align="right">Abby's Toy House-Students Name
General Ledger Trial Balance
As of Mar 31, 2004</td></tr>
</table>

		Abby's Toy House-Students Name General Ledger Trial Balance As of Mar 31, 2004	

Filter Criteria includes: Report order is by ID. Report is printed in Detail Format.

Account ID	Account Description	Debit Amt	Credit Amt
1110	Cash	8,890.00	
1120	Accounts Receivable	7,600.00	
1130	Inventory	6,712.00	
1140	Prepaid Rent	3,000.00	
1150	Delivery Truck	3,000.00	
2110	Accounts Payable		9,000.00
3110	Abby Ellen, Capital		13,000.00
4110	Sales		16,300.00
4140	Sales Discounts	48.00	
5050	Cost of Goods Sold	8,150.00	
5610	Salaries Expense	600.00	
5620	Cleaning Expense	300.00	
	Total:	38,300.00	38,300.00

Figure 7.5

Backing Up Your Company Data File

1. Select **Back up** from the **File** menu.

2. Click the check box to include the company name in the file name.

3. Select the **Save in** lookup box to find the location your instructor has identified for you to keep your backup file(s).

4. Click **Save**.

5. Click **OK**.

> ➢ **NOTE:** Refer to Chapter 1 for more detailed instructions on backing up files.

Exiting the Peachtree Complete Accounting 2006 program

1. Click **Exit** on the **File** menu to end the current work session and return to your Windows desktop.

2. If you are asked if you wish to save any unposted work, click the **Yes** button.

CHAPTER 8

Accounting Cycle for a Merchandise Company—The Corner Dress Shop

THIS WORKSHOP WILL HELP YOU REVIEW ALL THE KEY CONCEPTS OF A MERCHANDISE COMPANY

IT IS RECOMMENDED THAT YOU COMPLETE THE WORKSHOPS IN THE FOLLOWING CHAPTERS PRIOR TO COMPLETING THIS WORKSHOP:

> ➤ **CHAPTER 3—ADJUSTING JOURNAL ENTRIES**

> ➤ **CHAPTER 5—PAYROLL**

> ➤ **CHAPTER 6—ACCOUNTS RECEIVABLE AND ACCOUNTS PAYABLE**

Opening The Corner Dress Shop File

1. Double-click the **Peachtree** icon on your desktop to open the software program.

2. Click **Open an existing company** and then locate and select the **The Corner Dress Shop**.

3. Click **Open**.

> ➤ **NOTE:** Refer to Chapter 1 for more detailed instructions on opening company files.

Backing Up Your Company Data File

1. Select **Back up** from the **File** menu.

2. Click the check box to include the company name in the file name.

3. Add **Start** to the file name.

4. Select the **Save in** lookup box to find the location your instructor has identified for you to keep your backup file(s).

5. Click **Save**.

6. Click **OK**.

> ➤ **NOTE:** Refer to Chapter 1 for more detailed instructions on backing up files.

Adding Your Name to the Company Name

1. Click the **Maintain** menu option and then select **Company Information**. The program responds by bringing up the *Maintain Company Information* dialog box, which allows you to edit/add information about the company.

2. Click in the **Company Name** field and make sure your cursor is at the end of **The Corner Dress Shop**.

3. Add a dash and your name (-Student's Name).

4. Click the **OK** button.

> ➢ **NOTE**: Refer to Chapter 2 for more detailed instructions on adding your name to a company name.

Company Information

Since you are the accountant for The Corner Dress Shop, your task in this workshop is to complete the accounting cycle for March 2004.

The Corner Dress Shop, owned by Betty Loeb, is located at 1 Milgate Road, Marblehead, Massachusetts, 01945. Betty's employer identification number is 33-4158215. Peachtree automatically calculates federal income tax (FIT), state income tax (SIT), Social Security, Medicare, FUTA, and SUTA.

Employees are paid monthly. The payroll is recorded and paid on the last day of each month.

Printing the Beginning-of-the-Month Reports

1. Click the **General Ledger** [⊙ General Ledger] icon on the **Navigation Aids** toolbar at the bottom of your screen.

2. Select the **All General Ledger Reports** [All General Ledger Reports] icon from the section on the right of your screen. That opens the *Select a Report* dialog box.

3. Select **General Ledger Trial Balance** from the **Report List** section.

4. Click the **Options** [Options] icon, change the date to **2/29/04**, and click **OK**. The report shown in Figure 8.1 appears.

The Corner Dress Shop-Student Name
General Ledger Trial Balance
As of Feb 29, 2004

Filter Criteria includes: Report order is by ID. Report is printed in Detail Format.

Account ID	Account Description	Debit Amt	Credit Amt
1110	Cash	2,502.90	
1115	Petty Cash	35.00	
1120	Accounts Receivable	2,200.00	
1130	Inventory	5,600.00	
1140	Prepaid Rent	1,800.00	
1250	Delivery Truck	6,000.00	
1251	Accum. Dep-Delivery Truck		1,500.00
2110	Accounts Payable		1,900.00
2310	Federal Income Tax Payable		1,284.00
2320	State Income Tax Payable		756.00
2330	FICA- Soc. Sec. Payable		1,339.20
2335	FICA- Medicare Payable		313.20
2340	FUTA Payable		163.20
2350	SUTA Payable		979.20
2400	Unearned Rent		800.00
3110	Betty Loeb, Capital		9,103.10
	Total:	18,137.90	18,137.90

Figure 8.1

5. Click the **Print** icon to print the report.

6. Click the **Close** icon or button to exit the report.

7. From the *Select a Report* dialog box select **Accounts Receivable** from the **Report Area** section.

8. Double-click **Aged Receivables** in the **Report List** section.

9. Click the **Options** Options icon.

10. In the **Date** field select **Exact Date** as shown in Figure 8.2.

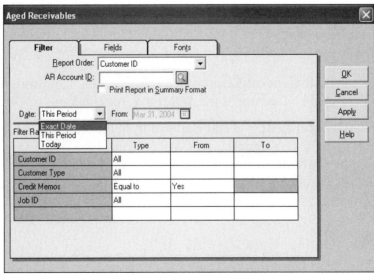

Figure 8.2

11. Change the **From** field to **3-1-04**.

12. Click **OK.** The report shown in Figure 8.3 appears.

		The Corner Dress Shop-Student Name Aged Receivables As of Mar 31, 2004				
Filter Criteria includes: Report order is by ID. Report is printed in Detail Format.						
Customer ID **Customer** **Contact** **Telephone 1**	**Invoice/CM #**	**0-30**	**31-60**	**61-90**	**Over 90 days**	**Amount Due**
001 Bing Company	12		2,200.00			2,200.00
001 Bing Company			2,200.00			2,200.00
Report Total			2,200.00			2,200.00

Figure 8.3

13. Click the **Print** icon.

14. Click the **Close** icon or button to close the Aged Receivables report and return to the *Select a Report* dialog box.

15. Click **Accounts Payable** in the **Report Area** section of the *Select a Report* dialog box.

16. Double-click **Aged Payables** in the **Report List** section.

17. Click the **Options** icon.

18. In the **Date** field select **Exact Date**.

19. Change the **From** field to **3-1-04**.

20. Click **OK**. The report shown in figure 8.4 appears.

		The Corner Dress Shop-Student Name Aged Payables As of Mar 1, 2004				
Filter Criteria includes: Report order is by ID. Report is printed in Detail Format.						
Vendor ID **Vendor** **Contact** **Telephone 1**	**Invoice/CM #**	**0 - 30**	**31 - 60**	**61 - 90**	**Over 90 days**	**Amount Due**
001 Blew Company	422	1,900.00				1,900.00
001 Blew Company		1,900.00				1,900.00
Report Total		1,900.00				1,900.00

Figure 8.4

21. Click the **Print** icon.

22. Click the **Close** button or icon to close the report.

Printing an Inventory Valuation Report

To see what inventory items The Corner Dress Shop has available, print a listing:

1. Click **Inventory** in the **Report Area** section of the *Select a Report* dialog box.

2. Double-click **Inventory Valuation Report** in the **Report List** section.

3. Click the **Options** icon.

4. In the **Date** field select **Exact Date**.

5. Change the **As of** box to **Period 2**.

6. Click **OK**. The report shown in Figure 8.5 appears.

The Corner Dress Shop-Student Name
Inventory Valuation Report
As of Feb 29, 2004

Filter Criteria includes: 1) Stock/Assembly. Report order is by ID. Report is printed with Truncated Long Descriptions.

Item ID Item Class	Item Description	Stocking U/M	Cost Method	Qty on Hand	Item Value	Avg Cost	% of Inv Value
1000 Stock item	Dress, Style 1000	Each	Average	30.00	750.00	25.00	13.39
2000 Stock item	Dress, Style 2000	Each	Average	25.00	750.00	30.00	13.39
3000 Stock item	Dress, Style 3000	Each	Average	25.00	875.00	35.00	15.63
4000 Stock item	Dress, Style 4000	Each	Average	25.00	1,000.00	40.00	17.86
5000 Stock item	Dress, Style 5000	Each	Average	25.00	1,125.00	45.00	20.09
6000 Stock item	Dress, Style 6000	Each	Average	22.00	1,100.00	50.00	19.64
					5,600.00		100.00

Figure 8.5

7. Click the **Print** icon.

8. You see that the company has six items in its inventory. In addition, you see the current cost on each item. Save this printed report to compare with a similar report you will print at the end of this practice set.

Maintaining Inventory Items

Peachtree's Inventory module allows you to easily add new items or make changes to existing items, such as recording price changes. You will be asked to change prices later in the practice set, so take a look at how that works now:

♦ Select **Inventory Items** from the **Maintain** menu, to open the *Maintain Inventory Items* dialog box (see Figure 8.6).

♦ In the **Item ID** field, select **6000** by using the look up button.

◆ In the **Description** field, you see the current description of this inventory item.

◆ Under the **General** tab is a **Description** field where you can enter a longer description of this item that will appear on sales and/or purchase invoices.

◆ The current selling price for this item is kept in the **Price Level 1** field. Peachtree has the capability of storing multiple prices for an item. When you click the arrow to the right of the **Price Level 1** field, a table is presented, which allows you to enter up to 10 different selling prices. You can assign different customers to different price levels in this manner. The company has only one price, so you can cancel the *Multiple Price Levels* dialog box to return to the *Maintain Inventory Items* window. When you are prompted to change prices later in the practice set, you simply change the price in the **Price Level 1** field rather than add multiple prices.

◆ The program automatically calculates to **Last Unit Cost** field, so that field is grayed out.

◆ The **Cost Method** field is where you select the cost assumption to use with this item: FIFO, LIFO, or Average. Once saved, the cost method *cannot* be changed.

◆ **Item Type, Location,** and **Stocking U/M** (unit measure) fields are sorting and information fields that can be used as needed and have no restrictions as to content except length.

◆ Peachtree uses default information to select the GL accounts needed for an inventory transaction. If there is some need to change these, you can select any account you need. Since there is no need to change these accounts, leave them at the default settings.

◆ The company could also establish a minimum stock level and have Peachtree warn you when you fall below this level. You can also establish a reorder point that Peachtree can use to generate an inventory reorder listing.

◆ The company can also select the preferred vendor from which you normally order this item. Peachtree uses this and all the information you can see in this window to work interactively with Peachtree's other modules and report features.

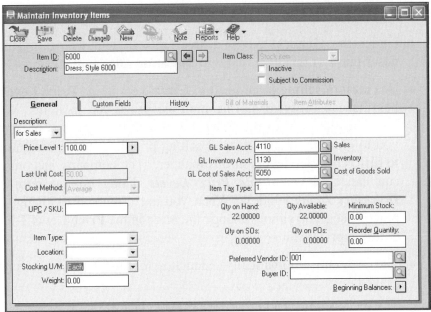

Figure 8.6

Recording Transactions for March

Record the following transactions using the appropriate entry window. The windows used in this workshop are *General Journal Entry* (G), *Sales/Invoicing* (S), *Receipts* (R), *Purchases/Receive Inventory* (PU), and *Payments* (PA).

Use the forms Invoice, Negative Invoice, Multi-purpose 2 stub Receipt (for receipts) and OCR Multi-Purp AP Laser (for checks).

If asked for a Cash account, select **Cash account 1110**. Accept the defaults for any field for which you are not given data.

Use the date of the transaction for the **Deposit Ticket ID** field.

Here are the transactions for March:

Mar.
2004

1   Received Check 7634 from the Bing Co., in the amount of $2,200, in payment of Invoice 12 ($2,200), dated January 1. Receipt 101 (R).

3   Purchased merchandise from the Morris Co. on account, $10,000, Invoice 1210, consisting of 184 Style 1000 and 180 Style 2000 dresses (P).

3   Sold merchandise to the Ronold Co. on account, $7,000, Invoice 51, consisting of 48 Style 1000, 30 Style 2000, 8 Style 3000, 9 Style 4000, 8 Style 5000 and 8 Style 6000 dresses (S).

7   Sold merchandise to the Ronold Co. on account, $5,000,

Invoice 52, consisting of 48 Style 1000, 24 Style 2000, 5 Style 3000, 3 Style 4000, 3 Style 5000 and 3 Style 6000 dresses (S).

10 Purchased merchandise from the Morris Co. on account, $5,000, Invoice 1286, consisting of 92 Style 1000 and 90 Style 2000 dresses (P).

10 Sold merchandise to the Ronold Co. on account $3,000, Invoice 53, consisting of 20 Style 1000, 20 Style 2000, 4 Style 3000, 2 Style 4000, and 4 Style 5000 dresses (S).

10 Paid cleaning service $300, Check 110, to Ronda's Cleaning Service. In the Payments window:

♦ Skip the Vendor ID field.

♦ Enter Ronda's name in the Name field.

♦ Enter a short description in the Description field on the Apply to Expenses tab.

♦ Select the correct GL account for this line (Cleaning Expense-5510).

♦ Enter the amount in the Amount column.

♦ Print the check as you did in Chapter 6 (PA).

11 Ronold Co. returned merchandise that the company sold to Ronold for $1,000 from Invoice 52, consisting of 4 Style 1000, 5 Style 2000, 2 Style 3000, 1 Style 4000, 2 Style 5000, and 1 Style 6000 dresses. The Corner Dress Shop issued Credit Memorandum CM 10 to the Ronald Co. for $1,000. Remember to use negative quantities and the Negative Invoice form for returns (S).

11 Purchased merchandise from the Jones Co. on account, $10,000, Invoice 4639, terms 1/15, n/60, consisting of 144 Style 3000 and 124 Style 4000 dresses (P).

12 Issued Check 111 to the Morris Co. in the amount of $9,800, in payment of Invoice 1210 ($10,000), dated March 2, less 2% discount ($200) (PA).

13 Sold $7,000 of merchandise for cash, consisting of 24 Style 1000, 30 Style 2000, 24 Style 3000, and 29 Style 4000 dresses. Skip the Customer ID field and type CASH in the name field and the Reference field. Change the Payment Method field to Cash. Receipt 102 (R).

14 Returned merchandise to the Jones Co. in the amount of $2,000, consisting of 32 Style 3000 and 22 Style 4000 dresses. Remember to use negative quantities for returns. Assign DM4 as the invoice number (P).

15 Look at your Trial Balance report that you printed at the

beginning of this workshop to determine how much to pay for each account. Pay FIT, Social Security, and Medicare taxes due for February payroll, Check 112, in the amount of $2,936.40. Skip the Vendor ID field and type IRS in the name field in the Pay to the Order Of section. Type 941 Payment in the Description field. Be sure to use the correct GL code for each payable account (PA).

15   Due to increased operating costs, The Corner Dress Shop must raise its selling prices, as follows:

Style 1000	$60.00
Style 2000	$70.00
Style 3000	$80.00
Style 4000	$90.00
Style 5000	$110.00
Style 6000	$120.00

Go to the Maintain menu and select Inventory Items. See the procedures discussed at the start of this practice set before continuing.

15   Sold merchandise for $29,000 cash, consisting of 124 Style 1000, 144 Style 2000, 72 Style 3000, 61 Style 4000, 1 Style 5000, and 1 Style 6000 dresses. Skip the Customer ID field. Type CASH in the Name and Reference fields. Receipt 103. If you do not end up with $29,000 as your total, check to make sure you accomplished the price changes correctly (R). If you get the message that the reference number has already been entered for this customer, click OK to continue.

15   Betty Loeb withdrew $100 for her own personal expenses, Check 113 (PA). Skip the Vendor ID and enter her name in the name field. Be sure to code to Owner's Withdrawals (3120).

15   Paid SIT tax for February payroll, Check 114. Skip the Vendor ID field. Make the check payable to the State of Massachusetts (using the name field). Type SIT Payment in the Description field. The check should be in the amount of $756.00 (PA).

17   Received Check 5432 from the Ronold Co. in the amount of $3,920, in payment of Invoice 52 ($5,000), dated March 7, less Credit Memo 10 (CM10) ($1,000), less 2% discount ($100 – 20 = $80, net sales discount). Receipt 104 (R).

17   Received Check 5447 from the Ronold Co. in the amount of $7,000, in payment of Invoice 51, dated March 3. Change the Payment Method to Check. Receipt 105 (R).

17   Sold merchandise to the Bing Co. on account, $3,200,

Invoice 54, consisting of 12 Style 1000, 10 Style 2000, 11 Style 3000, and 10 Style 4000 dresses. Be sure to change the invoice form when printing (S).

21 Purchased delivery truck on account from Moe's Garage, Invoice 7113, $17,200 (PU).

- ◆ Select Moe's Garage in the Vendor ID field.
- ◆ Enter the date and invoice number.
- ◆ Enter a description of the payment in that field.
- ◆ Select the correct GL account for this line (Delivery Truck).
- ◆ Enter the amount in the Amount column.
- ◆ Save.

22 Sold merchandise to the Ronold Co. on account $4,000, Invoice 55, consisting of 24 Style 1000, 24 Style 2000, 3 Style 3000, 2 Style 4000, 2 Style 5000, and 2- Style 6000 dresses (S).

23 Issued Check 115 to the Jones Co. in the amount of $7,920, in payment of Invoice 4639 ($10,000), dated March 11, less Debit Memo (DM4) ($2,000), less 1% discount ($100 – 20 = $80 net purchases discount) (PA).

24 Sold merchandise to the Bing Co. on account, $2,000, Invoice 56, consisting of 1 Style 2000, 10 Style 3000, 10 Style 4000, 1 Style 5000, and 1 Style 6000 dresses (S).

25 Purchased merchandise for $1,000 cash from the Jones Company, Check 116, consisting of 16 Style 3000 and 11 Style 4000 dresses. Skip the Vendor ID field and type Jones Company in the name field. Use the Quantity and Item fields in the PA window just as you would in the PU window.

27 Purchased merchandise from the Blew Co. on account, $6,000, Invoice 437, consisting of 60 Style 5000 and 66 Style 6000 dresses (PU).

28 Received Check 5562 from the Ronold Co. in the amount of $3,920, in payment of Invoice 55 ($4,000), dated March 22, less 2% discount ($80). Receipt 106 (R).

28 Received Check 8127 from the Bing Co. in the amount of $3,200, in payment of Invoice 54, dated March 16. Receipt 107 (R).

29 Purchased merchandise from the Morris Co. on account, $9,000, Invoice 1347, consisting of 150 Style 1000 and 150 Style 2000 dresses. The vendor has changed the prices on these items, so instead of accepting Peachtree's default for the unit prices, enter $28.00 and $32.00 for Style 1000 and

Style 2000, respectively (P).

30 Sold merchandise to the Bing Co. on account, $10,000, Invoice 57, consisting of 6 Style 3000, 5 Style 4000, 41 Style 5000, and 38 Style 6000 dresses (S).

30 The Auxiliary Petty Cash Record for March listed the following: Postage Expense, $5; Delivery Expense, $10; Cleaning Expense, $6; and Miscellaneous Expense, $10. Issued Check 117 for $31.00 to replenish the petty cash fund. Skip the Vendor ID field and type CASH in the name field (PA).

31 Issued payroll checks for March wages as follows:

Employee	March Wages	Check
Case, Mel	$3,325	118
Holl, Jane	4,120	119
Moore, Jackie	4,760	120

Use Select for Payroll Entry under the Tasks menu. Use 31 March as the pay end date as well as for the check date. Use Cash Account 1110 to issue the checks.

Printing the Reports

Print the reports shown in Figures 8.7 through 8.10, accepting the defaults.

The Corner Dress Shop-Student Name
General Ledger Trial Balance
As of Mar 31, 2004

Filter Criteria includes: Report order is by ID. Report is printed in Detail Format.

Account ID	Account Description	Debit Amt	Credit Amt
1110	Cash	26,450.74	
1115	Petty Cash	35.00	
1120	Accounts Receivable	15,000.00	
1130	Inventory	13,515.00	
1135	Inventory-Purchase Discounts		280.00
1140	Prepaid Rent	1,800.00	
1250	Delivery Truck	23,200.00	
1251	Accum. Dep-Delivery Truck		1,500.00
2110	Accounts Payable		39,100.00
2310	Federal Income Tax Payable		1,235.76
2320	State Income Tax Payable		586.80
2330	FICA- Soc. Sec. Payable		1,513.42
2335	FICA- Medicare Payable		353.94
2340	FUTA Payable		260.84
2350	SUTA Payable		1,565.04
2400	Unearned Rent		800.00
3110	Betty Loeb, Capital		9,103.10
3120	Betty Loeb, Withdrawals	100.00	
4110	Sales		69,200.00
4140	Sales Discounts	160.00	
5050	Cost of Goods Sold	31,085.00	
5100	Delivery Expense	10.00	
5400	Salaries Expense	12,205.00	
5420	Payroll Tax Expense	1,617.16	
5500	Postage Expense	5.00	
5510	Cleaning Expense	306.00	
5560	Miscellaneous Expense	10.00	
	Total:	125,498.90	125,498.90

Figure 8.7

The Corner Dress Shop-Student Name
Aged Receivables
As of Mar 31, 2004

Filter Criteria includes: Report order is by ID. Report is printed in Detail Format.

Customer ID Customer Contact Telephone 1	Invoice/CM #	0-30	31-60	61-90	Over 90 days	Amount Due
001	56	2,000.00				2,000.00
Bing Company	57	10,000.00				10,000.00
001 Bing Company		12,000.00				12,000.00
003 Ronold Company	53	3,000.00				3,000.00
003 Ronold Company		3,000.00				3,000.00
Report Total		15,000.00				15,000.00

Figure 8.8

The Corner Dress Shop-Student Name
Aged Payables
As of Mar 31, 2004

Filter Criteria includes: Report order is by ID. Report is printed in Detail Format.

Vendor ID Vendor Contact Telephone 1	Invoice/CM #	0 - 30	31 - 60	61 - 90	Over 90 days	Amount Due
001 Blew Company		7,900.00				7,900.00
003 Moe's Garage	7113	17,200.00				17,200.00
003 Moe's Garage		17,200.00				17,200.00
004	1286	5,000.00				5,000.00
Morris Company	1347	9,000.00				9,000.00
004 Morris Company		14,000.00				14,000.00
Report Total		39,100.00				39,100.00

Figure 8.9

The Corner Dress Shop-Student Name
Payroll Register
For the Period From Mar 1, 2004 to Mar 31, 2004
Filter Criteria includes: Report order is by Check Date. Report is printed in Detail Format.

Employee ID Employee SS No Reference Date	Pay Type	Pay Hrs	Pay Amt	Amount	Gross State SUI_ER	Fed_Income Soc_Sec_ER SDI_ER	Soc_Sec Medicare_ER	Medicare FUTA_ER
001 Mel Case 118 3/31/04	Salary		3,325.00	2,660.57	3,325.00 -148.40 -159.60	-261.67 -206.15	-206.15 -48.21	-48.21 -26.60
002 Jane Holl 119 3/31/04	Salary		4,120.00	3,190.20	4,120.00 -194.95 -197.76	-419.67 -255.44	-255.44 -59.74	-59.74 -32.96
003 Jackie Moore 120 3/31/04	Salary		4,760.00	3,597.99	4,760.00 -243.45 -228.48	-554.42 -295.12	-295.12 -69.02	-69.02 -38.08
Summary Total 3/1/04 thru 3/31/04	Salary		12,205.00	9,448.76	12,205.00 -586.80 -585.84	-1,235.76 -756.71	-756.71 -176.97	-176.97 -97.64

Figure 8.10

Recording the Adjusting Journal Entries

Record the following adjustments:

1. Open the *General Journal Entry* window from the **Tasks** menu.

2. In the **Date** field enter **3/31/04**.

3. In the **Reference Number** field enter **ADJ**.

4. Enter all the adjustments in the same entry window (see Figure 8.11):

    a. During March, rent expired, $600.

    b. Truck depreciated, $150.

    c. Rental income earned, $200 (debit to unearned rent).

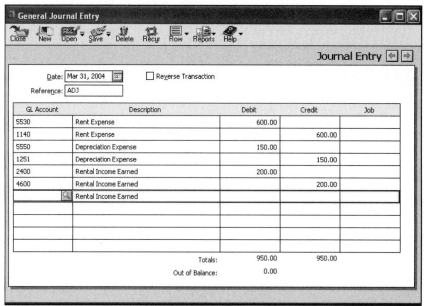

Figure 8.11

5. Review your entry before continuing. Make any corrections, if necessary.

6. Click the **Save** icon to post the journal entry.

7. Click the **Close** icon or button to exit the *General Journal Entry* window.

Displaying and Printing Reports

Print the reports shown in Figures 8.12 through 8.17, accepting all defaults.

The Corner Dress Shop-Student Name
General Journal
For the Period From Mar 1, 2004 to Mar 31, 2004

Filter Criteria includes: Report order is by Date. Report is printed with Accounts having Zero Amounts and with Truncated Transaction Descripti

Date	Account ID	Reference	Trans Description	Debit Amt	Credit Amt
3/31/04	5530	ADJ	Rent Expense	600.00	
	1140		Rent Expense		600.00
	5550		Depreciation Expense	150.00	
	1251		Depreciation Expense		150.00
	2400		Rental Income Earned	200.00	
	4600		Rental Income Earned		200.00
		Total		950.00	950.00

Figure 8.12

The Corner Dress Shop-Student Name
General Ledger Trial Balance
As of Mar 31, 2004

Filter Criteria includes: Report order is by ID. Report is printed in Detail Format.

Account ID	Account Description	Debit Amt	Credit Amt
1110	Cash	26,450.74	
1115	Petty Cash	35.00	
1120	Accounts Receivable	15,000.00	
1130	Inventory	13,515.00	
1135	Inventory-Purchase Discounts		280.00
1140	Prepaid Rent	1,200.00	
1250	Delivery Truck	23,200.00	
1251	Accum. Dep-Delivery Truck		1,650.00
2110	Accounts Payable		39,100.00
2310	Federal Income Tax Payable		1,235.76
2320	State Income Tax Payable		586.80
2330	FICA- Soc. Sec. Payable		1,513.42
2335	FICA- Medicare Payable		353.94
2340	FUTA Payable		260.84
2350	SUTA Payable		1,565.04
2400	Unearned Rent		600.00
3110	Betty Loeb, Capital		9,103.10
3120	Betty Loeb, Withdrawals	100.00	
4110	Sales		69,200.00
4140	Sales Discounts	160.00	
4600	Rental Income		200.00
5050	Cost of Goods Sold	31,085.00	
5100	Delivery Expense	10.00	
5400	Salaries Expense	12,205.00	
5420	Payroll Tax Expense	1,617.16	
5500	Postage Expense	5.00	
5510	Cleaning Expense	306.00	
5530	Rent Expense	600.00	
5550	Depreciation Exp.-Truck	150.00	
5560	Miscellaneous Expense	10.00	
	Total:	125,648.90	125,648.90

Figure 8.13

The Corner Dress Shop-Student Name
General Ledger
For the Period From Mar 1, 2004 to Mar 31, 2004
Filter Criteria includes: Report order is by ID. Report is printed with Truncated Transaction Descriptions and in Detail Format.

Account ID Account Description	Date	Reference	Jrnl	Trans Description	Debit Amt	Credit Amt	Balance
1110	3/1/04			Beginning Balance			2,502.90
Cash	3/1/04	7634	CRJ	Bing Company	2,200.00		
	3/10/04	110	CDJ	Rhonda's Cleaning Ser		300.00	
	3/12/04	111	CDJ	Morris Company		9,800.00	
	3/13/04	Cash	CRJ	Cash	7,000.00		
	3/15/04	112	CDJ	IRS		2,936.40	
	3/15/04	Cash	CRJ	Cash	29,000.00		
	3/15/04	113	CDJ	Betty Loeb		100.00	
	3/15/04	114	CDJ	State of Massachusetts		756.00	
	3/17/04	5432	CRJ	Ronold Company	3,920.00		
	3/17/04	5447	CRJ	Ronold Company	7,000.00		
	3/23/04	115	CDJ	Jones Company		7,920.00	
	3/25/04	116	CDJ	Jones Comany		1,000.00	
	3/28/04	5562	CRJ	Ronold Company	3,920.00		
	3/28/04	8127	CRJ	Bing Company	3,200.00		
	3/30/04	117	CDJ	Cash		31.00	
	3/31/04	118	PRJ	Mel Case		2,660.57	
	3/31/04	119	PRJ	Jane Holl		3,190.20	
	3/31/04	120	PRJ	Jackie Moore		3,597.99	
				Current Period Change	56,240.00	32,292.16	23,947.84
	3/31/04			Ending Balance			26,450.74
1115	3/1/04			Beginning Balance			35.00
Petty Cash	3/31/04			Ending Balance			35.00

Figure 8.14

The Corner Dress Shop-Student Name
Balance Sheet
March 31, 2004

ASSETS

Current Assets
Cash	$	26,450.74	
Petty Cash		35.00	
Accounts Receivable		15,000.00	
Inventory		13,515.00	
Inventory-Purchase Discounts		(280.00)	
Prepaid Rent		1,200.00	
Total Current Assets			55,920.74
Property and Equipment			
Delivery Truck		23,200.00	
Accum. Dep-Delivery Truck		(1,650.00)	
Total Property and Equipment			21,550.00
Other Assets			
Total Other Assets			0.00
Total Assets	$		77,470.74

LIABILITIES AND CAPITAL

Current Liabilities
Accounts Payable	$	39,100.00
Federal Income Tax Payable		1,235.76
State Income Tax Payable		586.80
FICA- Soc. Sec. Payable		1,513.42

Figure 8.15

The Corner Dress Shop-Student Name
Income Statement
For the Three Months Ending March 31, 2004

	Current Month		Year to Date	
Revenues				
Sales	$ 69,200.00	99.94	$ 69,200.00	99.94
Sales Returns & Allowances	0.00	0.00	0.00	0.00
Sales Discounts	(160.00)	(0.23)	(160.00)	(0.23)
Rental Income	200.00	0.29	200.00	0.29
Total Revenues	69,240.00	100.00	69,240.00	100.00
Cost of Sales				
Cost of Goods Sold	31,085.00	44.89	31,085.00	44.89
Total Cost of Sales	31,085.00	44.89	31,085.00	44.89
Gross Profit	38,155.00	55.11	38,155.00	55.11
Expenses				
Delivery Expense	10.00	0.01	10.00	0.01
Salaries Expense	12,205.00	17.63	12,205.00	17.63
Payroll Tax Expense	1,617.16	2.34	1,617.16	2.34
Postage Expense	5.00	0.01	5.00	0.01
Cleaning Expense	306.00	0.44	306.00	0.44
Rent Expense	600.00	0.87	600.00	0.87
Depreciation Exp.-Truck	150.00	0.22	150.00	0.22
Miscellaneous Expense	10.00	0.01	10.00	0.01
Total Expenses	14,903.16	21.52	14,903.16	21.52
Net Income	$ 23,251.84	33.58	$ 23,251.84	33.58

Figure 8.16

The Corner Dress Shop-Student Name
Inventory Valuation Report
As of Mar 31, 2004

Filter Criteria includes: 1) Stock/Assembly. Report order is by ID. Report is printed with Truncated Long Descriptions.

Item ID Item Class	Item Description	Stocking U/M	Cost Method	Qty on Hand	Item Value	Avg Cost	% of Inv Value
1000 Stock item	Dress, Style 1000	Each	Average	160.00	4,450.00	27.81	32.93
2000 Stock item	Dress, Style 2000	Each	Average	167.00	5,310.00	31.80	39.29
3000 Stock item	Dress, Style 3000	Each	Average	12.00	420.00	35.00	3.11
4000 Stock item	Dress, Style 4000	Each	Average	8.00	320.00 .	40.00	2.37
5000 Stock item	Dress, Style 5000	Each	Average	27.00	1,215.00	45.00	8.99
6000 Stock item	Dress, Style 6000	Each	Average	36.00	1,800.00	50.00	13.32
					13,515.00		100.00

Figure 8.17

Weighted-Average Inventory Cost

Compare the Inventory Valuation report you just printed (Figure 8.17) with the one created at the start of this workshop (Figure 8.5). Note that the first two items, the ones whose cost price changed when the company last purchased them, have neither the original prices of $25.00 and $30.00 nor the new prices of $28.00 and $32.00, respectively. Peachtree has created a weighted-average for these items.

Backing Up Your Company Data File

1. Select **Back up** from the **File** menu.

2. Click the check box to include the company name in the file name.

3. Add **EndMar** to the file name.

4. Select the **Save in** lookup box to find the location your instructor has identified for you to keep your backup file(s).

5. Click **Save**.

6. Click **OK**.

> NOTE: Refer to Chapter 1 for more detailed instructions on backing up files.

Advancing the Period to April

In order to close the accounting period, you then need to advance the period:

1. Click **System** in the **Tasks** menu and then select **Change Accounting Period**.

2. Using the list on the left, select **04- Apr 1, 2004 to Apr 30, 2004**.

3. Click the **OK** button.

4. Click **No** when asked whether to print reports before continuing. You have already printed your reports.

5. Note that the status bar at the bottom of the screen now reflects Period 4 (see Figure 8.18).

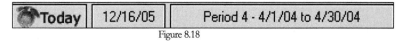

Figure 8.18

Backing Up Your Company Data File

1. Select **Backup** from the **File** menu.

2. Click the check box to include the company name in the file name.

3. Add **Final** to the file name.

4. Select the **Save in** lookup box to find the location your instructor has identified for you to keep your backup file(s).

5. Click **Save**.

6. Click **OK**.

> ➤ NOTE: Refer to Chapter 1 for more detailed instructions on backing up files.

Exiting the Peachtree Complete Accounting 2006 program

1. Click **Exit** from the **File** menu to end the current work session and return to your Windows desktop.

2. If you are asked if you wish to save any unposted work, click the **Yes** button.

CHAPTER 9

Perpetual Inventory System—The Paint Place

THIS WORKSHOP INCLUDES INFORMATION ON MAINTAINING PERPETUAL INVENTORY RECORDS AND ITEMS, ACCOUNTS RECEIVABLE, AND ACCOUNTS PAYABLE. THIS WORKSHOP DOES NOT COVER PAYROLL OR GENERAL JOURNAL ENTRIES.

IT IS RECOMMENDED THAT YOU COMPLETE THE WORKSHOP IN CHAPTER 6 BEFORE DOING THIS WORKSHOP.

Opening The Paint Place

1. Double-click the **Peachtree** icon on your desktop to open the software program.

2. Click **Open an existing company** and then locate and select **The Paint Place**.

3. Click **Open**.

   ➢ **NOTE:** Refer to Chapter 1 for more detailed instructions on opening files.

Backing Up Your Company Data File

1. Select **Backup** from the **File** menu.

2. Click the check box to include the company name in the file name.

3. Add **Start** to the file name.

4. Select the **Save in** lookup box to find the location your instructor has identified for you to keep your backup file(s).

5. Click **Save**.

6. Click **OK**.

   ➢ **NOTE:** Refer to Chapter 1 for more detailed instructions on backing up files.

Adding Your Name to the Company Name

1. Click the **Maintain** menu option and then select **Company Information**. The program responds by bringing up the *Maintain Company Information* dialog box, which allows you to edit/add information about the company.

2. Click in the **Company Name** field and make sure your cursor is at the end of **The Paint Place**.

3. Add a dash and your name (-Student's Name).

4. Click the **OK** button.

> **NOTE:** Refer to Chapter 2 for more detailed instructions on adding your name to a company name.

Overview of Perpetual Inventory

One of the most powerful features of a computerized accounting system is its ability to maintain perpetual inventory records easily and accurately. Earlier Peachtree workshops demonstrated this feature as you recorded purchases and sales of inventory. Peachtree Complete Accounting 2006 has the ability to maintain perpetual inventory records through its Inventory module. Peachtree Complete Accounting 2006 can calculate inventory by using FIFO, LIFO, or the weighted-average method as its inventory cost flow assumption. While a default assumption can be set, an assumption can also be designated for each inventory item individually.

In this workshop you will be working with the data files for a company called The Paint Place. The Paint Place uses the Sales/Invoicing, Receipts, Purchases, Payments, and Inventory modules of Peachtree Complete Accounting 2006 to maintain its accounting and perpetual inventory records.

The Paint Place extends terms of 2/10, n/30 to all its credit customers.

Printing the Beginning Balance Reports

> **NOTE:** For more detailed instructions on printing reports see Chapter 2.

Print the reports shown in Figures 9.1 through 9.4, changing the date to 2/29/04 or 3/1/04 under the Options menu. Compare the Accounts Receivable Aging, Accounts Payable Aging, and Inventory Valuation reports to the balances on the Trial Balance report. They should match.

The Paint Place
General Ledger Trial Balance
As of Feb 29, 2004

Filter Criteria includes: Report order is by ID. Report is printed in Detail Format.

Account ID	Account Description	Debit Amt	Credit Amt
1110	Cash	23,059.86	
1120	Accounts Receivable	8,259.95	
1130	Merchandise Inventory	28,928.67	
1140	Prepaid Rent	2,200.00	
1150	Store Supplies	1,622.30	
1250	Office Equipment	12,800.00	
1251	Accum. Dep-Office Equipment		1,469.44
1350	Store Equipment	13,500.00	
1351	Accum. Dep- Store Equipment		1,916.67
2110	Accounts Payable		4,142.12
3110	Mike Poole, Capital		37,728.86
3130	Retained Earnings		41,822.74
4110	Sales		3,290.95
	Total:	90,370.78	90,370.78

Figure 9.1

The Paint Place
Aged Receivables
As of Mar 1, 2004

Filter Criteria includes: Report order is by ID. Report is printed in Detail Format.

Customer ID Customer Contact Telephone 1	Invoice/CM #	0-30	31-60	61-90	Over 90 days	Amount Due
001 Elaine Anderson		2,293.05				2,293.05
002 Jake Kerns	5461	2,675.95				2,675.95
002 Jake Kerns		2,675.95				2,675.95
003 Wes Young	5468	3,290.95				3,290.95
003 Wes Young		3,290.95				3,290.95
Report Total		8,259.95				8,259.95

Figure 9.2

			The Paint Place			
			Aged Payables			
			As of Mar 1, 2004			

Filter Criteria includes: Report order is by ID. Report is printed in Detail Format.

Vendor ID Vendor Contact Telephone 1	Invoice/CM #	0 - 30	31 - 60	61 - 90	Over 90 days	Amount Due
001 Painter's Supply		975.34				975.34
002 Vantage Tints	5658	1,116.33				1,116.33
002 Vantage Tints		1,116.33				1,116.33
003 Wholesale Paints	56780	2,050.45				2,050.45
003 Wholesale Paints		2,050.45				2,050.45
Report Total		4,142.12				4,142.12

Figure 9.3

			The Paint Place			
			Inventory Valuation Report			
			As of Feb 29, 2004			

Filter Criteria includes: 1) Stock/Assembly. Report order is by ID. Report is printed with Truncated Long Descriptions.

Item ID Item Class	Item Description	Stocking U/M	Cost Method	Qty on Hand	Item Value	Avg Cost	% of Inv Value
001 Stock item	Latex Flat	Gallon	Average	642.00	4,795.74	7.47	16.58
002 Stock item	Latex Semi-Gloss	Gallon	Average	1066.00	7,963.02	7.47	27.53
003 Stock item	Latex High-Gloss	Gallon	Average	600.00	4,482.00	7.47	15.49
004 Stock item	Oil High-Gloss	Gallon	Average	801.00	7,184.97	8.97	24.84
005 Stock item	Oil Semi-Gloss	Gallon	Average	502.00	4,502.94	8.97	15.57
					28,928.67		100.00

Figure 9.4

Adding Inventory Items

Peachtree Complete Accounting 2006 allows you to quickly and easily add new inventory items or edit information about items currently in the inventory.

To add a new product to the inventory for **The Paint Place,** follow these steps:

1. Select **Inventory Items** from the **Maintain** menu.

2. In the **Item ID** field, type **006** and press Tab.

3. In the **Description** field, type Oil Flat and press Tab.

4. In the **Item class** field accept the default Stock Item because this will be a regular stocked item.

5. In the **Description** field you can enter a longer description of this item that will appear on sales and/or purchase invoices. For this item, the company will use the short description, so you can Tab to the **Price Level 1** field.

6. In the **Price Level 1** field enter **16.95**. This is the normal selling price for this item.

> ➤ **CHECK IT OUT:** Peachtree has the capability of storing multiple prices for an item. Click the arrow to the right of the **Price Level 1** field. You then see the *Multiple Price Level* window, where you can enter up to 10 different selling prices. Different customers can be given different price levels in this manner. Click **Cancel** to close the *Multiple Price Level* window since this company uses only one price level.

7. Tab to the **Cost Method** field. Select **Average** for the cost flow method for this item.

> ➤ **NOTE:** FIFO or LIFO could be selected as the cost flow method.

8. Tab through **GL accounts,** accepting the default account numbers for inventory transactions.

9. Tab through **Item Type** and **Location,** which are information fields that the company is not using at this time.

10. In the **Stocking U/M (Unit/Measure)** field enter **Gallon**. The company sells the paint in 1 gallon cans.

11. Accept Peachtree's default information on the rest of the fields in this window.

12. The company has not set up any Custom Fields and there is no History for this item, so you do not need to use those tabs in this workshop. Your screen should look like Figure 9.5.

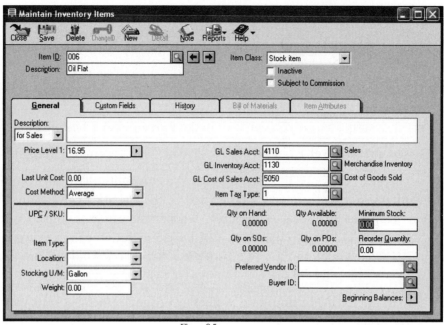

Figure 9.5

13. Click the **Save** icon to record this item in the inventory.

Editing Inventory Items

With the ***Maintain Inventory Items*** dialog box open, you can follow these steps to edit inventory items as necessary:

1. Click the lookup button (the magnifying glass) next to the **Item ID** field.

2. Click any item to display it on your screen.

3. Click any field and change information as needed.

4. Click the **Save** icon to save any changes you have made.

5. Click the **Close** button to exit the ***Maintain Inventory Items*** dialog box.

Recording Transactions for March

Record the following transactions, using the appropriate windows. This workshop uses the ***Sales/Invoicing*** (S), ***Receipts*** (R), ***Purchases/Receive Inventory*** (PU), and ***Payments*** (PA) windows.

Accept the defaults for any fields for which you are not given information.

Insert the appropriate number given in the transactions during the printing process for all print activities.

Mar. 2004	1	Sold 5 gallons of Oil High-gloss (Item 4) at $17.95 per gallon to Elaine Anderson on account, Invoice 5469 for $89.75 (S).
	3	Received Invoice 6892 from Wholesale Paints in the amount of $1,504 for the purchase of 200 gallons of Latex High-gloss (Item 3) at $7.52 per gallon. Don't forget to change the Unit Price (PU).
	3	Received Invoice CC675 from the Painter's Supply in the amount of $906, for the purchase of 100 gallons of Oil High-gloss (Item 4) at 9.06 per gallon. Don't forget to change the Unit Price (PU).
	4	Sold 5 gallons of Oil High-gloss paint (Item 4) at $17.95 per gallon to Jake Kerns on account, Invoice 5470, $89.75 (S).
	6	Received Check 8723 from Wes Young in the amount of $3,225.13 in payment of Invoice 5468 ($3,290.95), dated February 28, less 2% discount ($65.82). Receipt 101 (R).
	7	Issued Check 2345 to Vantage Tints in the amount of $1,082.84 in payment of Invoice 5658 ($1,116.33), dated February 28, less 3% discount ($33.49) (PA).
	14	Sold 10 gallons of Latex Semi-gloss (Item 2) at $16.95 per gallon to Elaine Anderson on account for $169.50, Invoice 5471 (S).
	17	Received Invoice 6943 from Wholesale Paints in the amount of $1,134 for the purchase of 150 gallons of Latex Semi-gloss (Item 2) at 7.56 per gallon. Don't forget to change the Unit Price. (PU).
	19	Received Invoice CC691 from Painter's Supply in the amount of $1,618.75 for the purchase of 175 gallons of Oil Semi-gloss (Item 5) at 9.25 per gallon. Don't forget to change the Unit Price (PU).
	21	Sold 10 gallons of Latex Semi-gloss (Item 2) at $16.95 per gallon to Jake Kerns on account, $169.50, Invoice 5472 (S).
	24	Sold 25 gallons of Oil Semi-gloss paint (Item 5) at $17.95 per gallon to Elaine Anderson on account for $448.75, Invoice 5473 (S).
	25	Received Invoice CC787 from Painter's Supply in the amount of $465 for the purchase of 50 gallons of Oil Semi-gloss (Item 5) at 9.30 per gallon. Don't forget to change the Unit Price, terms 2/10, n/30 (PU).
	31	Sold 25 gallons of Oil Semi-gloss (Item 5) at $17.95 per gallon to Jake Kerns on account, $448.75, Invoice 5474 (S).

Displaying and Printing the Inventory Unit Activity Report

You may wish to see how active the items in your inventory have been. Peachtree has a Unit Activity report that summarizes the units bought and sold for any selected period.

1. Select **Inventory** from the **Reports** menu.

2. From the *Select a Report* window select **Inventory Unit Activity Report**.

3. Accept all defaults. Your screen will look like Figure 9.6.

The Paint Place-Students Name
Inventory Unit Activity Report
For the Period From Mar 1, 2004 to Mar 31, 2004
Filter Criteria includes: 1) Stock/Assembly. Report order is by ID. Report is printed with Truncated Long Descriptions.

Item ID Item Description Item Class	Beg Qty	Units Sold	Units Purc	Adjust Qty	Assembly Qty	Qty on Hand
001 Latex Flat Stock item	642.00					642.00
002 Latex Semi-Gloss Stock item	1066.00	20.00	150.00			1196.00
003 Latex High-Gloss Stock item	600.00		200.00			800.00
004 Oil High-Gloss Stock item	801.00	10.00	100.00			891.00
005 Oil Semi-Gloss Stock item	502.00	50.00	225.00			677.00
006 Oil Flat Stock item						
		80.00	675.00			

Figure 9.6

4. Click the **Print** icon.

5. Click the **Close** icon or button to exit the report.

Displaying and Printing the Inventory Valuation Report

The Inventory Valuation report is one of the most valuable reports for inventory management.

1. From the *Select a Report* window select **Inventory Valuation Report.**

2. Accept all defaults. Your screen will look like Figure 9.7.

The Paint Place-Students Name
Inventory Valuation Report
As of Mar 31, 2004

Filter Criteria includes: 1) Stock/Assembly. Report order is by ID. Report is printed with Truncated Long Descriptions.

Item ID Item Class	Item Description	Stocking U/M	Cost Method	Qty on Hand	Item Value	Avg Cost	% of Inv Value
001 Stock item	Latex Flat	Gallon	Average	642.00	4,795.74	7.47	14.16
002 Stock item	Latex Semi-Gloss	Gallon	Average	1196.00	8,947.51	7.48	26.42
003 Stock item	Latex High-Gloss	Gallon	Average	800.00	5,986.00	7.48	17.68
004 Stock item	Oil High-Gloss	Gallon	Average	891.00	8,001.22	8.98	23.63
005 Stock item	Oil Semi-Gloss	Gallon	Average	677.00	6,134.11	9.06	18.11
006 Stock item	Oil Flat	Gallon	Average				
					33,864.58		100.00

Figure 9.7

3. Click the **Print** icon.

4. Click the **Close** icon or button to exit the report.

Printing the Reports for March

Print the following reports shown in Figures 9.8 through 9.12 for the month of March, accepting all defaults.

The Paint Place-Students Name
General Ledger Trial Balance
As of Mar 31, 2004

Filter Criteria includes: Report order is by ID. Report is printed in Detail Format.

Account ID	Account Description	Debit Amt	Credit Amt
1110	Cash	25,202.15	
1120	Accounts Receivable	6,385.00	
1130	Merchandise Inventory	33,831.09	
1140	Prepaid Rent	2,200.00	
1150	Store Supplies	1,622.30	
1250	Office Equipment	12,800.00	
1251	Accum. Dep-Office Equipment		1,469.44
1350	Store Equipment	13,500.00	
1351	Accum. Dep- Store Equipment		1,916.67
2110	Accounts Payable		8,653.54
3110	Mike Poole, Capital		37,728.86
3130	Retained Earnings		41,822.74
4110	Sales		4,706.95
4140	Sales Discounts	65.82	
5050	Cost of Goods Sold	691.84	
	Total:	96,298.20	96,298.20

Figure 9.8

The Paint Place-Students Name
Aged Receivables
As of Mar 31, 2004

Filter Criteria includes: Report order is by ID. Report is printed in Detail Format.

Customer ID Customer Contact Telephone 1	Invoice/CM #	0-30	31-60	61-90	Over 90 days	Amount Due
001	5441	2,293.05				2,293.05
Elaine Anderson	5469	89.75				89.75
	5471	169.50				169.50
	5473	448.75				448.75
001 Elaine Anderson		3,001.05				3,001.05
002	5461	2,675.95				2,675.95
Jake Kerns	5470	89.75				89.75
	5472	169.50				169.50
	5474	448.75				448.75
002 Jake Kerns		3,383.95				3,383.95
Report Total		6,385.00				6,385.00

Figure 9.9

The Paint Place-Students Name
Aged Payables
As of Mar 31, 2004

Filter Criteria includes: Report order is by ID. Report is printed in Detail Format.

Vendor ID Vendor Contact Telephone 1	Invoice/CM #	0 - 30	31 - 60	61 - 90	Over 90 days	Amount Due
001	4356	975.34				975.34
Painter's Supply	CC675	906.00				906.00
	CC691	1,618.75				1,618.75
	CC787	465.00				465.00
001 Painter's Supply		3,965.09				3,965.09
003	56780	2,050.45				2,050.45
Wholesale Paints	6892	1,504.00				1,504.00
	6943	1,134.00				1,134.00
003 Wholesale Paints		4,688.45				4,688.45
Report Total		8,653.54				8,653.54

Figure 9.10

The Paint Place-Students Name
Income Statement
For the Three Months Ending March 31, 2004

	Current Month		Year to Date	
Revenues				
Sales	$ 1,416.00	104.87	$ 4,706.95	101.42
Sales Returns & Allowances	0.00	0.00	0.00	0.00
Sales Discounts	(65.82)	(4.87)	(65.82)	(1.42)
Total Revenues	1,350.18	100.00	4,641.13	100.00
Cost of Sales				
Cost of Goods Sold	691.84	51.24	691.84	14.91
Total Cost of Sales	691.84	51.24	691.84	14.91
Gross Profit	658.34	48.76	3,949.29	85.09
Expenses				
Delivery Expense	0.00	0.00	0.00	0.00
Advertising Expense	0.00	0.00	0.00	0.00
Utilities Expense	0.00	0.00	0.00	0.00
Store Supplies Expense	0.00	0.00	0.00	0.00
Rent Expense	0.00	0.00	0.00	0.00
Deprec Exp.: Office Equipment	0.00	0.00	0.00	0.00
Deprec Exp.: Store Equipment	0.00	0.00	0.00	0.00
Miscellaneous Expense	0.00	0.00	0.00	0.00
Total Expenses	0.00	0.00	0.00	0.00
Net Income	$ 658.34	48.76	$ 3,949.29	85.09

Figure 9.11

The Paint Place-Students Name
Balance Sheet
March 31, 2004

ASSETS

Current Assets		
Cash	$ 25,202.15	
Accounts Receivable	6,385.00	
Merchandise Inventory	33,831.09	
Prepaid Rent	2,200.00	
Store Supplies	1,622.30	
Total Current Assets		69,240.54
Property and Equipment		
Office Equipment	12,800.00	
Accum. Dep-Office Equipment	(1,469.44)	
Store Equipment	13,500.00	
Accum. Dep- Store Equipment	(1,916.67)	
Total Property and Equipment		22,913.89
Other Assets		
Total Other Assets		0.00
Total Assets	$	92,154.43

LIABILITIES AND CAPITAL

Current Liabilities		
Accounts Payable	$ 8,653.54	
Total Current Liabilities		8,653.54

Figure 9.12

Backing Up Your Company Data File

1. Select **Back up** from the **File** menu.

2. Click the check box to include the company name in the file name.

3. Select the **Save in** lookup box to find the location your instructor has identified for you to keep your backup file(s).

4. Add **End** to the file name.

5. Click **Save**.

6. Click **OK**.

   ➢ **NOTE:** Refer to Chapter 1 for more detailed instructions on backing up files.

Exiting the Peachtree Complete Accounting 2006 Program

1. Click on **Exit** from the **File** menu to end the current work session and return to your Windows desktop.

2. If you are asked if you wish to save any unposted work, click the **Yes** button.

CHAPTER 10

Notes Receivable and Notes Payable--Lundquist Custom Woodworking

THIS WORKSHOP COVERS SHORT-TERM NOTES RECEIVABLE AND NOTES PAYABLES THAT ORIGINATE FROM ACCOUNTS RECEIVABLE AND ACCOUNTS PAYABLE BALANCES.

Peachtree Accounting does not have a specific provision for the recording of promissory notes from either the buyer's or the seller's prospective. Generally speaking, promissory note entries that do not involve accounts receivable or accounts payable, such as cash loans, can be entered through the General Journal Entry window.

Entries that involve accounts receivable and/or accounts payable must be entered through a window that will also perform a posting to the appropriate Subsidiary ledger. Using either the *Payments* window or *Receipts* window allows you to maintain the balance between the Subsidiary ledgers and their controlling accounts in the General ledger.

Peachtree does *not* automatically calculate interest, and you are still required to calculate interest manually.

Opening the Lundquist Custom Woodworking File

1. Double-click the **Peachtree** icon on your desktop to open the software program.

2. Click **Open an existing company** and then locate and select the **Lundquist Custom Woodworking**.

3. Click **Open**.

   ➢ **NOTE:** Refer to Chapter 1 for more detailed instructions on opening company files.

Backing Up Your Company Data File

1. Select **Back up** from the **File** menu.

2. Click the check box to include the company name in the file name.

3. Add **Start** to the file name.

4. Select the **Save in** lookup box to find the location your instructor has identified for you to keep your backup file(s).

5. Click **Save**.

6. Click **OK**.

> ➤ **NOTE:** Refer to Chapter 1 for more detailed instructions on backing up files.

Adding Your Name to the Company Name

1. Click **Maintain** menu option and then select **Company Information**. The program responds by bringing up the ***Maintain Company Information*** dialog box, which allows you to edit/add information about the company.

2. Click in the **Company Name** field and make sure your cursor is at the end of **Lundquist Custom Woodworking**.

3. Add a dash and your name (–**Student's Name**).

4. Click the **OK** button.

> ➤ **NOTE:** Refer to Chapter 2 for more detailed instructions on adding your name to a company name.

Printing the Beginning-of-the-Month Reports

Print the **General Ledger Trial Balance** report from the **General Ledger** report area section of the ***Select a Report*** dialog box:

1. With the report on your screen, click the **Options** [Options] icon.

2. Change the **As of date** to **Period 7 (7/31/04)**.

3. Click **OK**.

4. Click the **Print** icon.

5. Click **OK** to print the report, which is shown in Figure 10.1.

Lundquist Custom Woodworking-Name
General Ledger Trial Balance
As of Jul 31, 2004

Filter Criteria includes: Report order is by ID. Report is printed in Detail Format.

Account ID	Account Description	Debit Amt	Credit Amt
1110	Cash	30,000.00	
1120	Accounts Receivable	52,000.00	
1130	Notes Receivable	5,000.00	
1150	Shop Supplies	5,800.00	
1210	Shop Equipment	156,000.00	
1221	Accum. Depr- Shop Equipment		34,000.00
1230	Automobile	16,000.00	
1241	Accum. Depr- Automobile		4,000.00
2110	Accounts Payable		2,000.00
2130	Notes Payable		3,000.00
3110	Vernon Lunquist, Capital		10,000.00
3130	Retained Earnings		211,800.00
	Total:	264,800.00	264,800.00

Figure 10.1

Print the **Aged Receivables** report from the **Accounts Receivable** report area section of the *Select a Report* dialog box:

1. With the report on your screen, click the **Options** ⬛ icon.

2. Change the **Date** field to **Exact Date**.

3. In the **From** field enter **7/31/04**.

4. Click **OK.**

5. Click the **Print** icon and click **OK** to print the report, which is shown in Figure 10.2.

		Lundquist Custom Woodworking-Name				
		Aged Receivables				
		As of Jul 31, 2004				
Filter Criteria includes: Report order is by ID. Report is printed in Detail Format.						
Customer ID **Customer** **Contact** **Telephone 1**	**Invoice/CM #**	**0-30**	**31-60**	**61-90**	**Over 90 days**	**Amount Due**
BB Betty's Boutique Betty	98734351	4,000.00				4,000.00
BB Betty's Boutique		4,000.00				4,000.00
CAS Carl's Accounting Service Carl	98734352	6,000.00				6,000.00
CAS Carl's Accounting Service		6,000.00				6,000.00
SSD Salinas School District Helen	98734353	42,000.00				42,000.00
SSD Salinas School District		42,000.00				42,000.00

Figure 10.2

Print the **Aged Payables** report from the **Accounts Payable** report area section of the *Select a Report* dialog box:

1. With the report on your screen, click the **Options** ⬛ icon.

2. Change the **Date** field to **Exact Date**.

3. In the **From** field enter **7/31/04**.

4. Click **OK.**

5. Click the **Print** icon and click **OK** to print the report, which is shown in Figure 10.3.

		Lundquist Custom Woodworking-Name				
		Aged Payables				
		As of Jul 31, 2004				
Filter Criteria includes: Report order is by ID. Report is printed in Detail Format.						
Vendor ID Vendor Contact Telephone 1	Invoice/CM #	0 - 30	31 - 60	61 - 90	Over 90 days	Amount Due
ELS Elmer Lumber Supply Elmer	5688B	800.00				800.00
ELS Elmer Lumber Supply		800.00				800.00
OSH Orchard Supply Hardware Nick	A3456782-6	1,200.00				1,200.00
OSH Orchard Supply Hardware		1,200.00				1,200.00
Report Total		2,000.00				2,000.00

Figure 10.3

Recording a Note Receivable in Settlement of an Accounts Receivable Balance

A common reason for issuing a promissory note is to extend the amount of time for settlement of an account receivable. To illustrate how easily notes can be added, you will add a new note receivable to Lundquist Custom Woodworking.

You will transfer the amount owed to the company from one Asset account (Accounts Receivable) to another Asset account (Notes Receivable). While you could accomplish this in Peachtree quickly and easily with a General Journal entry, the balance owed to the company would continue to show in the Subsidiary Accounts Receivable ledger. Instead of using the General Journal entry window, you will use the *Receipts* window, changing the debit to Cash into a debit to Notes Receivable.

> **TRANSACTION: On August 15, 2004, Betty's Boutique, a customer of Lundquist Custom Woodworking, will settle her accounts receivable balance of $4,000.00 by issuing a 12% 60-day note.**

1. Select **Receipts** from the **Tasks** menu.
2. In the **Deposit ticket ID** field enter **081504**.
3. Using the lookup icon, select **Betty's Boutique** in the **Customer ID** field.
4. In the **Reference** field type **12%, 60 Day**.
5. In the **Receipt Number** field type **101**.
6. In the **Date** field enter or select **8/15/04**.

7. Using the lookup icon select account **1130 Notes Receivable** in the **Cash Account** field. This forces the debit to account 1130 instead of the cash account, 1110.

> **Important Warning:** By changing the Cash account to 1130, you cause Peachtree to use this account number again in the next transaction entered through the *Receipts* window. Be sure to change the Cash account back to 1110 the next time this window is used.

8. Click the **Apply to Invoices** tab.

9. In the **Pay** column, select the $4,000 invoice by clicking in the box (see Figure 10.4).

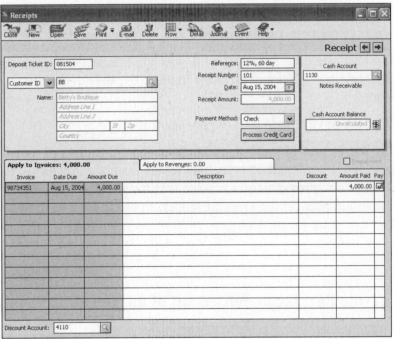

Figure 10.4

10. To view the impact of the transaction, click the **Journal** [Journal] icon. The window shown in Figure 10.5 appears.

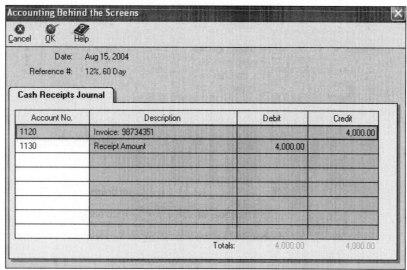

Figure 10.5

11. You now see how Peachtree will post the transaction to the General ledger (Debits and Credits). Click the **Cancel** button on the *Accounting Behind the Screens* window.

12. Click the **Save** icon to post the transaction.

To view the impact of your transaction on the Subsidiary Accounts Receivable ledger, you may look at an **Aged Receivables** report from the **Accounts Receivable** report area of the *Select a Report* dialog box. Note that the invoice is no longer listed on this report. To view the impact on the General ledger, you can look at the **Cash Receipts Journal** found in the same menu. You can view these reports on your screen or print them for later examination.

Recording a Note Payable in Settlement of an Accounts Payable Balance

When one business records a promissory note as a note receivable, another business will be recording the same note as a note payable. The second company, known as the *maker* of the note, is extending the time it has for payment of debt. You will be moving the amount the company owes from one liability account (Accounts Payable) to another liability account (Notes Payable). Again, you could accomplish this with a General Journal entry, but you are faced with the problem of having the Subsidiary ledger out of balance with the General ledger. To prevent this, use the *Payments* window, changing the credit to Cash into a credit to Notes Payable.

> **TRANSACTION: On August 18, 2004, Lundquist Custom Woodworking extended the time for payment of the balance due to Elmer Lumber Supply. Lundquist Custom Woodworking will settle its accounts payable by issuing an $800.00 12% 60-day note.**

1. Select **Payments** from the **Tasks** menu.

2. Using the lookup icon, select **Elmer Lumber Supply** in the **Vendor ID** field.

3. In the **Check Number** field type **NP01**.

4. Enter or select **8/18/04** as the date and press **Tab**.

5. In the **Memo** field, enter **12%, 60 Day**.

6. Using the lookup icon, select account **2130 Notes Payable** in the field marked **Cash Account**. This forces the credit to account 2130 instead of account 1110.

➤ **Important Warning:** By changing the Cash account to 2130, you cause Peachtree to use this account number again in the next transaction entered through the *Payments* window. Be sure to change the Cash account back to 1110 the next time this window is used.

7. Click the **Apply to Invoices** tab.

8. In the **Pay** column, select the $800 invoice by clicking in the box (see Figure 10.6).

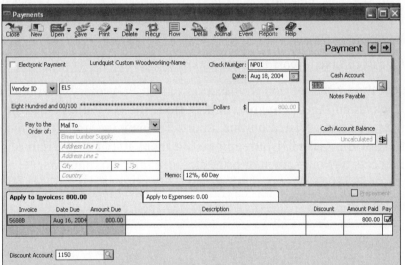

Figure 10.6

9. To view the impact of the transaction, Click the **Journal** icon. The screen shown in Figure 10.7 appears.

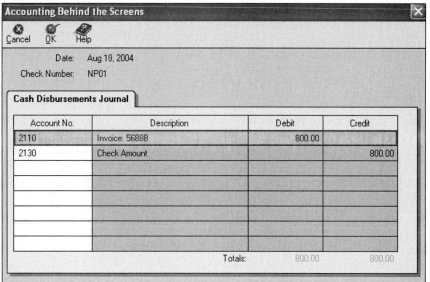

Figure 10.7

10. You see how Peachtree will post the transaction to the General ledger (Debits and Credits). Click the **Cancel** icon to close the *Accounting Behind the Screens* window.

11. Click on **Save** to post the transaction.

To view the impact of your transaction on the Subsidiary Accounts Payable ledger, you may look at an **Aged Payables** report from the **Accounts Payable Report** menu. The invoice is no longer listed on this report. To view the impact on the General ledger, you can look at the **Cash Disbursements Journal** found in the same menu. You can view these reports on your screen or print them for later examination.

Recording the Receipt of a Note Receivable Payment

Once recorded, a promissory note no longer has an impact on the Subsidiary ledgers. You could record the receipt of the note in the General journal; however, cash receipts collected for notes receivables are best entered through the *Receipts* window. Peachtree does not calculate the interest for you. You calculate the interest in the same manner as you would in a manual accounting system, by using this formula:

$$I = P \times R \times T$$

> **TRANSACTION: On August 15, 2004, the company receives a payment from Erin's Design for the existing Note Receivable principal of $5,000.00 plus $100.00 interest (I = $5,000.00 X 12% X 60/360 = $100.00). The company accepted a 12% 60-day note on June 15, 2004. It is now August 15, 2004, 60 days later, and payment in full has been received.**

1. Select **Receipts** from the **Tasks** menu.

2. In the **Deposit Ticket ID** field enter **08152004**.

3. Since this payment is not a payment on an account receivable, leave the **Customer ID** field blank.

4. In the **Name** field enter **Erin's Design**.

5. In the **Reference** field enter **1501**, the number of the check Erin has sent the company.

6. In the **Receipt Number** field type **102**.

7. Enter or select **8/15/04** as the date.

8. Accept the default of **Check** in the **Payment Method** field.

9. Make sure the **Cash Account** field contains **1110**, the cash account. (It may still be set to **1130 Notes Receivable** from the prior transaction.)

10. Click in the **Description** column of the first row and type **Payment for note receivable**.

11. In the **GL Account** field use the lookup icon to select account **1130 Notes Receivable** since you are applying this cash receipt in part to the Notes Receivable account.

12. Enter **5000.00** in the **Amount** column; this was the original amount of the note.

13. Type **Interest revenue** in the **Description** field.

14. Using the lookup icon, select account **4200 Interest Revenue**.

15. Enter **100.00** in the **Amount** column (see Figure 10.8). The amount of interest revenue is calculated using the interest formula above.

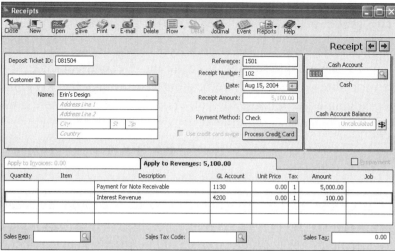

Figure 10.8

16. To view the impact of the transaction, click the **Journal** 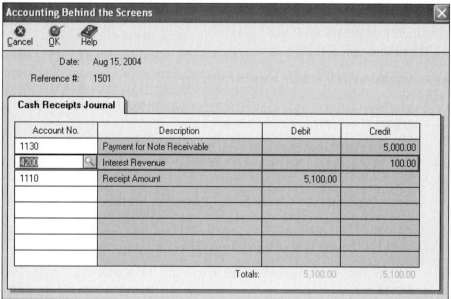 icon. The screen shown in Figure 10.9 appears.

Figure 10.9

17. You now see how Peachtree will post the transaction to the General ledger (Debits and Credits). Click the **Cancel** icon to close the *Accounting Behind the Screens* window.

18. Click the **Save** icon to post the transaction.

Recording the Payment of a Note Payable

Once recorded, a promissory note no longer has an impact on the subsidiary ledgers. You could record the payment of the note in the General journal. However, cash payments paid on notes payables are best made through the *Payments* window. Peachtree does not calculate the interest for you. You calculate the interest in the same manner as you would in a manual accounting system by using this formula:

$$I = P \times R \times T$$

TRANSACTION: On August 18, 2004, Lundquist Custom Woodworking paid off a $3,000.00 12% 60-day note dated June 18, 2004, to the Bank of Salinas. Interest expense would be I = $3,000.00 X 12% X 60/360 = $60.00.

---

1. Select **Payments** from the **Tasks** menu.

2. Since this payment is not a payment on an account payable, skip the **Vendor ID** field.

3. In the **Pay to the Order of** field enter **Bank of Salinas**.

4. Enter or select **8/18/04** as the date.

5. Make sure the **Cash Account** field contains **1110**, the cash account. (It may still be set to **2130 Notes Payable** from the prior transaction.)

6. Click the **Apply to Expenses** tab.

7. Click in the **Description** column of the first row and type **Payment of note payable**.

8. Using the lookup icon, select account **2130 Notes Payable** since you are applying this cash payment in part to the Notes Payable account.

9. Enter 3000.00 in the **Amount** column; this was the original amount of the note.

10. Type **Interest expense** in the **Description** field.

11. Using the lookup icon, select account **5200 Interest Expense**.

12. Enter **60.00** in the **Amount** column (see Figure 10.10). This is the amount calculated using the interest formula.

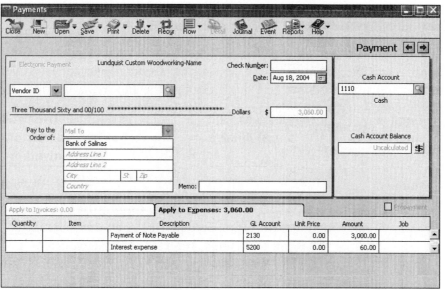

Figure 10.10

13. After verifying that the check is correct, click the **Print** icon to print it.

14. You are presented with the ***Print Forms: Disbursement Checks*** dialog box. Use the default form **OCR Multi-Purp AP Detail Laser**.

15. Enter **103** as the check number.

16. Select **Print**.

17. Close the ***Payments*** dialog box.

Many other situations could also involve notes payables or notes receivable. In every case, you manipulate the ***Receipts*** and ***Payments*** windows of Peachtree to accommodate your needs.

Printing the August Reports

Print the reports shown if Figures 10.11 through 10.15, accepting all defaults.

> ➤ **NOTE:** Refer to Chapter 2 for more detailed instructions on printing.

Account ID	Account Description	Debit Amt	Credit Amt
	Lundquist Custom Woodworking-Name		
	General Ledger Trial Balance		
	As of Aug 31, 2004		

Filter Criteria includes: Report order is by ID. Report is printed in Detail Format.

Account ID	Account Description	Debit Amt	Credit Amt
1110	Cash	32,040.00	
1120	Accounts Receivable	48,000.00	
1130	Notes Receivable	4,000.00	
1150	Shop Supplies	5,800.00	
1210	Shop Equipment	156,000.00	
1221	Accum. Depr- Shop Equipment		34,000.00
1230	Automobile	16,000.00	
1241	Accum. Depr- Automobile		4,000.00
2110	Accounts Payable		1,200.00
2130	Notes Payable		800.00
3110	Vernon Lunquist, Capital		10,000.00
3130	Retained Earnings		211,800.00
4200	Interest Revenue		100.00
5200	Interest Expense	60.00	
	Total:	261,900.00	261,900.00

Figure 10.11

Lundquist Custom Woodworking-Name
Aged Receivables
As of Aug 31, 2004

Filter Criteria includes: Report order is by ID. Report is printed in Detail Format.

Customer ID Customer Contact Telephone 1	Invoice/CM #	0-30	31-60	61-90	Over 90 days	Amount Due
CAS Carl's Accounting Service Carl	98734352	6,000.00				6,000.00
CAS Carl's Accounting Service		6,000.00				6,000.00
SSD Salinas School District Helen	98734353	42,000.00				42,000.00
SSD Salinas School District		42,000.00				42,000.00
Report Total		48,000.00				48,000.00

Figure 10.12

Lundquist Custom Woodworking-Name
Cash Receipts Journal
For the Period From Aug 1, 2004 to Aug 31, 2004
Filter Criteria includes: Report order is by Check Date. Report is printed in Detail Format.

Date	Account ID	Transaction Ref	Line Description	Debit Amnt	Credit Amnt
8/15/04	1120	12%, 60 Day	Invoice: 98734351		4,000.00
	1130		Betty's Boutique	4,000.00	
8/15/04	1130	1501	Payment for Note Receivable		5,000.00
	4200		Interest Revenue		100.00
	1110		Erin's Design	5,100.00	
				9,100.00	9,100.00

Figure 10.13

Lundquist Custom Woodworking-Name
Aged Payables
As of Aug 31, 2004
Filter Criteria includes: Report order is by ID. Report is printed in Detail Format.

Vendor ID Vendor Contact Telephone 1	Invoice/CM #	0 - 30	31 - 60	61 - 90	Over 90 days	Amount Due
OSH Orchard Supply Hardware Nick	A3456782-6	1,200.00				1,200.00
OSH Orchard Supply Hardware		1,200.00				1,200.00
Report Total		1,200.00				1,200.00

Figure 10.14

Lundquist Custom Woodworking-Name
Cash Disbursements Journal
For the Period From Aug 1, 2004 to Aug 31, 2004
Filter Criteria includes: Report order is by Date. Report is printed in Detail Format.

Date	Check #	Account ID	Line Description	Debit Amount	Credit Amount
8/18/04	103	2130	Payment of Note Payable	3,000.00	
		5200	Interest expense	60.00	
		1110	Bank of Salinas		3,060.00
8/18/04	NP01	2110	Invoice: 5688B	800.00	
		2130	Elmer Lumber Supply		800.00
	Total			3,860.00	3,860.00

Figure 10.15

Backing Up Your Company Data File

1. Select **Back up** from the **File** menu.

2. Click the check box to include the company name in the file name.

3. Add **Final** to the file name.

4.   Select the **Save in** lookup box to find the location your instructor has identified for you to keep your backup file(s).

5.   Click **Save**.

6.   Click **OK**.

   ➢ **NOTE:** Refer to Chapter 1 for more detailed instructions on backing up files.

Exiting the Peachtree Complete Accounting 2006 Program

1.   Click **Exit** from the **File** menu to end the current work session and return to your Windows desktop.

2.   If you are asked if you wish to save any unposted work, click the **Yes** button.

CHAPTER 11

System Requirements, Installation, Ordering Trial Software, and Opening, Backing up, and Restoring Company Data files

System Requirements

The recommended minimum software and hardware requirements your computer system needs to run both Windows and QuickBooks Pro 2006:

♦ At least 1 GHz Intel Pentium III (or equivalent) with 256 MB of RAM for single-user or 512 MB of RAM for multiple concurrent users

♦ 500 MHz Intel Pentium II (or equivalent) with 128 MB of RAM for single-user or 256 MB of RAM for multiple concurrent users

♦ Windows 2000/XP

♦ 850 MB of disk space for QuickBooks installation

♦ Internet Explorer 6.0 required. Microsoft Internet Explorer 6.0 is provided on the CD. Requires an additional 70 MB of disk space.

♦ Microsoft .NET Framework CLR 1.1. It is provided on the CD. Requires an additional 150 MB of disk space.

♦ At least 256–color SVGA video

♦ Optimized for 1024X768 resolution, but support for 800X600 with small fonts

♦ 2x CD-ROM

♦ All online features/services require Internet access with at least a 56 Kbps modem

Integration/compatibility requirements:

♦ Word and Excel integration requires Microsoft Word and Excel 2000, 2002, or 2003

Multiuser environment:

♦ Multiuser mode is optimized for Windows 2000 Server or Windows Server 2003 client server networks and Windows 2000/XP peer-to-peer networks. Novell NetWare is supported but not recommended.

♦ Use in a terminal server environment is supported for Windows XP Pro/2000 Server/Server 2003 Terminal Services.

Using QuickBooks Pro 2006 on a Network

Intuit has the QuickBooks: Pro Education Site Licenses in 10-, 25-, and 50-user packs. The QuickBooks Pro 2006 version is available. To order the site license, call 888-729-1996.

QuickBooks Pro 2006 can be used in a network environment as long as each student uses a separate student data file source to store his or her data files. Students should consult with their instructors and/or network administrators for specific procedures regarding program installation and any special printing procedures required for proper network operation.

QuickBooks will run most efficiently if the student data files are installed on a hard drive. This can occur on the local hard drive or in a unique student folder on a network drive. Because it is possible that student files may be tampered with between class sessions, it is recommended that students backup and restore their files with a floppy disk (or jump drive) each class day. The QuickBooks backup and restore functions are quick and easy to follow.

Ordering the QuickBooks Trial Version Software

The QuickBooks software is not included with this text book. However, you can order a trial version of the QuickBooks software to use on your home computer by using these instructions:

1. With your Internet browser open, go to http://quickbooks.intuit.com.

2. Type Trials in the Search box, as shown in Figure 11.1.

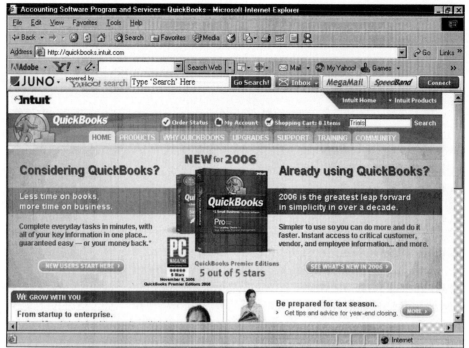

Figure 11.1

3. Click the **QuickBooks Trial Products** 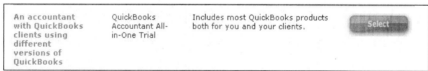 link.

4. In the *QuickBooks 2006 Trials* screen, scroll down until you reach the QuickBooks Accountant All-in-One Trial, as shown below in Figure 11.2.

An accountant with QuickBooks clients using different versions of QuickBooks	QuickBooks Accountant All-in-One Trial	Includes most QuickBooks products both for you and your clients.	Select

Figure 11.2

5. Click the **Select** button.

6. In the *Checkout* screen you will need to create an account.

7. Click the **Continue** button (see Figure 11.3).

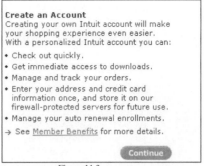

Figure 11.3

8. Complete the required information on the ***Account Setup*** screen.

    ➢ **NOTE:** You do not need to provide your credit card information. It is optional.

9. Click **Continue** to complete your order. You will be presented with a confirmation screen like the partial screen shown in Figure 11.4.

Figure 11.4

Your order should be shipped within two weeks, if not sooner. When you receive the software, follow the instructions for installing QuickBooks 2006 All-in-One Trial for Accountants. The trial version is good for 90 days.

Installing QuickBooks 2006

To install QuickBooks 2006 All-in-One Trial for Accountants on your hard disk (i.e., c: drive), follow these steps:

1. Start Windows.

2. Make sure no other programs on your system are running.

3. Insert the **QuickBooks 2006 All-in-One Trial for Accountants,** and follow the instructions on your screen to load the software.

4. The program installs in the default folder C:\Program Files\Intuit\QuickBooks 2006, with the sample companies installed the same directory, as shown in Figure 11.5.

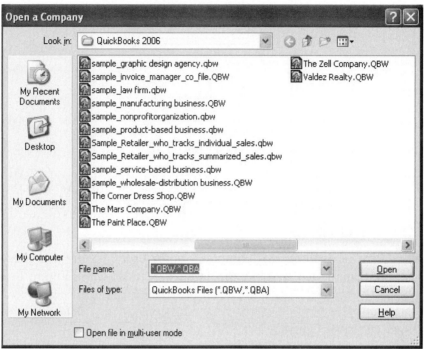

Figure 11.5

Installing Student Data Files

After the QuickBooks 2006 All-in-One Trial for Accountants software is loaded, you need to copy the company data files to your c: drive. The company data files are located on the textbook website.

1. Open your browser and go to www.prenhall.com/compaccounting.

2. Double-click the **QuickBooks** link.

3. Double-click the **Getting Started with QuickBooks Pro 2006 student resources** link.

4. You see the zipped data files. Download the data files to C:\Program Files\Intuit\QuickBooks 2006.

5. Close your browser.

6. Double-click the **My Computer** icon on your desktop.

7. Locate the zipped files in the C:\Program Files\Intuit\QuickBooks 2006 directory.

8. Right-click the zipped data files and select **Extract**. Extract the files to the same directory that you downloaded them to.

Opening a Company Data File

1. Double-click the **QuickBooks** icon on your desktop, and you will see the *No Company Open* dialog box as shown in Figure 11.6.

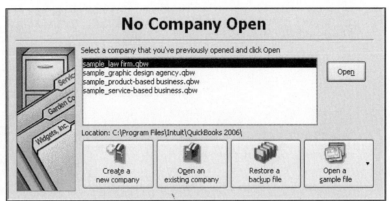

Figure 11.6

2. Click the **Open an existing company** icon.

3. QuickBooks brings up the *Open a Company* dialog box, where you can direct QuickBooks to the location of the company data files you need, as shown in Figure 11.6. If you do not see these files when you first open the dialog box, you may need to change the directory or drive to one your instructor specifies. If you followed the instructions above for installation of the directory, you can find the data files in C:\Program Files\Intuit\QuickBooks 2006. The directory should contain the company data files as shown in Figure 11.7.

Figure 11.7

4. Click **Atlas.QBW** and then click the **Open** button.

5. You are presented with the *Home* screen, as shown in Figure 11.8.

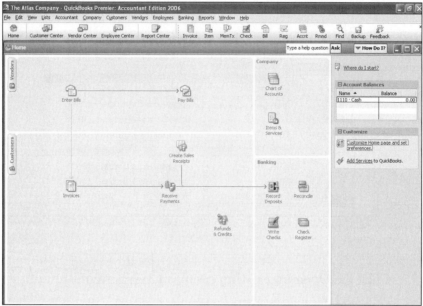

Figure 11.8

Backing Up a Company Data File

Before starting any assignment, it is suggested that you create a backup of the company data file in the event that you need to restore the original file (i.e., start the assignment over).

QuickBooks has the capability to quickly and easily backup your data to protect against accidental loss. To backup The Atlas Company file, follow these instructions:

1. Select the **Backup** Backup icon from the **Icon** toolbar above the *Home* screen.

2. You are presented with the *QuickBooks Backup* dialog box (see Figure 11.9).

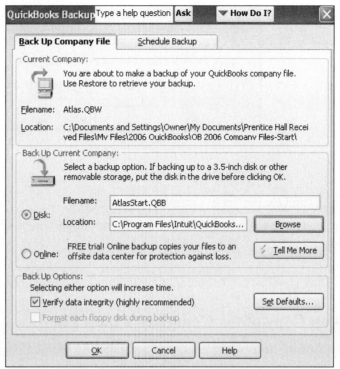

Figure 11.9

3. Click in the **File name** box and put your cursor between the *s* (at the end of the name *Atlas*) and the period. Add **Start** to the file name, as shown in Figure 11.9.

4. Click the **OK** button to continue. QuickBooks 2006 defaults the backup location to the last location the file was backed up to. You can change the location to save the backup file by clicking the **Browse** button. Your instructor may want you to save your backup to a specific location, such as a floppy disk or another storage medium.

5. You are presented with a warning regarding backing up your file to the same drive, as shown in Figure 11.10.

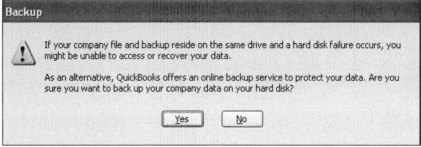

Figure 11.10

6. Click the **Yes** button to continue the backup process.

7. You are presented with the *QuickBooks Information* dialog box (see Figure 11.11).

Figure 11.11

8. Click the **OK** button to complete the process.

9. Select **Close Company** from the **File** menu.

10. You return to the *No Company Open* dialog box.

Using the Backup Copy of the Company's Data File

At certain times in the assignments, you are asked to make a backup copy of a company's data files. There are several reasons you might want to access the backup copy of a company's data file. For example, you might not have printed a required report in an assignment before adding additional transactions. You might have several errors and simply want to start an assignment over or at a specific point prior to the errors instead of correcting the mistakes.

➢ **NOTE:** You should consider saving a file every day you work on it to protect yourself against possible loss. If you backup your data using a different file name each day, you will have the option of restoring from any of these files. It would be wise to indicate in the file name the point in the text (e.g., p125) at which you created each backup so you will know what transactions have been entered.

Restoring a Backup File

You always have the option to repeat an assignment for additional practice or to start an assignment over. You simply restore the company data files back to their original state, using a backup created at the start or during the assignment. Follow these instructions to restore the AtlasStart.QBB (QuickBooks Backup) file you just created:

1. In the *No Company Open* dialog box click the **Restore a backup file** icon.

2. You are presented with the *Restore Company Backup* dialog box, shown in Figure 11.12.

Figure 11.12

3. Click the **Browse** button in the **Get Company Backup From** section to bring up the *Restore From* dialog box, shown in Figure 11.13.

Figure 11.13

> ➤ **NOTE:** If you are keeping your backups on a floppy or on a drive/path other than the one QuickBooks is defaulting to, click the **Browse** button to change the drive and select the correct path. You may have several backups made at different points in time so be sure to select the correct one. At this point, you should have

only one backup file (the one from earlier in this workshop) to select. So select AtlasStart.QBB.

4. In the **Look in** box go to C:\Program Files\Intuit\QuickBooks 2006 and select the AtlasStart.QBB (QuickBooks backup) file.

5. Click **Open**.

6. Click the **Browse** button in the **Restore Company Backup To** section to bring up the *Restore To* dialog box.

7. In the **look in** box go to C:\Program Files\Intuit\QuickBooks 2006, or another location specified by your instructor.

8. Click **Save**.

9. Click **Restore**.

10. If you get the warning shown in Figure 11.14, click **Yes**.

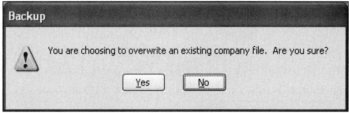

Figure 11.14

11. You should now see the confirmation screen shown in Figure 11.15. Click the **OK** button to continue.

Figure 11.15

You are now ready to continue with the workshop in Chapter 12.

QUICKBOOKS
Workshop

CHAPTER 12

Journalizing, Posting, and Printing Reports—The Atlas Company

THIS WORKSHOP COVERS JOURNALIZING; POSTING; AND PRINTING THE: GENERAL LEDGER, TRIAL BALANCE, AND CHART OF ACCOUNTS

> ➤ **NOTE:** If you just completed Chapter 11, skip to **"Toggling to the QuickBooks Pro 2006 Version"** on the next page.

Opening the Company Data Files

1. Double Click the **QuickBooks** icon on your desktop.

2. Double-click on **Atlas.QBW** in the *No Company Open* dialog box, shown in Figure 12.1.

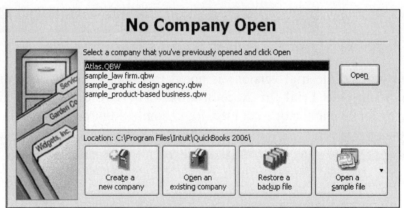

Figure 12.1

3. When the company data file opens, you see the *Home* dialog box (see Figure 12.2).

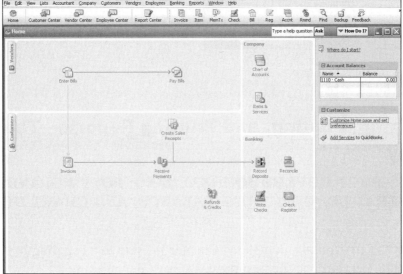

Figure 12.2

Toggling to the QuickBooks Pro 2006 Version

If you are using the QuickBooks Pro 2006 version on campus, you may skip this section as long as your title bar looks like Figure 12.3.

Figure 12.3

If you ordered the trial version, as noted in Chapter 11, you are using a **QuickBooks 2006 All-in-One Trial for Accountants**. You can determine which edition you are using by looking at the title bar (see, for example, Figures 12.3 and 12.4).

The Atlas Company - QuickBooks Premier: Accountant Edition 2006

Figure 12.4

So that you see the same screenshots in on your screen as in this text, you need to toggle to the QuickBooks Pro Edition. The following instructions walk you through this process:

1. Select **Toggle to Another Edition** from the **File** menu.

2. Click the radio button next to **QuickBooks Pro** to select it (see Figure 12.5).

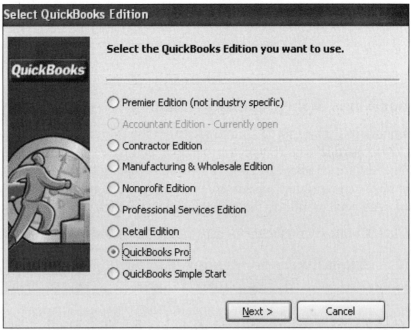

Figure 12.5

3. Click **Next**.

4. You are presented with the screen shown in Figure 12.6. Click the **Toggle** button.

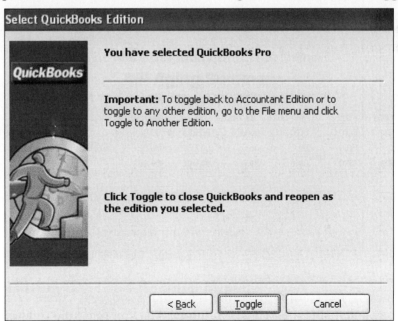

Figure 12.6

5. It takes a few seconds for the process to complete. Your title bar then looks like Figure 12.7.

The Atlas Company - QuickBooks Pro 2006 (via Accountant Edition)

Figure 12.7

Adding Your Name to the Company Name

It is important for you to be able to identify the reports you print for each assignment as your own, particularly if you are using a computer that shares a printer with other computers. QuickBooks Pro 2006 prints the company name at the top of each report. To personalize your printed reports so that you can identify both the company and your reports, you need to modify the company so it includes your name:

1. Click **Company** on the menu bar (Figure 12.8) and select **Company Information**.

File   Edit   View   Lists   Company   Customers   Vendors   Employees   Banking   Reports   Window   Help

Figure 12.8

The program will respond by bringing up the ***Company Information*** dialog box which allows you to edit/add information about the company.

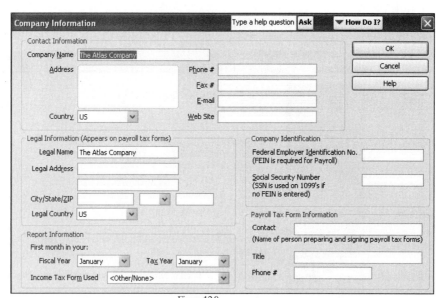

Figure 12.9

2. Click in the **Company Name** field and place your cursor at the end of **The Atlas Company**. If it is already highlighted, you can press the right-arrow key to get to the end of the field.

3. Add a dash and your name (**–Student's Name**) or initials to the end of the company name. Your screen will look similar to Figure 12.10, except of course that it will have your name or initials instead of **Student's Name**.

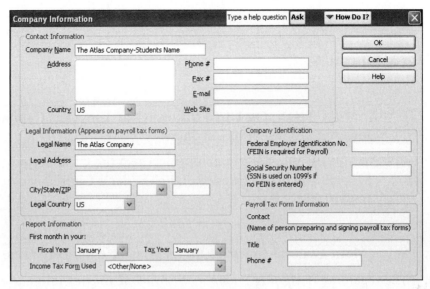

Figure 12.10

4. Click the **OK** button to return to the *Home* screen.

Recording a Journal Entry

> **TRANSACTION: On 1/1/04 the owner of The Atlas Company invested $10,000 in the business.**
>
> **ANALYSIS: You need to debit (increase) the Cash account (1110) for $10,000 and credit (increase) the Owner's Capital account (3110) for $10,000.**

1. Select **Make General Journal Entries** from the **Company** menu on the menu bar.

2. The regarding *Assigning Numbers to Journal Entries* information box appears (see Figure 12.11).

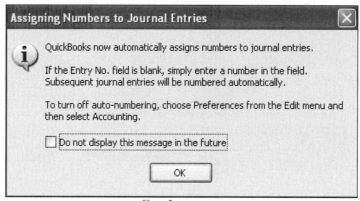

Figure 5

3. Click the check box next to **Do not display this message in the future** to select it.

4. Click **OK**.

5. For this workshop, you need to assign the first journal entry and allow QuickBooks to continue numbering automatically.

6. In the **Date** field enter **1/1/04** and then press the **Tab** key.

7. In the **Entry No.** field enter **101**. Press the **Tab** key.

8. In the **Account** (general ledger account) field, Click the lookup icon (magnifying glass icon) and click **1110 Cash**. Tab to the **Debit** field.

9. In the **Debit** field enter **10000**. Press the **Tab** key twice to move to the **Credit** field.

10. In the **Memo** field enter **Initial investment of cash by owner** and press Tab twice.

11. In the **Account** field click the lookup icon and then click **3110 Owner's Capital**. Use the scrollbar if the account is not visible in the lookup list.

12. In the **Credit** field enter 10000. **Tab** to the **Memo** field.

13. Tab through the next three fields, back to the **Account** field. The program automatically enters the same description as the first line (even if you do not see it on your screen). This completes the data you need to enter into the *Make General Journal Entries* dialog box for the journal entry. Your screen should look like Figure 12.12.

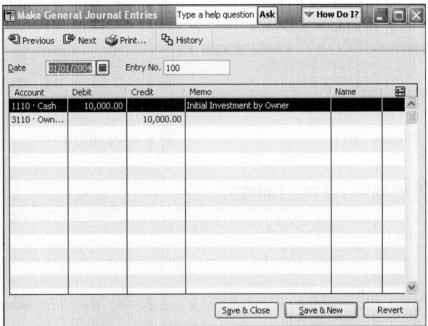

Figure 12.12

14. Before posting this transaction, verify that the information is correct by reviewing the journal entry. If you have made an error, use the following editing techniques to correct the error.

Editing a Journal Entry

♦ Using your mouse, click in the field that contains the error. This highlights the selected text box information so that you can change it.

♦ Type the correct information and then press the **Tab** key to enter it. You can then either Tab to other fields that need corrections or again use the mouse to click in the proper field.

♦ If you have selected an incorrect account, use the pull-down menu to select the correct account. This replaces the incorrect account with the correct account.

♦ To discard an entry and start over, click the **Revert** button. You are not given the opportunity to verify this step, so make sure you want to delete the transaction before selecting this option.

> ➢ **NOTE:** Even though the **Save & Close** and **Save & New** buttons are available if the entry is out of balance (total debits must equal total credits), the program does not allow you to post the transaction until the entry is in balance. You see the warning box shown in Figure 12.13 if your entry is not balanced.

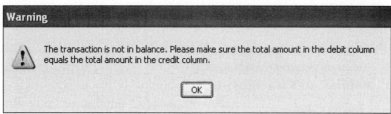

Figure 12.13

♦ Review the journal entry for accuracy after making any corrections.

Posting (Saving) a Journal Entry

1. After you verify that a journal entry is correct, click the **Save & New** icon to post this transaction to the General ledger.

2. Leave the *Make General Journal Entries* dialog box open to record additional journal entries.

> ➢ **TIP:** To move between the journal entries, use the arrow buttons on the *Make General Journal Entries* screen (see Figure 12.14). To look at the entry you just entered, click the **Previous** icon.

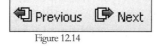

Figure 12.14

Entering Additional Journal Entries

1. Enter the date listed for each transaction. You can use the + key to advance the date or use the calendar icon next to the field to select the date from a calendar.

2. Accept the additional number that QuickBooks adds to **101** in the **Entry No.** by pressing the **Tab** key. if it is showing in the **Entry No** field.

Enter these transactions for January:

2004		
Jan.	1	Paid rent for two months in advance, $400.
	3	Purchased office supplies with cash, $100.
	9	Received $1,500 for fees earned (cash sale).
	13	Paid telephone bill, $180.
	20	Owner withdrew $500 from the business.
	27	Received $450 for fees earned (cash sale).

> 31   Paid salaries expense, $700.

3.   After you have entered the additional journal entries, click the **Close** button  to exit the ***Make General Journal Entries*** dialog box.

Displaying and Printing a General Journal

1.   Click the **Report Center** [Report Center] icon.

2.   Click on **Accountant & Taxes** in the list on the left of the screen (see Figure 12.15).

Reports

Company & Financial

Customers & Receivables

Sales

Jobs, Time & Mileage

Vendors & Payables

Employees & Payroll

Banking

Accountant & Taxes

Budgets

List

Figure 12.15

3.   The right side of your screen should look like Figure 12.16.

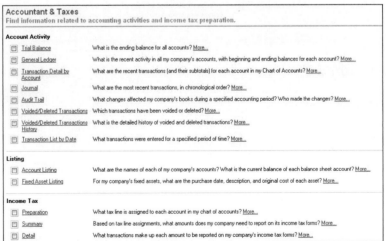

Figure 12.16

4.   Click **Journal** in the ***Report Center*** dialog box. QuickBooks defaults to the current month-to-date for the report, as shown in Figure 12.17.

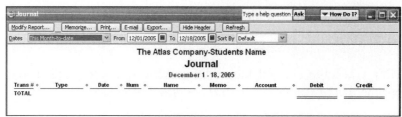

Figure 12.17

5. Tab to the **From** field and enter **1/1/04**. Tab to the **To** field and enter **1/31/04**. (See Figure 12.18).

Figure 12.18

6. To adjust the columns so that the information is more readable, select the diamond on the right side of the Memo field and drag it to the right until you can see the entire description.

7. Do the same thing for the **Account** field.

8. For the **Name** field (since there is no information in that field), select the diamond on the right side of the field and drag it to the left until the column is not showing at all. Your report should look like Figure 12.19.

The Atlas Company-Students Name
Journal
January 2004

Trans #	Type	Date	Num	Memo	Account	Debit	Credit
2	General Journal	01/01/2004	101	Prepaid 2 months rent	1140 · Prepaid Rent	400.00	
				Prepaid 2 months rent	1110 · Cash		400.00
						400.00	400.00
3	General Journal	01/03/2004	102	Purchased Office supplies with Cash	1150 · Office Supplies	100.00	
				Purchased Office supplies with Cash	1110 · Cash		100.00
						100.00	100.00
4	General Journal	01/09/2004	103	Received cash for fees earned	1110 · Cash	1,500.00	
				Received cash for fees earned	4110 · Fees Earned		1,500.00
						1,500.00	1,500.00
5	General Journal	01/13/2004	104	Paid Telephone bill	5150 · Telephone Expense	180.00	
				Paid Telephone bill	1110 · Cash		180.00
						180.00	180.00
6	General Journal	01/20/2004	105	Owner Withdrawal	3120 · Owner's Withdrawals	500.00	
				Owner Withdrawal	1110 · Cash		500.00
						500.00	500.00
7	General Journal	01/27/2004	106	Received Cash for Fees Earned	1110 · Cash	450.00	
				Received Cash for Fees Earned	4110 · Fees Earned		450.00
						450.00	450.00
8	General Journal	01/31/2004	107	Paid Salaries	5120 · Salaries Expense	700.00	
				Paid Salaries	1110 · Cash		700.00
						700.00	700.00
TOTAL						**13,830.00**	**13,830.00**

Figure 12.19

9. Click the **Print** button ⟦Print...⟧ to print the Journal report.

If you experience any difficulties with your printer (for example, the type size is too small), refer to the Appendix B of this text book for information on how to adjust the print and display settings.

Correcting a Posted General Journal Entry

Compare your printed Journal report to Figure 12.19. If you note an error at this point, you can easily fix it:

1. With the Journal report on your screen, place your cursor over the incorrect entry. (It will resemble a magnifying glass with a *z* in the center.)

2. Double-click the entry you want to correct, and you are taken to the *Make General Journal Entries* dialog box that contains the entry.

3. Edit any posted transaction using the same procedures as for editing an unposted transaction.

4. After making the necessary changes, click the **Save & Close** button to save your changes. You are returned to your Journal report, where you can view the changes made.

5. If you made any changes, reprint the Journal report.

6. Click the **Close** button to exit the Journal report.

7. If you are prompted with the warning screen shown in Figure 12.20, check the box next to **Do not display this message in the future** and Click the **No** button.

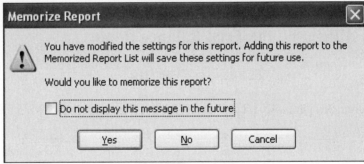

Figure 12.20

Displaying and Printing the General Ledger Report

1. Click the **General Ledger** report from the **Accountant & Taxes** reports.

2. Change the dates to **1/1/04** and **1/31/04** as you did for the Journal report.

3. Adjust the columns, as needed, to show the entire details of each field. Remove the Name column. You do not see the entire report on the screen (see Figure 12.21). You can use the scrollbars to advance the display to view other portions of the report. You can also double-click any transaction to bring up the entry window for that transaction if corrections need to be made.

The Atlas Company-Students Name
General Ledger
As of January 31, 2004

Type	Date	Num	Memo	Split	Amount	Balance
1110 · Cash						0.00
General Journal	01/01/2004	100	Initial Investment by Owner	3110 · Owner's Capital	10,000.00	10,000.00
General Journal	01/01/2004	101	Prepaid 2 months rent	1140 · Prepaid Rent	-400.00	9,600.00
General Journal	01/03/2004	102	Purchased Office supplies with Cash	1150 · Office Supplies	-100.00	9,500.00
General Journal	01/09/2004	103	Received cash for fees earned	4110 · Fees Earned	1,500.00	11,000.00
General Journal	01/13/2004	104	Paid Telephone bill	5150 · Telephone Expense	-180.00	10,820.00
General Journal	01/20/2004	105	Owner Withdrawal	3120 · Owner's Withdrawals	-500.00	10,320.00
General Journal	01/27/2004	106	Received Cash for Fees Earned	4110 · Fees Earned	450.00	10,770.00
General Journal	01/31/2004	107	Paid Salaries	5120 · Salaries Expense	-700.00	10,070.00
Total 1110 · Cash					10,070.00	10,070.00
1120 · Accounts Receivable						0.00
Total 1120 · Accounts Receivable						0.00
1140 · Prepaid Rent						0.00
General Journal	01/01/2004	101	Prepaid 2 months rent	1110 · Cash	400.00	400.00
Total 1140 · Prepaid Rent					400.00	400.00
1150 · Office Supplies						0.00
General Journal	01/03/2004	102	Purchased Office supplies with Cash	1110 · Cash	100.00	100.00
Total 1150 · Office Supplies					100.00	100.00
1210 · Office Equipment						0.00
Total 1210 · Office Equipment						0.00
1221 · Accum. Dep.-Office Equipment						0.00
Total 1221 · Accum. Dep.-Office Equipment						0.00
1230 · Automobile						0.00
Total 1230 · Automobile						0.00

Figure 12.21

4. Click the **Print** icon to print the General Ledger report.

5. Click the **Close** button to exit the General Ledger report.

Displaying and Printing the Trial Balance Report

1. In the *Reports* dialog box click the **Trial Balance** report from the **Accountant & Taxes** reports.

2. Change the Dates to **1/1/04** and **1/31/04**. The report shown in Figure 12.22 appears.

The Atlas Company-Students Name
Trial Balance
As of January 31, 2004

	Jan 31, 04	
	Debit	Credit
1110 · Cash	10,070.00	
1140 · Prepaid Rent	400.00	
1150 · Office Supplies	100.00	
3110 · Owner's Capital		10,000.00
3120 · Owner's Withdrawals	500.00	
4110 · Fees Earned		1,950.00
5120 · Salaries Expense	700.00	
5150 · Telephone Expense	180.00	
TOTAL	11,950.00	11,950.00

Figure 12.22

3. Click the **Print** button to print the Trial Balance report.

4. Click **Close** button to exit the Trial Balance report.

Displaying and Printing the Chart of Accounts Report

1. Select **Account Listing** from the *Reports* window for **Accountants & Taxes** reports.

2. Adjust the column widths to show the entire fields (see Figure 12.23).

The Atlas Company-Students Name
Account Listing
December 18, 2005

Account	Type	Balance Total	Description	Accn...	Tax Line
1110 · Cash	Bank	10,070.00		1110	<Unassigned>
1120 · Accounts Receivable	Accounts Receivable	0.00		1120	<Unassigned>
1140 · Prepaid Rent	Other Current Asset	400.00		1140	<Unassigned>
1150 · Office Supplies	Other Current Asset	100.00		1150	<Unassigned>
1210 · Office Equipment	Fixed Asset	0.00		1210	<Unassigned>
1221 · Accum. Dep.-Office Eq...	Fixed Asset	0.00		1221	<Unassigned>
1230 · Automobile	Fixed Asset	0.00		1230	<Unassigned>
1241 · Accum. Dep.-Automobile	Fixed Asset	0.00		1241	<Unassigned>
1250 · Store Equipment	Fixed Asset	0.00		1250	<Unassigned>
1261 · Accum. Dep.-Store Equ...	Fixed Asset	0.00		1261	<Unassigned>
2110 · Accounts Payable	Accounts Payable	0.00		2110	<Unassigned>
2100 · Payroll Liabilities	Other Current Liability	0.00		2100	<Unassigned>
3000 · Opening Bal Equity	Equity	0.00		3000	<Unassigned>
3110 · Owner's Capital	Equity	10,000.00		3110	<Unassigned>
3120 · Owner's Withdrawals	Equity	-500.00		3120	<Unassigned>
3900 · Retained Earnings	Equity			3900	<Unassigned>
4110 · Fees Earned	Income			4110	<Unassigned>
5110 · Rent Expense	Expense			5110	<Unassigned>
5120 · Salaries Expense	Expense			5120	<Unassigned>
5150 · Telephone Expense	Expense			5150	<Unassigned>
6560 · Payroll Expenses	Expense			6560	<Unassigned>

Figure 12.23

3. Click the **Print** button to print the Chart of Accounts report.

4. Click the **Close** button to exit the Chart of Accounts report.

Backing Up Your Company Data File

1. Click the **Backup** 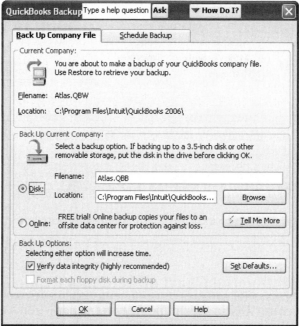 icon. The dialog box shown in Figure 12.24 appears.

Figure 12.24

2. Click the **Browse** button in the **Back Up Current Company** section. You see the screen shown in Figure 12.25.

Figure 12.25

3. Change the file name to **AtlasFinal** and click **Save** Click **OK** on the ***QuickBooks Backup*** dialog box.

4. When the backup has completed, you see the confirmation shown in Figure 12.26. Click **OK**.

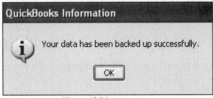

Figure 12.26

Exiting the QuickBooks Pro 2006 Program

1. Select **Close Company** from the **File** menu.

2. Select **Exit** from the **File** menu to end the current work session and return to your Windows desktop.

CHAPTER 13

Compound Journal Entries, Adjusting Entries, and Printing Financial Reports—The Zell Company

THIS WORKSHOP COVERS COMPOUND JOURNAL ENTRIES, ADJUSTING JOURNAL ENTRIES, AND PRINTING FINANCIAL REPORTS.

Opening The Zell Company

1. Double-click the QuickBooks icon on your desktop to open the software program.

2. Click the **Open an existing company** icon and then locate and select **The Zell Company**.

3. Click **Open**.

    ➢ **NOTE:** Refer to Chapter 11 for more detailed instructions on opening files.

Backing Up Your Company Data File

1. Select **Backup** from the **File** menu or click the **Backup** icon.

2. Click the **Browse** button to find the location where your instructor has told you to keep your backup file(s).

3. Add **Start** to the company name so you can identify the backup (see Figure 13.1).

Figure 13.1

4. Click **OK** on the *QuickBooks Backup* dialog box.

5. Click **OK** on the confirmation dialog box.

 ➤ **NOTE:** Refer to Chapter 11 for more detailed instructions on backing up files.

Toggling to the QuickBooks Pro 2006 Version

If you are using the QuickBooks Pro 2006 version and not the Accountant Edition 2006 you may skip this section.

If you ordered the trial version, as noted in Chapter 11, you are using Accountant Edition 2006. So that you see the same screenshots on your screen as in this text, you need to toggle to the QuickBooks Pro Edition. The following instructions walk you through the toggling process:

1. Select **Toggle to Another Edition** from the **File** menu.

2. Click the radio button next to **QuickBooks Pro** to select it.

3. Click **Next**.

4. Click the **Toggle** button.

5. It takes a few second for the process to complete. Your title bar then says **(via Accountant Edition)**.

Adding Your Name to the Company Name

1. Click the **Company** menu option and select **Company Information**. The program responds by bringing up the *Company Information* dialog box, which allows you to edit/add information about the company.

2. Click in the **Company Name** field and make sure your cursor is at the end of **The Zell Company**.

3. Add a dash and your name **(-Student's Name)**.

4. Click the **OK** button. The title bar now looks like Figure 13.2.

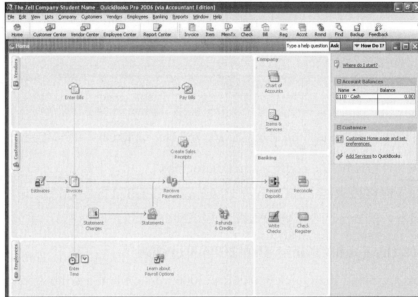

Figure 13.2

Recording Compound Journal Entries

Compound journal entries are also recorded in the *Make General Journal Entries* dialog box.

> **TRANSACTION: The owner of The Zell Company made an investment in the business consisting of $5,000 in cash and an automobile valued at $12,000 on 1/1/04.**
>
> **ANALYSIS: Cash will increase so you need to debit the Cash account (1110) for $5,000. The Automobile account will increase, so you need to debit the Automobile account (1230) for $12,000. The owner's capital will increase, so you need credit the Owner's Capital account (3110) for $17,000.**

1. Select **Make General Journal Entries** from the **Company** menu.

2. If you see the dialog box, shown in Figure 13.3 select the check box **Do not display this message in the future**. Then click **OK**. The screen shown in Figure 13.4 appears.

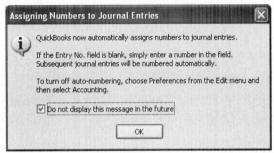

Figure 13.3

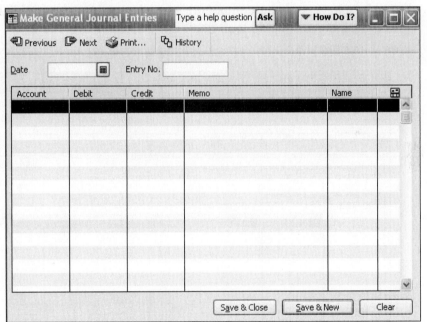

Figure 13.4

3. In the **Date** field enter **1/1/04** (the transaction date) and press the **Tab** key.

4. In the **Entry No.** field enter **Memo1** and press the **Tab** key.

5. In the **Account No.** field click the lookup icon and then click on **1110 Cash**. Tab to the **Debit** field.

6. In the **Debit** field enter **5000.00** and press **Tab** twice to move to the **Memo** field.

7. In the **Memo** field enter **Initial investment by owner** and press the **Tab** key twice.

8. In the **Account No.** field, click the lookup icon and double-click **1230 Automobile** Tab to the **Debit** field.

9. In the **Debit** field enter **12000.00**. Click the **Tab** key twice to move to the **Memo** field.

10. The **Memo** field should repeat the description from the first line by default. It does not show on your screen, but it appears in your reports. Press the **Tab** key twice. You should now have two debit entries.

11. In the **Account No.** field, click the lookup icon and then click **3110 Owner's Capital**. Press **Tab** twice to move to the **Credit** field.

12. In the **Credit** field enter **17000.00**. Click the **Tab** key three times to move back to the **Account No.** field.

This completes the data you need to enter in the *Make General Journal Entries* dialog box to record the compound journal entry for the initial investment by the owner. Your screen should look like Figure 13.5.

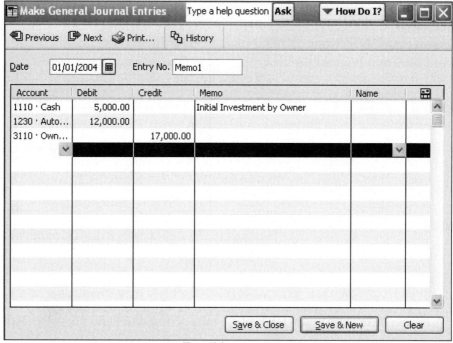

Figure 13.5

13. Review the compound journal entry for accuracy, making any corrections required by following the instructions in Chapter 12 for correcting journal entries.

14. Click the **Save & New** button to post this transaction.

15. If you are presented with the screen shown in Figure 13.6, click the check box next to **Do not display this message in the future**. Click **OK**.

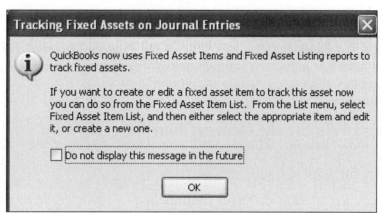

Figure 13.6

16. You now have a blank *Make General Journal Entries* dialog box open to record additional journal entries.

Recording Additional Journal Entries

Analyze and record the following additional journal entries:

1. In the **Date** field enter the date listed for each transaction. You can use the + key to advance the date or use the calendar icon next to the field to select the date from a calendar.

2. In the **Entry No.** field accept additional number that QuickBooks adds to **Memo** by pressing the **Tab** key. Record these entries:

2004		
Jan.	1	Paid rent for two months in advance, $500.
	3	Purchased from Office Supplies, Inc. office supplies ($200) and office equipment ($1,100)—both on account (compound journal entry). Be sure to use the Asset accounts. QuickBooks requires a vendor name for the Accounts Payable module. For the Accounts Payable line for the Name column, select Office Supplies, Inc.
	9	Billed Wayne Andrews for fees earned, $2,000. In the Name field for the Accounts Receivable line, you need to select Andrews, Wayne.
	13	Paid telephone bill, $150.
	20	Owner withdrew $475 from the business for personal

		use.
	27	Received $600 cash for fees earned.
	31	Paid salaries expense, $800.

3. Click the **Close** button to exit the ***Make General Journal Entries*** dialog box after you have entered all the transactions. This returns you to the ***Home*** window.

Displaying and Printing the General Journal

1. Click the **Report Center** 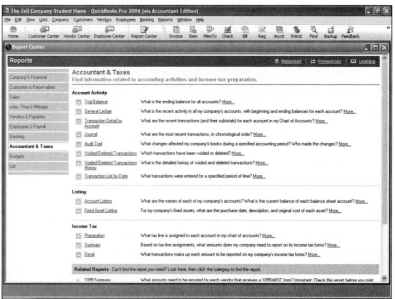 button.

2. Select **Accountant & Taxes** from the list on the left side of your screen (see Figure 13.7).

Figure 13.7

3. Click the **Journal** report.

4. Change the dates to **1/1/04** and **1/31/04**.

5. Adjust the column width as shown in Chapter 12, using the diamonds between the titles so that all the relevant information shows (see Figure 13.8).

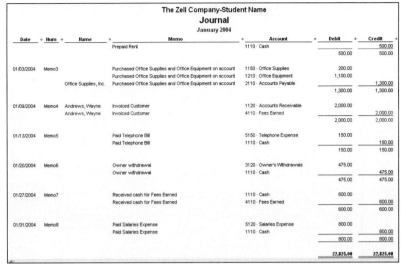

Figure 13.8

6. Click the **Print** Print... button to bring up the ***Print Reports*** dialog box, shown in Figure 13.9.

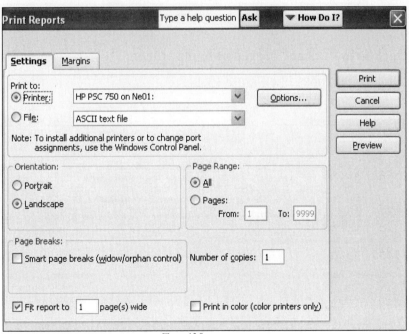

Figure 13.9

7. Click the **Preview** button to view your report before you print it (see Figure 13.10). If your report needs to be adjusted before printing, click the **Close** button and make the necessary changes on the ***Print Reports*** screen.

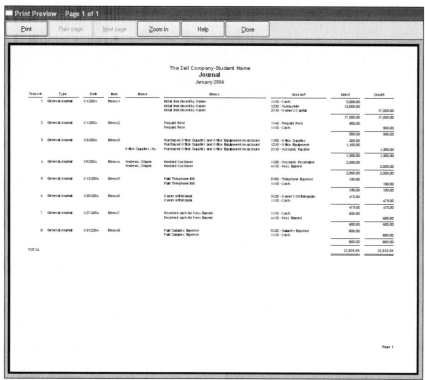

Figure 13.10

8. Click **Print** to send your report to the printer.

9. Your screen looks like Figure 13.11.

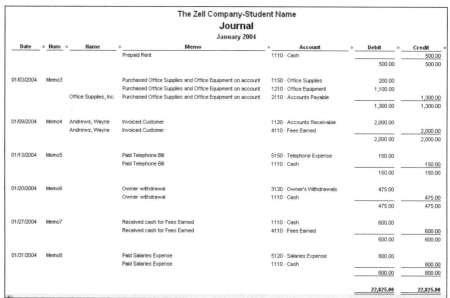

Figure 13.11

10. Compare the transactions on your screen to those in Figure 13.11. If a posted transaction needs to be changed, zoom in on the transaction to make the correction, as you did in Chapter 12.

11. Click the **Close** button to exit the Journal report screen.

12. If asked if you would like to memorize the report, click **No**.

Displaying and Printing the Trial Balance Report

1. Click **Trial Balance** in the *Reports* dialog box.

2. Change the dates to **1/1/04** and **1/31/04**. Your screen looks like Figure 13.12.

The Zell Company-Student Name
Trial Balance
As of January 31, 2004

	Jan 31, 04	
	Debit	Credit
1110 · Cash	3,675.00	
1120 · Accounts Receivable	2,000.00	
1140 · Prepaid Rent	500.00	
1150 · Office Supplies	200.00	
1210 · Office Equipment	1,100.00	
1230 · Automobile	12,000.00	
2110 · Accounts Payable		1,300.00
3110 · Owner's Capital		17,000.00
3120 · Owner's Withdrawals	475.00	
4110 · Fees Earned		2,600.00
5120 · Salaries Expense	800.00	
5150 · Telephone Expense	150.00	
TOTAL	20,900.00	20,900.00

Figure 13.12

3. Compare your screen to Figure 13.12. If your figures do not match, make corrections to your journal entries. You can double-click any of the numbers to bring up the list of transactions for that account. From there, you can double-click any individual entry in the account and go to the *Make General Journal Entries* dialog box to make the correction(s). Then you can click **Save & Close.**

4. Click the **Print** icon to print the Trial Balance report.

5. Click the **Close** button to exit the Trial Balance report.

6. Click the **Close** button to close the *Reports* dialog box. You should once again be looking at the *Home* window.

Adjusting Journal Entries

1. Select **Make General Journal Entries** from the **Company** menu.

2. In the **Date** field enter **1/31/04**.

3. In the **Entry No.** field enter **ADJ**.

4. You can enter all the adjustments on the same page before posting (see Figure 13.13):

   a. One month's rent has expired.
   b. An inventory shows $25 of office supplies remaining.
   c. Depreciation on office equipment, $50.
   d. Depreciation on automobile, $150.

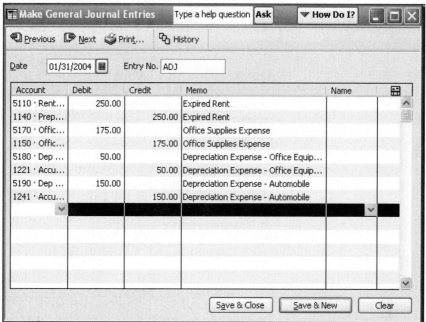

Figure 13.13

5. Click the **Save & Close** button.

Displaying and Printing the General Journal, General Ledger, Trial Balance Reports

1. Click the **Report Center** Report Center icon.

2. From the **Accountants & Taxes** list print the reports shown in Figures 13.14 through 13.16.

The Zell Company-Student Name

Journal

January 2004

Type	Date	Item	Name	Memo	Account	Debit	Credit
General Journal	01/13/2004	Memo5		Paid Telephone Bill	5150 · Telephone Expense	150.00	
				Paid Telephone Bill	1110 · Cash		150.00
						150.00	150.00
General Journal	01/20/2004	Memo6		Owner withdrawal	3120 · Owner's Withdrawals	475.00	
				Owner withdrawal	1110 · Cash		475.00
						475.00	475.00
General Journal	01/27/2004	Memo7		Received cash for Fees Earned	1110 · Cash	600.00	
				Received cash for Fees Earned	4110 · Fees Earned		600.00
						600.00	600.00
General Journal	01/31/2004	Memo8		Paid Salaries Expense	5120 · Salaries Expense	800.00	
				Paid Salaries Expense	1110 · Cash		800.00
						800.00	800.00
General Journal	01/31/2004	ADJ		Expired Rent	5110 · Rent Expense	250.00	
				Expired Rent	1140 · Prepaid Rent		250.00
				Office Supplies Expense	5170 · Office Supplies Expense	175.00	
				Office Supplies Expense	1150 · Office Supplies		175.00
				Depreciation Expense - Office Equipment	5180 · Dep Expense-Office Equi...	50.00	
				Depreciation Expense - Office Equipment	1221 · Accum Dep-Office Equipm...		50.00
				Depreciation Expense - Automobile	5190 · Dep Expense-Automobile	150.00	
				Depreciation Expense - Automobile	1241 · Accum Dep-Automobile		150.00
						625.00	625.00
						23,450.00	23,450.00

Figure 13.14

The Zell Company-Student Name

General Ledger

As of January 31, 2004

Type	Date	Item	Name	Memo	Split	Amount	Balance
1110 · Cash							0.00
General Journal	01/01/2004	Memo1		Initial Investment by Owner	-SPLIT-	5,000.00	5,000.00
General Journal	01/01/2004	Memo2		Prepaid Rent	1140 · Prepaid Rent	-500.00	4,500.00
General Journal	01/13/2004	Memo5		Paid Telephone Bill	5150 · Telephone Expense	-150.00	4,350.00
General Journal	01/20/2004	Memo6		Owner withdrawal	3120 · Owner's Withdrawals	-475.00	3,875.00
General Journal	01/27/2004	Memo7		Received cash for Fees Earned	4110 · Fees Earned	600.00	4,475.00
General Journal	01/31/2004	Memo8		Paid Salaries Expense	5120 · Salaries Expense	-800.00	3,675.00
Total 1110 · Cash						3,675.00	3,675.00
1120 · Accounts Receivable							0.00
General Journal	01/09/2004	Memo4	Andrews, Wayne	Invoiced Customer	4110 · Fees Earned	2,000.00	2,000.00
Total 1120 · Accounts Receivable						2,000.00	2,000.00
1140 · Prepaid Rent							0.00
General Journal	01/01/2004	Memo2		Prepaid Rent	1110 · Cash	500.00	500.00
General Journal	01/31/2004	ADJ		Expired Rent	5110 · Rent Expense	-250.00	250.00
Total 1140 · Prepaid Rent						250.00	250.00
1150 · Office Supplies							0.00
General Journal	01/03/2004	Memo3		Purchased Office Supplies and Of...	-SPLIT-	200.00	200.00
General Journal	01/31/2004	ADJ		Office Supplies Expense	5110 · Rent Expense	-175.00	25.00
Total 1150 · Office Supplies						25.00	25.00
1210 · Office Equipment							0.00
General Journal	01/03/2004	Memo3		Purchased Office Supplies and Of...	1150 · Office Supplies	1,100.00	1,100.00
Total 1210 · Office Equipment						1,100.00	1,100.00

Figure 13.15

The Zell Company-Student Name
Trial Balance
As of January 31, 2004

	Jan 31, 04	
	Debit	Credit
1110 · Cash	3,675.00	
1120 · Accounts Receivable	2,000.00	
1140 · Prepaid Rent	250.00	
1150 · Office Supplies	25.00	
1210 · Office Equipment	1,100.00	
1221 · Accum Dep-Office Equipment		50.00
1230 · Automobile	12,000.00	
1241 · Accum Dep-Automobile		150.00
2110 · Accounts Payable		1,300.00
3110 · Owner's Capital		17,000.00
3120 · Owner's Withdrawals	475.00	
4110 · Fees Earned		2,600.00
5110 · Rent Expense	250.00	
5120 · Salaries Expense	800.00	
5150 · Telephone Expense	150.00	
5170 · Office Supplies Expense	175.00	
5180 · Dep Expense-Office Equipment	50.00	
5190 · Dep Expense-Automobile	150.00	
TOTAL	21,100.00	21,100.00

Figure 13.16

3. Change the dates to **1/1/04** to **1/31/04** on each report.

4. Adjust the column widths as necessary.

5. Review your printed reports. If you have made an error in a posted journal entry, make the necessary changes and reprint the reports, as needed.

Displaying and Printing the Income Statement (Profit & Loss)

1. Select the **Company & Financial** from the list on the left side of the **Reports** dialog box (see Figure 13.17).

Figure 13.17

2. Click on **Standard** in the **Profit & Loss** section.

3. Change the dates to **1/1/04** to **1/31/04**.

4. Adjust the column widths as necessary

5. Your report should look like Figure 13.18.

The Zell Company-Student Name **Profit & Loss** January 2004	
	◊ **Jan 04** ◊
Income	
4110 · Fees Earned	▶ 2,600.00 ◀
Total Income	2,600.00
Expense	
5110 · Rent Expense	250.00
5120 · Salaries Expense	800.00
5150 · Telephone Expense	150.00
5170 · Office Supplies Expense	175.00
5180 · Dep Expense-Office Equipment	50.00
5190 · Dep Expense-Automobile	150.00
Total Expense	1,575.00
Net Income	**1,025.00**

Figure 13.18

6. Click the **Print** icon.

7. Verify in the *Print Reports* dialog box, shown in Figure 13.19, that the report orientation is **Portrait** and that the check box next to **Fit Report to 1 page(s) wide** is checked.

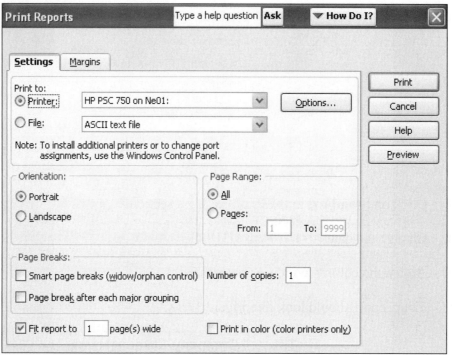

Figure 13.19

8. Click the **Print** icon.

9. Click the **Close** button. You will be returned to the *Reports* dialog box.

Displaying and Printing the Balance Sheet

1. In the **Balance Sheet & Net Worth** section of the **Company & Financial** reports, click **Standard.**

2. Change the date to **1/31/04**.

3. Adjust the column widths as necessary (see Figure 13.20).

```
                    The Zell Company-Student Name
                           Balance Sheet
                        As of January 31, 2005
                                                          ◇ Jan 31, 05 ◇
            ASSETS
               Current Assets
                  Checking/Savings
                     1110 · Cash                      ▶    3,675.00  ◀
                  Total Checking/Savings                   3,675.00

                  Accounts Receivable
                     1120 · Accounts Receivable            2,000.00
                  Total Accounts Receivable                2,000.00

                  Other Current Assets
                     1140 · Prepaid Rent                     250.00
                     1150 · Office Supplies                   25.00
                  Total Other Current Assets                 275.00

               Total Current Assets                        5,950.00

               Fixed Assets
                     1210 · Office Equipment               1,100.00
                     1221 · Accum Dep-Office Equipment       -50.00
                     1230 · Automobile                    12,000.00
                     1241 · Accum Dep-Automobile            -150.00
                  Total Fixed Assets                      12,900.00

            TOTAL ASSETS                                  18,850.00
```

Figure 13.20

> ➤ **NOTE:** You can use the scrollbars to advance the display to the Owner's Equity section of the balance sheet. The statement of owner's equity appears on the balance sheet when you select the Standard Balance Sheet report.

4. Click the **Print** button.

5. Verify in the ***Print Reports*** dialog box that the report orientation is **Portrait** and that the check box next to **Fit Report to 1 page(s) wide** is checked.

6. Click the **Close** button to close the Balance Sheet report.

7. Click the **Close** button to exit the ***Reports*** window.

Backing Up Your Company Data File

1. Click the **Backup** [Backup] icon.

2. Click the **Browse** button in the **Backup Current Company** section to specify a location to keep your backup files.

3. Add **Final** to the file name. Click **Save**.

4. Click **OK**.

5. When the backup is complete, click **OK**.

> ➢ **NOTE:** For more detailed instructions on backing up files, refer to Chapter 11.

Exiting the QuickBooks Pro 2006 Program

1. Select **Close Company** from the **File** menu.

2. Select **Exit** from the **File** menu to end the current work session and return to your Windows desktop.

CHAPTER 14

The Closing Process—Valdez Realty

IN THIS WORKSHOP YOU WILL COMPLETE THE ACCOUNTING CYCLE FOR VALDEZ REALTY TWICE, USING GENERAL JOURNAL ENTRIES AND ADJUSTING JOURNAL ENTRIES.

On June 1, Juan Valdez opened a real estate office called Valdez Realty.

Opening the Valdez Realty File

1. Double-click the **QuickBooks** icon on your desktop to open the software program.

2. Click **Open an existing company** and then locate and select **Valdez Realty**.

3. Click **Open**.

   ➢ **NOTE:** Refer to Chapter 11 for more detailed instructions on opening files.

Backing Up Your Company Data File

1. Click the **Backup** [Backup] icon.

2. Click the **Browse** button in the **Backup Current Company** section to specify a location to keep your backup files.

3. Add **Start** to the file name. Click **Save**.

4. Click **OK**.

5. When the backup is complete, click **OK**.

   ➢ **NOTE:** For more detailed instructions on backing up files, refer to Chapter 11.

Adding Your Name to the Company Name

1. Click the **Company** menu option and select **Company Information**. The program responds by bringing up the *Company Information* dialog box, which allows you to edit/add information about the company.

2. Click in the **Company Name** field and make sure your cursor is at the end of **Valdez Realty**.

3. Add a dash and your name (**-Student's Name**).

4. Click the **OK** button. The title bar should look like Figure 14.1.

Valdez Realty-Student Name - QuickBooks Pro 2006 (via Accountant Edition)

Figure 14.1

Valdez Realty—The June Accounting Cycle

Recording the June General Journal Entries

1. Click the **Company** menu and select **Make General Journal Entries** to open the *Make General Journal Entries* window.

2. In the **Date** field enter the date listed for each transaction.

3. In the **Entry No.** field for the first entry, enter **Memo 1**. For the rest of the transactions accept the number that QuickBooks adds to **Memo 1** by pressing the **Tab** key. Record these entries:

2004		
Jun.	1	Juan Valdez invested $7,000 cash in the real estate agency, along with $3,000 in office equipment.
	1	Rented office space and paid three months' rent in advance, $2,100.
	1	Bought an automobile from Country Auto Sales on account for $12,000. On the Accounts Payable line make sure to select Country Auto Sales in the Name field.
	4	Purchased office supplies for cash, $300.
	5	Purchased office supplies from Supplies, Etc., on account, $150. On the Accounts payable line make sure to select Supplies, Etc. in the Name field.
	6	Sold a house and collected a $6,000 commission.
	8	Paid gas bill, $22.
	15	Paid the salary of the office secretary, $350.
	17	Sold a building lot to Eric Bailey and earned a commission, $6,500. Expect to be paid on 7/8/04. On the Accounts Receivable line make sure to select Bailey, Eric in the Name field.
	20	Juan Valdez withdrew $1,000 from the business to pay personal expenses.
	21	Sold a house and collected a $3,500 commission.
	22	Paid gas bill, $25.
	24	Paid $600 to repair automobile.
	30	Paid the salary of the office secretary, $350.

| | 30 | Paid the June telephone bill, $510. |
| | 30 | Received advertising bill from County Newspaper for June in the amount of $1,200. The bill is to be paid on 7/2/04. On the Accounts Payable line make sure to select County Newspaper in the Name field. |

4. Review the journal entries and make any corrections, following the instructions in Chapter 12 for editing a journal entry.

5. Click the **Close** button to exit the *Make General Journal Entries* window.

Displaying and Printing the Working Reports for June

> **NOTE:** See Chapter 12 for more detailed instructions regarding printing reports.

1. In the *Home* window click the **Report Center** Report Center icon.

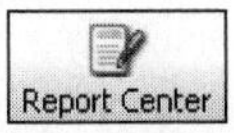

2. Select **Accountant & Taxes** from the list on the left side of your screen.

3. Click **Journal** to display the Journal report on your screen.

4. Change the dates to **6/1/04** and **6/30/04**.

5. Adjust your column widths by dragging the diamonds located between the field titles to show the entire fields (see Figure 14.2).

Figure 14.2

6. Click the **Print** button.

7. Verify the print setup and then click **Print**.

8. Click the **Close** button to return to the *Reports* window.

9. Click the **Trial Balance** report in the *Reports* window.

10. Change the dates to **6/1/04** and **6/30/04**.

11. Adjust your column widths by dragging the diamonds located between the field titles to show the entire fields (see Figure 14.3).

12. Click the **Print** icon.

Valdez Realty-Student Name

Trial Balance

As of June 30, 2004

	Jun 30, 04	
	Debit	Credit
1110 · Cash	11,243.00	
1120 · Accounts Receivable	6,500.00	
1140 · Prepaid Rent	2,100.00	
1150 · Office Supplies	450.00	
1210 · Office Equipment	3,000.00	
1230 · Automobile	12,000.00	
2110 · Accounts Payable		13,350.00
3110 · Juan Valdez, Capital		10,000.00
3120 · Juan Valdez, Withdrawals	1,000.00	
4110 · Commissions Earned		16,000.00
5120 · Salaries Expense	700.00	
5130 · Gas Expense	47.00	
5140 · Repairs Expense	600.00	
5150 · Telephone Expense	510.00	
5160 · Advertising Expense	1,200.00	
TOTAL	39,350.00	39,350.00

Figure 14.3

13. Verify the print setup and then click **Print**.

14. Click the **Close** button to return to the *Reports* window.

15. Review your printed reports. If you have made an error in a posted journal entry, correct the error and reprint the reports before proceeding.

16. Click the **Close** button in the *Reports* window.

Adjusting Journal Entries for June

Use the Trial Balance report you just printed to adjust the following journal entries:

1. Click the **Company** menu and select **Make General Journal Entries** to open the *Make General Journal Entries* dialog box.

2. In the **Date** field enter **June 30, 2004**.

3. In the **Entry No.** field enter **ADJ JUNE**.

4. Enter all the adjustments as a single journal entry:

    a. One month's rent has expired.

b. An inventory shows $50 of office supplies remaining.

c. Depreciation on office equipment, $100.

d. Depreciation on automobile, $200.

5. Review your journal entry and make any necessary corrections. The total should be $1,400.00.

6. Click the **Save & Close** button.

Printing the Final Reports for June

1. Print the Journal, General Ledger, and Trial Balance reports from the **Accountant & Taxes *Report*** dialog box (see Figures 14.4 through 14.6).

2. Print the Income Statement and Balance Sheet reports from the **Company & Financial *Report*** dialog box (see Figures 14.7-14.8).

3. Change the dates to **6/1/04** and **6/30/04**.

4. Adjust the column widths as necessary.

➤ **HINT:** See the detailed instructions in Chapter 12 for printing reports.

Figure 14.4

Valdez Realty-Student Name
General Ledger
As of June 30, 2004

Type	Date	Num	Name	Memo	Split	Amount	Balance
1110 · Cash							**0.00**
General Journal	06/01/2004	Memo 1		Owner Investment	-SPLIT-	7,000.00	7,000.00
General Journal	06/01/2004	Memo 2		Paid 3 months advance rent	1140 · Prepaid Rent	-2,100.00	4,900.00
General Journal	06/04/2004	Memo 4		Cash Purchase of Office Supplies	1150 · Office Supplies	-300.00	4,600.00
General Journal	06/06/2004	Memo 6		Received 6000 Commission	4110 · Commissions Earned	6,000.00	10,600.00
General Journal	06/08/2004	Memo 7		Paid Gas Bill	5130 · Gas Expense	-22.00	10,578.00
General Journal	06/15/2004	Memo 8		Paid Office secretary salary	5120 · Salaries Expense	-350.00	10,228.00
General Journal	06/20/2004	Memo 10		Owner Withdrawal	3120 · Juan Valdez, Withdrawals	-1,000.00	9,228.00
General Journal	06/21/2004	Memo 11		Received Commission	4110 · Commissions Earned	3,500.00	12,728.00
General Journal	06/22/2004	Memo 12		Paid gas bill	5130 · Gas Expense	-25.00	12,703.00
General Journal	06/24/2004	Memo 13		Repairs on Automobile	5140 · Repairs Expense	-600.00	12,103.00
General Journal	06/30/2004	Memo 14		Paid Salaries	5120 · Salaries Expense	-350.00	11,753.00
General Journal	06/30/2004	Memo 15		Paid telephone bill	5150 · Telephone Expense	-510.00	11,243.00
Total 1110 · Cash						11,243.00	11,243.00
1120 · Accounts Receivable							**0.00**
General Journal	06/17/2004	Memo 9	Bailey, Eric	Earned commission to collect in July	4110 · Commissions Earned	6,500.00	6,500.00
Total 1120 · Accounts Receivable						6,500.00	6,500.00
1140 · Prepaid Rent							**0.00**
General Journal	06/01/2004	Memo 2		Paid 3 months advance rent	1110 · Cash	2,100.00	2,100.00
General Journal	06/30/2004	ADJ JUNE		Expired Rent	5110 · Rent Expense	-700.00	1,400.00
Total 1140 · Prepaid Rent						1,400.00	1,400.00
1150 · Office Supplies							**0.00**
General Journal	06/04/2004	Memo 4		Cash Purchase of Office Supplies	1110 · Cash	300.00	300.00
General Journal	06/05/2004	Memo 5		Purchased Office supplies on acc...	2110 · Accounts Payable	150.00	450.00
General Journal	06/30/2004	ADJ JUNE		Office supplies used	5110 · Rent Expense	-400.00	50.00
Total 1150 · Office Supplies						50.00	50.00

Figure 14.5

Valdez Realty-Student Name
Trial Balance
As of June 30, 2004

	Jun 30, 04	
	Debit	**Credit**
1110 · Cash	11,243.00	
1120 · Accounts Receivable	6,500.00	
1140 · Prepaid Rent	1,400.00	
1150 · Office Supplies	50.00	
1210 · Office Equipment	3,000.00	
1221 · Accum Dep-Office Equipment		100.00
1230 · Automobile	12,000.00	
1241 · Accum Dep-Automobile		200.00
2110 · Accounts Payable		13,350.00
3110 · Juan Valdez, Capital		10,000.00
3120 · Juan Valdez, Withdrawals	1,000.00	
4110 · Commissions Earned		16,000.00
5110 · Rent Expense	700.00	
5120 · Salaries Expense	700.00	
5130 · Gas Expense	47.00	
5140 · Repairs Expense	600.00	
5150 · Telephone Expense	510.00	
5160 · Advertising Expense	1,200.00	
5170 · Office Supplies Expense	400.00	
5180 · Dep Expense-Office Equipment	100.00	
5190 · Dep Expense-Automobile	200.00	
TOTAL	**39,650.00**	**39,650.00**

Figure 14.6

Valdez Realty-Student Name
Profit & Loss
June 2004

	Jun 04
Income	
4110 · Commissions Earned	▶ 16,000.00 ◀
Total Income	16,000.00
Expense	
5110 · Rent Expense	700.00
5120 · Salaries Expense	700.00
5130 · Gas Expense	47.00
5140 · Repairs Expense	600.00
5150 · Telephone Expense	510.00
5160 · Advertising Expense	1,200.00
5170 · Office Supplies Expense	400.00
5180 · Dep Expense-Office Equipment	100.00
5190 · Dep Expense-Automobile	200.00
Total Expense	4,457.00
Net Income	**11,543.00**

Figure 14.7

```
                    Valdez Realty-Student Name
                        Balance Sheet
                      As of June 30, 2004

                                          ◇ Jun 30, 04 ◇
  ASSETS
    Current Assets
      Checking/Savings
        1110 · Cash                       ▶  11,243.00 ◀
      Total Checking/Savings                  11,243.00


      Accounts Receivable
        1120 · Accounts Receivable             6,500.00
      Total Accounts Receivable                6,500.00


      Other Current Assets
        1140 · Prepaid Rent                    1,400.00
        1150 · Office Supplies                    50.00
      Total Other Current Assets               1,450.00


    Total Current Assets                      19,193.00


    Fixed Assets
      1210 · Office Equipment                  3,000.00
      1221 · Accum Dep-Office Equipment         -100.00
      1230 · Automobile                       12,000.00
      1241 · Accum Dep-Automobile              -200.00
    Total Fixed Assets                        14,700.00


  TOTAL ASSETS                                33,893.00
```

Figure 14.8

5. Review your printed reports.

6. If you have made errors in posted journal entries, make any necessary corrections.

7. Reprint all reports if you make corrections.

Preparing to Close the Books for June

Computerized accounting systems maintain all their input in compartments called *periods*. Some systems identify periods with the name of the month or with a simple numeric designation, such as 1, 2, 3, and so on. Valdez Realty is currently in Period 6, the June period.

You need to change the current period to the July period prior to inputting the July transactions. You must always tell QuickBooks to move to the next accounting period before starting on the transactions for a new month. This process is the equivalent of closing in a manual accounting system although the temporary accounts are not really closed until the end of the year. You advance the period after you back up your June accounting records.

Backing Up Your Company Data File

1. Click the **Backup** 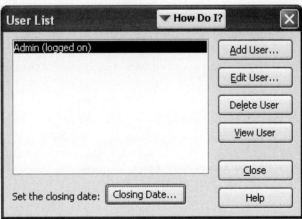 icon .

2. Click the **Browse** button in the **Backup Current Company** section to specify a location to keep your backup files.

3. Add **ENDJUNE** to the file name. Click **Save**.

4. Click **OK**.

5. When the backup is complete, click **OK**.

> ➤ **NOTE:** For more detailed instructions on backing up files, refer to Chapter 11.

Advancing the Accounting Period to July

You must now advance the period to prepare QuickBooks for the July transactions:

1. Select **Set up users** from the **Company** menu. The dialog box shown in Figure 14.9 appears.

Figure 14.9

2. Click the **Closing Date** button. The dialog box shown in Figure 14.10 appears.

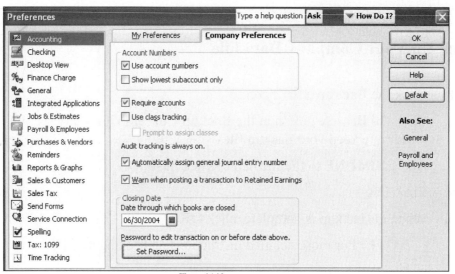

Figure 14.10

3. In the **Closing Date** section, enter **6/30/04**.

4. Click the **OK** button.

5. You are presented with the screen shown in Figure 14.11.

Figure 14.11

6. Select the check box next to **Do not display this message in the future**.

7. Click the **No** button.

8. Click the **C**lose button to exit the *User List* dialog box.

Exiting the QuickBooks Pro 2006 program

1. Select **Close Company** from the **File** menu.

2. Select **Exit** from the **File** menu to end the current work session and return to your Windows desktop.

    ➢ **ALTERNATIVE:** Continue with Recording the July General Journal Entries.

Valdez Realty—The July Accounting Cycle

Opening Valdez Realty File

1. Double-click the **QuickBooks** icon on your desktop to open the software program.

2. Click **Open an existing company** and then locate and select **Valdez Realty**.

3. Click **Open**.

> ➤ **NOTE:** Refer to Chapter 11 for more detailed instructions on opening files.

Recording the July General Journal Entries

1. From the **Company** menu select **Make General Journal Entries**. You should now be looking at the *Make General Journal Entries* dialog box.

2. In the **Date** field enter the date listed for each transaction.

3. In the **Entry No.** field enter **Memo 17** for the first transaction and then accept the number that QuickBooks adds to **Memo** by pressing **Tab** for the rest of the transactions:

2004		
Jul.	1	Purchased additional office supplies from Supplies, Etc., on account, $700.
	2	Paid advertising bill for June, $1200.
	3	Sold a house and collected a commission, $6,600.
	6	Paid gas expense, $29.
	8	Received $6,500 commission from Eric Bailey for the sale of building lot on 6/17/04 (collected the accounts receivable).
	12	Paid $300 to send employees to realtors' workshop (miscellaneous expense).
	15	Paid the salary of the office secretary, $350.
	17	Sold a house to Mike Tung and earned a commission of $2,400. Expected receipt on 8/10/04. (Add a new customer by clicking on the lookup arrow in the name field; select <Add New>. Click OK in the Select Name Type dialog box. In the First Name field enter Mike, in the Last Name field enter Tung. Click OK to add the customer.)
	18	Sold a building lot and collected a commission of $7,000.
	22	Sent a check for $40 to help sponsor a local road race to

		aid the public (miscellaneous expense).
✓	24	Paid for repairs to automobile, $590.
✓	28	Juan Valdez withdrew $1,800 from the business to pay personal expenses.
✓	30	Paid the salary of the office secretary, $350.
✓	30	Paid the July telephone bill, $590.
✓	30	Advertising bill from County Newspaper for July, $1,400. The bill is to be paid on 8/2/04.

4. After you have posted (saved) all the journal entries, click the **Close** button to exit the *Make General Journal Entries* dialog box.

Printing the Working Reports for July

1. Print the General Journal and Trial Balance reports.

2. Change the dates to **7/1/04** and **7/31/04**.

3. Adjust the columns so that all the information shows (see Figures 14.12 and 14.13).

Figure 14.12

Valdez Realty-Student Name
Trial Balance
As of July 31, 2004

	Jul 31, 04	
	Debit	Credit
1110 · Cash	26,094.00	
1120 · Accounts Receivable	2,400.00	
1140 · Prepaid Rent	1,400.00	
1150 · Office Supplies	750.00	
1210 · Office Equipment	3,000.00	
1221 · Accum Dep-Office Equipment		100.00
1230 · Automobile	12,000.00	
1241 · Accum Dep-Automobile		200.00
2110 · Accounts Payable		14,250.00
3110 · Juan Valdez, Capital		10,000.00
3120 · Juan Valdez, Withdrawals	2,800.00	
4110 · Commissions Earned		32,000.00
5110 · Rent Expense	700.00	
5120 · Salaries Expense	1,400.00	
5130 · Gas Expense	76.00	
5140 · Repairs Expense	1,190.00	
5150 · Telephone Expense	1,100.00	
5160 · Advertising Expense	2,600.00	
5170 · Office Supplies Expense	400.00	
5180 · Dep Expense-Office Equipment	100.00	
5190 · Dep Expense-Automobile	200.00	
5210 · Miscellaneous Expense	340.00	
TOTAL	56,550.00	56,550.00

Figure 14.13

4. Review your printed reports. If you made an error in a posted journal entry, correct the error before proceeding.

5. Reprint the reports, if necessary.

Adjusting Journal Entries for July

Using the Trial Balance report you just printed for July, analyze and enter the following journal entries for the end of July:

1. Open the *Make General Journal Entries* dialog box from the **Company** menu.

2. In the **Date** field enter **7/31/04**.

3. In the **Entry No.** field enter **ADJ JULY**.

4. Enter the following adjustments as one General journal entry:

    a. One month's rent has expired.

    b. An inventory shows $90 of office supplies remaining.

      c.   Depreciation on office equipment, $100.

      d.   Depreciation on automobile, $200.

5.   Click the **Save & Close** button.

6.   Click the **Close** button to exit the *Make General Journal Entries* window.

Printing the Final Reports for July

1.   Print the Journal, Trial Balance, General Ledger reports from the **Accountant & Taxes** reports (see Figures 14.14 through 14.16).

2.   Print the Income Statement and Balance Sheet reports from the **Company & Financial** reports (see Figures 14.17 and 14.18).

3.   Change the dates to **7/1/04** to **7/31/04**.

4.   Adjust the column widths as necessary.

Valdez Realty-Student Name
Journal
July 2004

Type	Date	Num	Name	Memo	Account	Debit	Credit
General Journal	07/28/2004	Memo 28		Owner withdrawal	3120 · Juan Valdez, Withdrawals	1,800.00	
				Owner withdrawal	1110 · Cash		1,800.00
						1,800.00	1,800.00
General Journal	07/30/2004	Memo 29		Paid office salary	5120 · Salaries Expense	350.00	
				Paid office salary	1110 · Cash		350.00
						350.00	350.00
General Journal	07/30/2004	Memo 30		Paid Telephone bill	5150 · Telephone Expense	590.00	
				Paid Telephone bill	1110 · Cash		590.00
						590.00	590.00
General Journal	07/30/2004	Memo 31		Advertising bill from County Newspaper	5160 · Advertising Expense	1,400.00	
			County Newspaper	Advertising bill from County Newspaper	2110 · Accounts Payable		1,400.00
						1,400.00	1,400.00
General Journal	07/30/2004	Memo 32		Expired Rent	5110 · Rent Expense	700.00	
				Expired Rent	1140 · Prepaid Rent		700.00
				Office supplies used	5170 · Office Supplies Expense	660.00	
				Office supplies used	1150 · Office Supplies		660.00
				Depreciation of office equipment	5180 · Dep Expense-Office Equipm...	100.00	
				Depreciation of office equipment	1221 · Accum Dep-Office Equipme...		100.00
				Depreciation of automobile	5190 · Dep Expense-Automobile	200.00	
				Depreciation of automobile	1241 · Accum Dep-Automobile		200.00
						1,660.00	1,660.00
						31,509.00	31,509.00

Figure 14.14

Valdez Realty-Student Name
Trial Balance
As of July 31, 2004

	Jul 31, 04	
	Debit	Credit
1110 · Cash	26,094.00	
1120 · Accounts Receivable	2,400.00	
1140 · Prepaid Rent	700.00	
1150 · Office Supplies	90.00	
1210 · Office Equipment	3,000.00	
1221 · Accum Dep-Office Equipment		200.00
1230 · Automobile	12,000.00	
1241 · Accum Dep-Automobile		400.00
2110 · Accounts Payable		14,250.00
3110 · Juan Valdez, Capital		10,000.00
3120 · Juan Valdez, Withdrawals	2,800.00	
4110 · Commissions Earned		32,000.00
5110 · Rent Expense	1,400.00	
5120 · Salaries Expense	1,400.00	
5130 · Gas Expense	76.00	
5140 · Repairs Expense	1,190.00	
5150 · Telephone Expense	1,100.00	
5160 · Advertising Expense	2,600.00	
5170 · Office Supplies Expense	1,060.00	
5180 · Dep Expense-Office Equipment	200.00	
5190 · Dep Expense-Automobile	400.00	
5210 · Miscellaneous Expense	340.00	
TOTAL	56,850.00	56,850.00

Figure 14.15

Valdez Realty-Student Name
General Ledger
As of July 31, 2004

Type	Date	Num	Name	Memo	Split	Amount	Balance
1110 · Cash							11,243.00
General Journal	07/02/2004	Memo 18	County Newspaper	Paid advertising bill from June	2110 · Accounts Payable	-1,200.00	10,043.00
General Journal	07/03/2004	Memo 19		Received commission	4110 · Commissions Earned	6,600.00	16,643.00
General Journal	07/06/2004	Memo 20		Gas expense	5130 · Gas Expense	-29.00	16,614.00
General Journal	07/08/2004	Memo 21	Bailey, Eric	Received payment from Eric Bailey	1120 · Accounts Receivable	6,500.00	23,114.00
General Journal	07/12/2004	Memo 22		Employee realtor workshop	5210 · Miscellaneous Expense	-300.00	22,814.00
General Journal	07/15/2004	Memo 23		Paid salary of office secretary	5120 · Salaries Expense	-350.00	22,464.00
General Journal	07/18/2004	Memo 25		Received commission	4110 · Commissions Earned	7,000.00	29,464.00
General Journal	07/22/2004	Memo 26		Sponsor a local road race	5210 · Miscellaneous Expense	-40.00	29,424.00
General Journal	07/24/2004	Memo 27		Automobile repairs	5140 · Repairs Expense	-590.00	28,834.00
General Journal	07/28/2004	Memo 28		Owner withdrawal	3120 · Juan Valdez, Withdrawals	-1,800.00	27,034.00
General Journal	07/30/2004	Memo 29		Paid office salary	5120 · Salaries Expense	-350.00	26,684.00
General Journal	07/30/2004	Memo 30		Paid Telephone bill	5150 · Telephone Expense	-590.00	26,094.00
Total 1110 · Cash						14,851.00	26,094.00
1120 · Accounts Receivable							6,500.00
General Journal	07/08/2004	Memo 21	Bailey, Eric	Received payment from Eric Bailey	1110 · Cash	-6,500.00	0.00
General Journal	07/17/2004	Memo 24	Mike Tung	Earned Commission	4110 · Commissions Earned	2,400.00	2,400.00
Total 1120 · Accounts Receivable						-4,100.00	2,400.00
1140 · Prepaid Rent							1,400.00
General Journal	07/30/2004	Memo 32		Expired Rent	5110 · Rent Expense	-700.00	700.00
Total 1140 · Prepaid Rent						-700.00	700.00
1150 · Office Supplies							50.00
General Journal	07/01/2004	Memo 17		Purchased Office Supplies	2110 · Accounts Payable	700.00	750.00
General Journal	07/30/2004	Memo 32		Office supplies used	5110 · Rent Expense	-660.00	90.00
Total 1150 · Office Supplies						40.00	90.00

Figure 14.16

```
┌─────────────────────────────────────────────────────────┐
│              Valdez Realty-Student Name                   │
│                 Profit & Loss                             │
│                   July 2004                               │
│                                          ◇  Jul 04  ◇     │
│   Income                                                  │
│      4110 · Commissions Earned         ▶ 16,000.00 ◀      │
│   Total Income                           16,000.00        │
│                                                           │
│   Expense                                                 │
│      5110 · Rent Expense                    700.00        │
│      5120 · Salaries Expense                700.00        │
│      5130 · Gas Expense                      29.00        │
│      5140 · Repairs Expense                 590.00        │
│      5150 · Telephone Expense               590.00        │
│      5160 · Advertising Expense           1,400.00        │
│      5170 · Office Supplies Expense         660.00        │
│      5180 · Dep Expense-Office Equipment    100.00        │
│      5190 · Dep Expense-Automobile          200.00        │
│      5210 · Miscellaneous Expense           340.00        │
│   Total Expense                           5,309.00        │
│                                                           │
│   Net Income                             10,691.00        │
└─────────────────────────────────────────────────────────┘
```

Figure 14.17

```
                    Valdez Realty-Student Name
                         Balance Sheet
                        As of July 31, 2004
                                                    ◇ Jul 31, 04 ◇

        ASSETS
          Current Assets
            Checking/Savings
              1110 · Cash                         ▶ 26,094.00 ◀
            Total Checking/Savings                  26,094.00


            Accounts Receivable
              1120 · Accounts Receivable             2,400.00
            Total Accounts Receivable                2,400.00


            Other Current Assets
              1140 · Prepaid Rent                      700.00
              1150 · Office Supplies                    90.00
            Total Other Current Assets                 790.00


          Total Current Assets                       29,284.00


          Fixed Assets
            1210 · Office Equipment                   3,000.00
            1221 · Accum Dep-Office Equipment          -200.00
            1230 · Automobile                        12,000.00
            1241 · Accum Dep-Automobile                -400.00
          Total Fixed Assets                         14,400.00


        TOTAL ASSETS                                 43,684.00
```

Figure 14.18

5. Review your printed reports. If you have made errors in posted journal entries, use the procedures detailed in Chapter 12 to make any necessary corrections. Reprint all reports if you make corrections.

Backing Up Your Company Data File

1. Click the **Backup** [Backup] icon.

2. Click the **Browse** button in the **Back Up Current Company** section to specify a location to keep your backup files.

3. Add **EndJuly** to the file name. Click **Save**.

4. Click **OK**.

5. When the backup is complete, click **OK**.

> ➢ **NOTE:** For more detailed instructions on backing up files, refer to Chapter 11.

Advancing the Accounting Period to August

You must now advance the period to prepare QuickBooks for the August transactions:

1. Select **Set up users** from the **Company** menu.

2. Click the **Closing Date** button.

3. In the Closing Date section enter **7/31/04**.

4. Click the **OK** button.

5. Click the **Close** button to exit the *User List* dialog box.

Exiting the QuickBooks Pro 2006 Program

1. Select **Close Company** from the **File** menu

2. Select **Exit** from the **File** menu to end the current work session and return to your Windows desktop.

CHAPTER 15

Payroll Requirements for the First Quarter—Pete's Market

IN THIS WORKSHOP YOU WILL YOU WILL ENTER THE PAYROLL TRANSACTIONS FOR FIRST QUARTER–JANUARY THROUGH MARCH, 2004, FOR PETE'S MARKET.

Company Information

Pete's Market, owned by Pete Reel, is located at 4 Sun Avenue, Swampscott, Massachusetts, 01970. His employer identification number is 42-4583312.

QuickBooks offers several options for processing payroll:

1. Do-It-Yourself—Provides tax tables for a fee.

2. Assisted Payroll—Charges a fee and provides tax tables, makes tax payments, and prepares W-2 and W-3 forms.

3. Complete Payroll—Involves paying a fee and is a fully outsourced payroll service.

4. Manual—Lets you enter all information in each paycheck, using government publications.

All options except Manual involve fees. To avoid paying for the payroll service, this assignment uses the Manual method for completing the payroll. The amounts of federal income tax (FIT), state income tax (SIT), Social Security, Medicare, FUTA, and SUTA are all provided for you, and you must enter these when processing the payroll.

When transactions are recorded for the monthly payroll, the program automatically updates the employee records, records the journal entry, and posts all accounts affected in the General ledger.

Opening the Pete's Market File

1. Double-click the **QuickBooks** icon on your desktop to open the software program.

2. Click **Open an existing company** and then locate and select **Pete's Market**.

3. Click **Open**.

> ➢ **NOTE:** Refer to Chapter 11 for more detailed instructions on opening files.

Backing Up Your Company Data File

1. Click the **Backup** 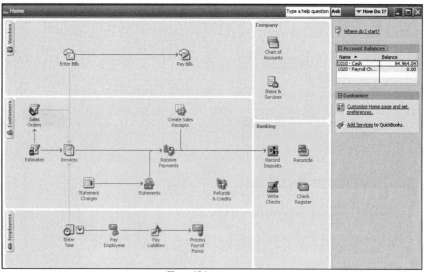 icon.

2. Click **Browse** button in the **Backup Current Company** section to specify a location to keep your backup files.

3. Add **Start** to the file name. Click **Save**.

4. Click **OK**.

5. When the backup is complete, click **OK**.

    ➢ **NOTE:** For more detailed instructions on backing up files, refer to Chapter 11.

Adding Your Name to the Company Name

1. Click the **Company** menu option and select **Company Information**. The program responds by bringing up the ***Company Information*** dialog box, which allows you to edit/add information about the company.

2. Click in the **Company Name** field and make sure that your cursor is at the end of **Pete's Market**.

3. Add a dash and your name **(-Student's Name)**.

4. Click the **OK** button. You should now be looking at the ***Home*** window, which is shown in Figure 15.1.

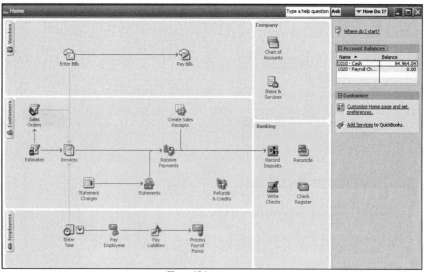

Figure 15.1

The trial balance for Pete's Market as of 1/1/04 appears in Figure 15.2.

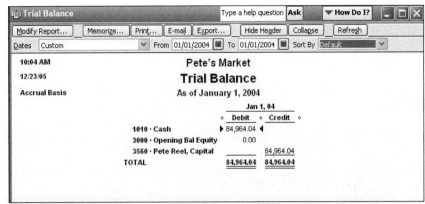

Figure 15.2

Paying Employees

1. Click the **Pay Employees** 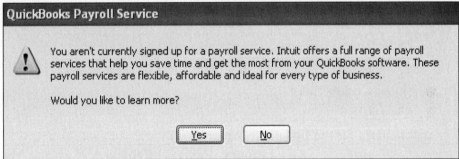 icon in the **Payroll Section** of the *Home* window.

2. On the *QuickBooks Payroll Service* warning screen, click **No** (see Figure 15.3).

Figure 15.3

3. On the *Pay Employees* dialog box, click the **Pay Employees anyway** button (see Figure 15.4).

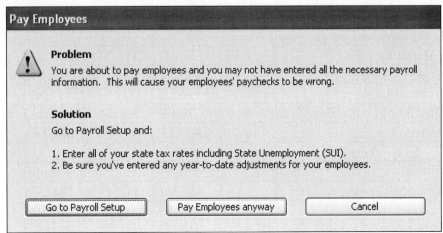

Figure 15.4

4. On the *Select Employees to Pay* window select **1020 Payroll Checking Cash** in the **Bank Account** field.

5. Verify that the check date and pay period ending date are both 1/31/04.

6. Click **Mark All** to select all the employees. Your screen should look like Figure 15.5.

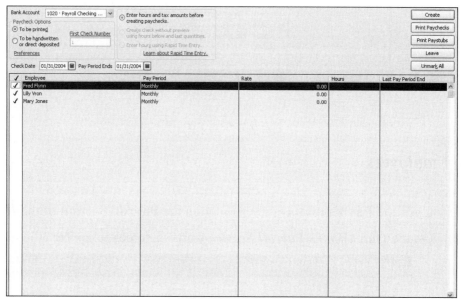

Figure 15.5

7. Click the **Create** button.

The following are the employees of Pete's Market and their monthly wages and withholding for the first payroll quarter:

	January	February	March
Fred Flynn			
Salary	$2,500.00	$2,590.00	$2,475.00
Social Security Company	155.00	160.58	153.45
Medicare Company	36.25	37.56	35.89
Federal Unemployment	20.00	20.72	15.28
MA-Unemployment Company	122.50	126.91	121.28
Federal Withholding	365.00	390.00	358.00
Social Security Employee	155.00	160.58	153.45
Medicare Employee	36.25	37.56	35.89
MA Withholding	136.00	140.00	135.00
Net Pay	**1,807.25**	**1,861.86**	**1,792.66**
Lilly Vron			
Salary	3,000.00	3,000.00	4,000.00
Social Security Company	186.00	186.00	248.00
Medicare Company	43.50	43.50	58.00
Federal Unemployment	24.00	24.00	8.00
MA-Unemployment Company	147.00	147.00	196.00

Federal Withholding	375.00	375.00	450.00
Social Security Employee	186.00	186.00	248.00
Medicare Employee	43.50	43.50	58.00
MA Withholding	140.00	140.00	198.00
Net Pay	**2,255.50**	**2,255.50**	**3,046.00**
Mary Jones			
Salary	3,000.00	3,000.00	4,260.00
Social Security Company	186.00	186.00	264.12
Medicare Company	43.50	43.50	61.77
Federal Unemployment	24.00	24.00	8.00
MA-Unemployment Company	147.00	147.00	208.74
Federal Withholding	440.00	440.00	593.00
Social Security Employee	186.00	186.00	264.12
Medicare Employee	43.50	43.50	61.77
MA Withholding	144.00	144.00	218.00
Net Pay	**2,186.50**	**2,186.50**	**3,123.11**

8. The **_Preview Paycheck_** screen for Fred Flynn appears.

9. Enter the salary and withholding information from the chart for Fred for January. Your screen should look like Figure 15.6.

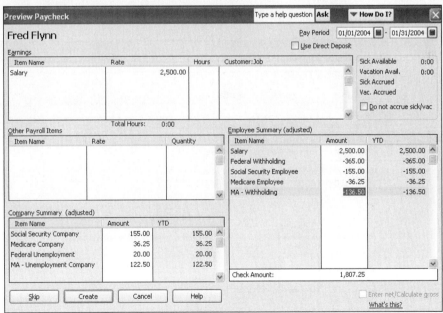

Figure 15.6

10. Review the information entered for Fred Flynn. If everything is correct, click the **Create** button.

11. Enter the information for Lilly Vron and Mary Jones from the table above and create their paychecks.

12. The net pay for Lilly Vron and Mary Jones should be $2,255.50 and $2,186.50, respectively.

13. After verifying that the payroll entries are correct and returning to the *Select Employees to Pay* screen, click the **Print Paychecks** button. The screen shown in Figure 15.7 appears.

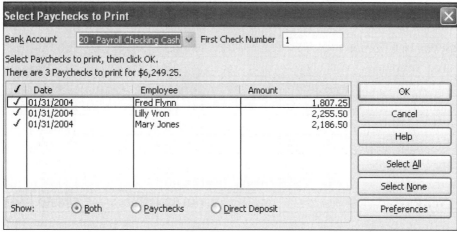

Figure 15.7

14. Make sure that all three employees have check marks in the checkmark column.

15. **First Check Number** should be **1**. If it is not, click in the field and change it.

16. Click the **OK** button. The window shown in Figure 15.8 appears.

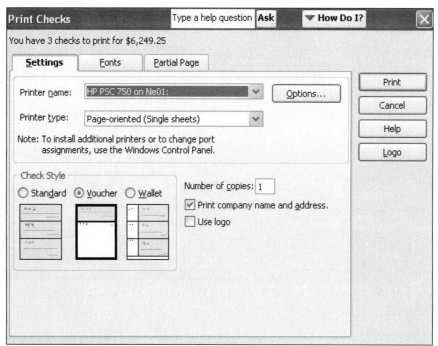

Figure 15.8

17. In the **Check Style** section select **Voucher** and check the box to print the company name and address on the checks.

18. Click the **Print** button.

19. When the checks have finished printing, you see the ***Did check(s) print OK?*** dialog box (see Figure 15.9). This feature allows you to print them a second time if something interfered with the printing process the first time through. Click **OK**.

20. Upon confirming a successful run, you are taken back to the ***Select Employees to Pay*** screen. Click the **Leave** button.

Figure 15.9

21. If the ***Set Check Reminder*** screen appears (see Figure 15.10), select the box next to **Do not display this message in the future** and click **No**.

Figure 15.10

22. Click the **Close** button to exit the ***Select Employees to Pay*** dialog box.

Printing the Payroll Summary

1. Click the **Report Center** Report Center icon.
2. Select **Employees & Payroll** from the list on the left side of the screen.
3. Select **Payroll Summary** to bring up the payroll deductions and withholdings for the checks you just issued.
4. Change the date to **1/1/04** to **1/31/04**. Your screen should look like Figure 15.11.

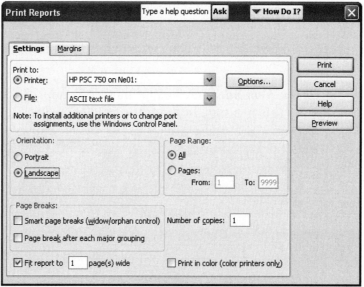

12:12 PM 12/23/05	Pete's Market-Student Name **Payroll Summary** January 2004											
		Fred Flynn			Lilly Vron			Mary Jones			TOTAL	
	◇ Hours ◇	Rate ◇	Jan 04 ◇	Hours ◇	Rate ◇	Jan 04 ◇	Hours ◇	Rate ◇	Jan 04 ◇	Hours ◇	Rate ◇	Jan 04 ◇
Employee Wages, Taxes and Adjustments												
Gross Pay												
Salary			▶ 2,500.00 ◀			3,000.00			3,000.00			8,500.00
Total Gross Pay			2,500.00			3,000.00			3,000.00			8,500.00
Adjusted Gross Pay			2,500.00			3,000.00			3,000.00			8,500.00
Taxes Withheld												
Federal Withholding			-365.00			-375.00			-440.00			-1,180.00
Medicare Employee			-36.25			-43.50			-43.50			-123.25
Social Security Employee			-155.00			-186.00			-186.00			-527.00
MA - Withholding			-136.50			-140.00			-144.00			-420.50
Total Taxes Withheld			-692.75			-744.50			-813.50			-2,250.75
Net Pay			**1,807.25**			**2,255.50**			**2,186.50**			**6,249.25**
Employer Taxes and Contributions												
Federal Unemployment			20.00			24.00			24.00			68.00
Medicare Company			36.25			43.50			43.50			123.25
Social Security Company			155.00			186.00			186.00			527.00
MA - Unemployment Company			122.50			147.00			147.00			416.50
Total Employer Taxes and Contributions			333.75			400.50			400.50			1,134.75

Figure 15.11

5. Click the **Print** icon. The dialog box shown in Figure 15.12 appears.

Figure 15.12

6. Make sure the orientation is **Landscape** and that there is a check mark by **Fit report to 1 page(s) wide**.

7. Click **Print**.

8. Review your report and make any necessary corrections. If you make corrections, reprint the Payroll Summary report before continuing.

Transferring Funds from One Checking Account to Another

You use the Payroll Summary report to determine the net pay for the payroll period. This amount must be transferred to the Payroll Checking account since the paychecks are drawn on that account. It must be funded prior to issuing the checks to the employees. The total in the **Net Pay** row on the Payroll Summary report is **$6,249.25**.

1. Select **Transfer funds** from the **Company** menu.

2. Enter the date **1/31/04** in the **Date** field.

3. In the **Transfer Funds From** box click the drop-down list arrow and select **1010 Cash**.

4. In the **Transfer Funds To** box click the drop-down list arrow and select **1020 Payroll Checking Cash**.

5. In the **Transfer Amount** enter **6249.25**.

6. The **Memo** field automatically shows **Funds Transfer** (see Figure 15.13).

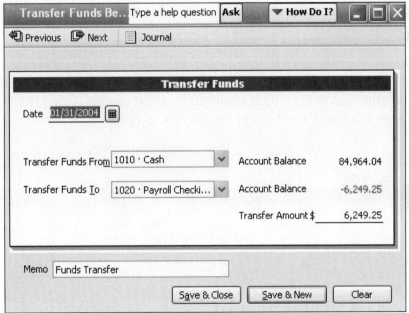

Figure 15.13

7. Click **Save & New** to complete the transfer and post the transaction.

8. Click the **Previous** ![Previous] button to review your posted transaction. As you can see in Figure 155.14 the account balances have changed.

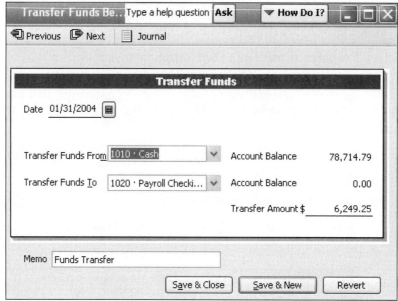

Figure 15.14

9. Click the **Journal** ▤ Journal icon. Your screen looks like Figure 15.15 (except the column widths have been adjusted). As you can see, QuickBooks has made a journal entry (Debits & Credits) for the transfer of funds.

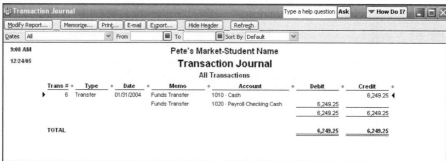

Figure 15.15

10. Click the **Close** button to exit the ***Transaction Journal*** dialog box.

11. Click the **Close** button to exit the ***Transfer of Funds*** dialog box.

Reviewing the Paychecks to make corrections or to see the detail

If you want to see details about any of the employees or make changes to an employee's paycheck, you need to go to the individual check for the employee and make changes to the paycheck.

1. Click the **Register** Reg button.

2. In the *Use Register* dialog box, click the drop-down list arrow and select **1020 Payroll Checking Cash** (see Figure 15.16).

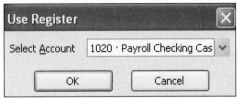

Figure 15.16

3. Click **OK**. The window shown in Figure 15.17 appears.

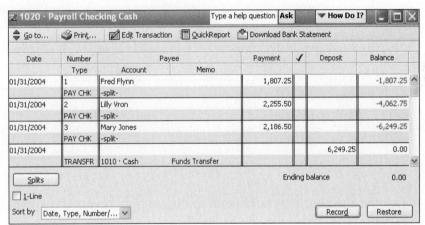

Figure 15.17

4. Double-click the paycheck for Fred Flynn (see Figure 15.18).

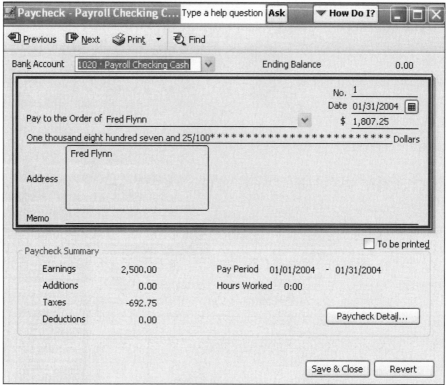

Figure 15.18

5. Click the **Paycheck Detail** button to display the ***Review Paycheck*** screen (see Figure 15.19).

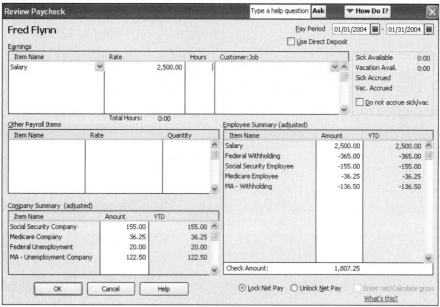

Figure 15.19

6. Change any of the numbers presented in the white fields of the ***Review Paycheck*** dialog box by highlighting the number you wish to change and entering a new number. Accept all the information as given.

7. Click the **Cancel** button since you made no changes.

8. Click the **Close** button to exit the *Payroll – Paycheck* dialog box.

9. Click the **Close** button to close the Payroll register.

Printing Reports

1. Click the **Report Center** Report Center icon.

2. Click **Accountant & Taxes** from the list on the left of your screen.

3. Select and print the General Journal and Trial Balance reports (see Figures 15.20 and 15.21).

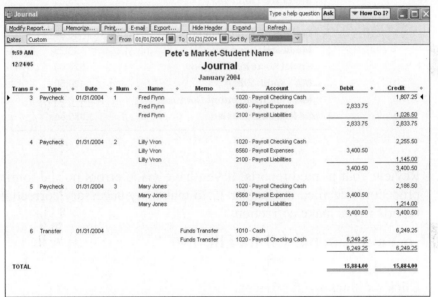

Figure 15.20

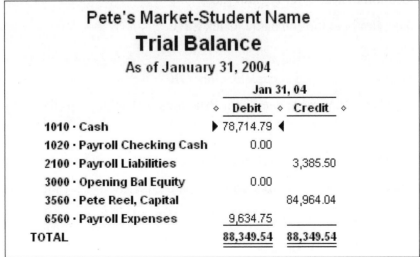

Figure 15.21

4. Change the dates to **1/1/04** and **1/31/04**.

5. Adjust the columns to show the entire fields.

6. Select **Employees & Payroll** from the *Report Center* dialog box.

7. Print the Payroll Liability Balances report for January (see Figure 15.22).

Pete's Market-Student Name
Payroll Liability Balances
January 2004

	◇ BALANCE ◇
Payroll Liabilities	
Federal Withholding	▶ 1,180.00 ◀
Medicare Employee	123.25
Social Security Employee	527.00
Federal Unemployment	68.00
Medicare Company	123.25
Social Security Company	527.00
MA - Withholding	420.50
MA - Unemployment Company	416.50
Total Payroll Liabilities	**3,385.50**

Figure15.22

8. Review your printed reports. If you have made errors posted journal entries, use the procedures detailed in Chapter 12 to make any necessary corrections. Reprint all the reports if you make corrections.

Backing Up Your Company Data File

1. Click the **Backup** [Backup] icon.

2. Click the **Browse** button in the **Backup Current Company** section to specify a location to keep your backup files.

3. Add **Jan04** to the file name. Click **Save**.

4. Click **OK**.

5. When the backup is complete, click **OK**.

   ➢ **NOTE:** For more detailed instructions on backing up files, refer to Chapter 11.

Advancing the Accounting Period to February

You must now advance the period to prepare QuickBooks for the February transactions:

1. Select **Set up users** from the **Company** menu.

2. Click the **Closing Date** button.

3. In the **Closing Date** section, enter **1/31/04**.

4. Click the **OK** button.

5. Click the **Close** button to exit the *User List* dialog box.

6. Click the **Home** Home icon.

Paying the January Payroll Liability

Record the following payment of payroll liabilities:

2004		
Feb.	15	Record the payment of Social Security, Medicare, and FIT from last month's payroll.

1. Click the **Pay Liabilities** Pay Liabilities icon.

2. Enter the date range for liabilities from **01/01/04** through **01/31/04** (see Figure 15.23).

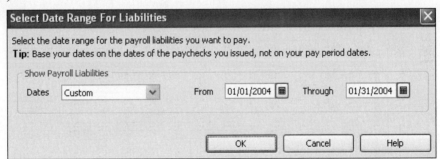

Figure 15.23

3. Click **OK**.

4. On the Pay Liabilities screen, make sure the Checking Account is "1010 Cash".

5. Enter **02/15/04** for **Payment Date**.

6. The dates for **Show Payroll Liabilities** should be from **01/01/04** through **01/31/04**.

7. Make sure that **Review liability check to enter expenses/penalties** is selected.

8. Click in the checkmark column next to Federal Withholding, Medicare, and Social Security to mark these items for payment.

9. Your screen now looks like Figure 15.24.

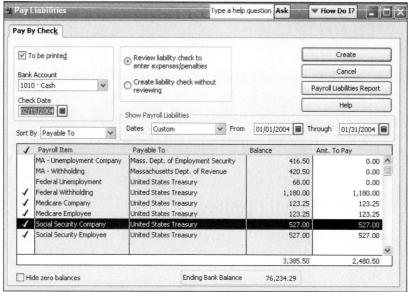

Figure 15.24

10. Click the **Create** button. When the check appears on the screen (see Figure 15.25), review it for accuracy.

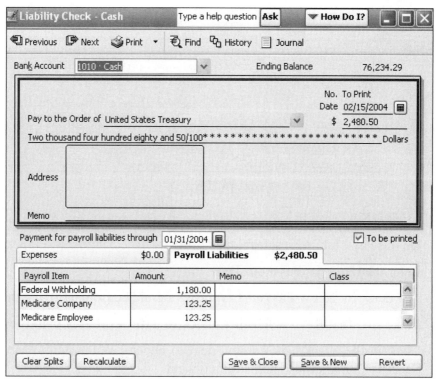

Figure 15.25

11. Click the **Print** icon.

12. Change the check number to **101**.

13. Click **OK**.

14. Click **Print**.

15. Click **Save & Close** to post the check.

Recording the February Payroll

Select **Pay Employees** to pay the February payroll for all three employees: Fred Flynn, Lilly Vron, and Mary Jones.

1. Enter the amounts shown for the employees from the table on page 210.

2. Follow the same procedure for creating and printing checks that you used in January except use the date **February 29**.

3. When printing the checks, the starting check number should be **4**.

4. Be sure to transfer the net pay into the Payroll Checking Cash account.

Printing February Reports

1. In the *Report Center* dialog box select **Employees & Payroll**.

2. Print the payroll summary dated 2/1/04 to 2/29/04 (see Figure 15.26).

| | Fred Flynn | | | Lilly Vron | | | Mary Jones | | | TOTAL | | |
	Hours	Rate	Feb 04	Hours	Rate	Feb 04	Hours	Rate	Feb 04	Hours	Rate	Feb 04
Employee Wages, Taxes and Adjustments												
Gross Pay												
Salary			2,590.00			3,000.00			3,000.00			8,590.00
Total Gross Pay			2,590.00			3,000.00			3,000.00			8,590.00
Adjusted Gross Pay			2,590.00			3,000.00			3,000.00			8,590.00
Taxes Withheld												
Federal Withholding			-390.00			-375.00			-440.00			-1,205.00
Medicare Employee			-37.56			-43.50			-43.50			-124.56
Social Security Employee			-160.58			-186.00			-186.00			-532.58
MA - Withholding			-140.00			-140.00			-144.00			-424.00
Total Taxes Withheld			-728.14			-744.50			-813.50			-2,286.14
Net Pay			1,861.86			2,255.50			2,186.50			6,303.86
Employer Taxes and Contributions												
Federal Unemployment			20.72			24.00			24.00			68.72
Medicare Company			37.56			43.50			43.50			124.56
Social Security Company			160.58			186.00			186.00			532.58
MA - Unemployment Company			126.91			147.00			147.00			420.91
Total Employer Taxes and Contributions			345.77			400.50			400.50			1,146.77

Pete's Market-Student Name
Payroll Summary
February 2004
2:08 PM 12/24/05

Figure 15.26

3. Print the payroll liabilities balance dated 1/1/04 to 2/29/04 (see Figure 15.27).

Pete's Market-Student Name

Payroll Liability Balances

January through February 2004

	Jan 04	Feb 04	BALANCE
Payroll Liabilities			
Federal Withholding	0.00	1,205.00	1,205.00
Medicare Employee	0.00	124.56	124.56
Social Security Employee	0.00	532.58	532.58
Federal Unemployment	68.00	68.72	136.72
Medicare Company	0.00	124.56	124.56
Social Security Company	0.00	532.58	532.58
MA - Withholding	420.50	424.00	844.50
MA - Unemployment Company	416.50	420.91	837.41
Total Payroll Liabilities	**905.00**	**3,432.91**	**4,337.91**

Figure 15.27

4. In the ***Report Center*** dialog box select **Accountant & Taxes**.
5. Print the General Journal and the Trial Balance reports (see Figures 15.28 and 15.29).
6. Use the dates **02/01/04** to **02/29/04**.

2:29 PM
12/24/05

Pete's Market-Student Name

Journal

February 2004

Trans #	Type	Date	Num	Name	Memo	Account	Debit	Credit
7	Liability Check	02/15/2004	4	United States Treasury		1010 · Cash		2,480.50
				United States Treasury		2100 · Payroll Liabilities	2,480.50	
							2,480.50	2,480.50
8	Paycheck	02/29/2004		Fred Flynn		1020 · Payroll Checking Cash		1,861.86
				Fred Flynn		6560 · Payroll Expenses	2,935.77	
				Fred Flynn		2100 · Payroll Liabilities		1,073.91
							2,935.77	2,935.77
9	Paycheck	02/29/2004		Lilly Vron		1020 · Payroll Checking Cash		2,255.50
				Lilly Vron		6560 · Payroll Expenses	3,400.50	
				Lilly Vron		2100 · Payroll Liabilities		1,145.00
							3,400.50	3,400.50
10	Paycheck	02/29/2004		Mary Jones		1020 · Payroll Checking Cash		2,186.50
				Mary Jones		6560 · Payroll Expenses	3,400.50	
				Mary Jones		2100 · Payroll Liabilities		1,214.00
							3,400.50	3,400.50
11	Transfer	02/29/2004			Funds Transfer	1010 · Cash		6,303.86
					Funds Transfer	1020 · Payroll Checking Cash	6,303.86	
							6,303.86	6,303.86
TOTAL							**18,521.13**	**18,521.13**

Figure 15.28

```
                  Pete's Market-Student Name
                        Trial Balance
                   As of February 29, 2004

                                          Feb 29, 04
                                     ◇   Debit  ◇   Credit  ◇
       1010 · Cash                    ▶ 69,930.43 ◀
       1020 · Payroll Checking Cash        0.00
       2100 · Payroll Liabilities                     4,337.91
       3000 · Opening Bal Equity           0.00
       3560 · Pete Reel, Capital                     84,964.04
       6560 · Payroll Expenses         19,371.52
       TOTAL                           89,301.95    89,301.95
```

Figure 15.29

Backing Up Your Company Data File

1. Click the **Backup** [Backup] icon.

2. Click the **Browse** button in the **Backup Current Company** section to specify a location to keep your backup files.

3. Add **Feb04** to the file name. Click **Save**.

4. Click **OK**.

5. When the backup is complete, click **OK**.

   ➢ **NOTE:** For more detailed instructions on backing up files, refer to Chapter 11.

Advancing the Accounting Period to March

You must now advance the period to prepare QuickBooks for the March transactions:

1. Select **Set up users** from the **Company** menu.

2. Click the **Closing Date** button.

3. In the **Closing Date** section enter **2/28/04**.

4. Click the **OK** button.

5. Click the **Close** button to exit the *User List* dialog box.

Paying the Payroll Liabilities for February

Record the following payment of payroll liabilities:

2004		
Mar.	15	Record the payment of Social Security, Medicare, and FIT from last month's payroll. Print the payment on Check 102. Use account 1010 Cash.

1. Click the **Pay Liabilities** 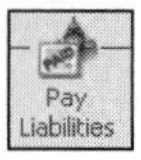

icon.
2. Use the dates **1/1/04** to **2/29/04**.
3. Use **Cash account 1010** and date the check **3/15/04**.
4. Mark the Federal Withholding, the Social Security, and Medicare items in the checkmark column. The total check should be $2,519.28. Use Check 102 from Account 1010 Cash.

Recording the March Payroll

Select **Pay Employees** to record the March payroll for all three employees: Fred Flynn, Lilly Vron, and Mary Jones.

1. Enter the amounts shown for the employees in the table on page 210.
2. Follow the same procedure for creating and printing checks as you used in January, except use the date **March 31**.
3. When printing the checks, the starting check number should be **7**.
4. Be sure to transfer the net pay into the Payroll Checking Cash account.

Printing March Reports

1. In the ***Report Center*** dialog box select **Employees & Payroll**.
2. Print the payroll summary report dated 3/1/04 to 3/31/04 (see Figure 15.30).
3. Print the payroll liabilities balance report dated 1/1/04 to 3/31/04 (see Figure 15.31).

3:22 PM
12/24/05

Pete's Market-Student Name
Payroll Summary
March 2004

	Fred Flynn			Lilly Vron			Mary Jones			TOTAL		
	Hours	Rate	Mar 04	Hours	Rate	Mar 04	Hours	Rate	Mar 04	Hours	Rate	Mar 04
Employee Wages, Taxes and Adjustments												
Gross Pay												
Salary			2,475.00			4,000.00			4,260.00			10,735.00
Total Gross Pay			2,475.00			4,000.00			4,260.00			10,735.00
Adjusted Gross Pay			2,475.00			4,000.00			4,260.00			10,735.00
Taxes Withheld												
Federal Withholding			-358.00			-450.00			-593.00			-1,401.00
Medicare Employee			-35.89			-58.00			-61.77			-155.66
Social Security Employee			-153.45			-248.00			-264.12			-665.57
MA - Withholding			-135.00			-198.00			-218.00			-551.00
Total Taxes Withheld			-682.34			-954.00			-1,136.89			-2,773.23
Net Pay			1,792.66			3,046.00			3,123.11			7,961.77
Employer Taxes and Contributions												
Federal Unemployment			15.28			8.00			8.00			31.28
Medicare Company			35.89			58.00			61.77			155.66
Social Security Company			153.45			248.00			264.12			665.57
MA - Unemployment Company			121.28			196.00			208.74			526.02
Total Employer Taxes and Contributions			325.90			510.00			542.63			1,378.53

Figure 15.30

Pete's Market-Student Name
Payroll Liability Balances
January through March 2004

Payroll Liabilities	Jan 04	Feb 04	Mar 04	BALANCE
Federal Withholding	0.00	0.00	1,401.00	1,401.00
Medicare Employee	0.00	0.00	155.66	155.66
Social Security Employee	0.00	0.00	665.57	665.57
Federal Unemployment	68.00	68.72	31.28	168.00
Medicare Company	0.00	0.00	155.66	155.66
Social Security Company	0.00	0.00	665.57	665.57
MA - Withholding	420.50	424.00	551.00	1,395.50
MA - Unemployment Company	416.50	420.91	526.02	1,363.43
Total Payroll Liabilities	**905.00**	**913.63**	**4,151.76**	**5,970.39**

Figure 15.31

4. In the *Report Center* dialog box select **Accountant & Taxes**.

5. Print the General Journal and the Trial Balance reports (see Figures 15.32 and 15.33).

6. Use the dates **03/01/04** to **3/31/04**.

3:29 PM
12/24/05

Pete's Market-Student Name
Journal
March 2004

Tra...	Type	Date	Num	Name	Account	Debit	Credit
12	Liability Check	03/15/2004	5	United States Treasury	1010 · Cash		2,519.28
				United States Treasury	2100 · Payroll Liabilities	2,519.28	
						2,519.28	2,519.28
13	Paycheck	03/31/2004		Fred Flynn	1020 · Payroll Checking Cash		1,792.66
				Fred Flynn	6560 · Payroll Expenses	2,800.90	
				Fred Flynn	2100 · Payroll Liabilities		1,008.24
						2,800.90	2,800.90
14	Paycheck	03/31/2004		Lilly Vron	1020 · Payroll Checking Cash		3,046.00
				Lilly Vron	6560 · Payroll Expenses	4,510.00	
				Lilly Vron	2100 · Payroll Liabilities		1,464.00
						4,510.00	4,510.00
15	Paycheck	03/31/2004		Mary Jones	1020 · Payroll Checking Cash		3,123.11
				Mary Jones	6560 · Payroll Expenses	4,802.63	
				Mary Jones	2100 · Payroll Liabilities		1,679.52
						4,802.63	4,802.63
16	Transfer	03/31/2004			1010 · Cash		7,961.77
					1020 · Payroll Checking Cash	7,961.77	
						7,961.77	7,961.77
TOTAL						**22,594.58**	**22,594.58**

Figure 15.32

Pete's Market-Student Name

Trial Balance

As of March 31, 2004

	Mar 31, 04	
	Debit	Credit
1010 · Cash	59,449.38	
1020 · Payroll Checking Cash	0.00	
2100 · Payroll Liabilities		5,970.39
3000 · Opening Bal Equity	0.00	
3560 · Pete Reel, Capital		84,964.04
6560 · Payroll Expenses	31,485.05	
TOTAL	90,934.43	90,934.43

Figure 15.33

Backing Up Your Company Data File

1. Click the **Backup** [Backup] icon.

2. Click the **Browse** button in the **Backup Current Company** section to specify a location to keep your backup files.

3. Add **Mar04** to the file name. Click **Save**.

4. Click **OK**.

5. When the backup is complete, click **OK**.

> ➤ **NOTE:** For more detailed instructions on backing up files, refer to Chapter 11.

Advancing the Accounting Period to April

You must now advance the period to prepare QuickBooks for the April transactions:

1. Select **Set up users** from the **Company** menu.

2. Click the **Closing Date** button.

3. In the **Closing Date** section enter **3/31/04**.

4. Click the **OK** button.

5. Click the **Close** button to exit the *User List* dialog box.

Paying the March Payroll Liabilities

Record the following payment(s) of payroll liabilities:

2004		
Apr.	15	Record the payment of Social Security, Medicare, and FIT from last month's payroll. Print the payment on Check 103.
	30	Record the payment of SUTA, FUTA and state withholding. Check numbers 104, 105, and 106

1. Click **Pay Liabilities** icon.

2. Use the dates **1/1/04** and **3/31/04**.

3. The check date should be **4/15/04** for the federal tax payment

4. Select **Federal Withholding**, **Social Security** and **Medicare**.

5. Click **Create**.

6. Click the **Print** icon on the *Liability Check – Payroll* screen.

7. Make sure your check number is **103**.

8. Click **Pay Liabilities** icon.

9. Use the dates **1/1/04** and **3/31/04**.

10. The check date should be **4/30/04**.

11. Select **MA – Unemployment**, **Federal Unemployment** and **MA state withholding**.

12. Click **Create**.

13. Click **Save & Close** on the *Liability Check – payroll* screen.

14. From the **File** menu select **Print Forms** and then select **Checks**.

15. You should see three checks dated 4/30/04 on the *Select Checks to Print* dialog box. Make sure they are all selected. The starting check number should be **104**.

16. Click **OK**.

Printing the Reports for April

Print the reports shown in Figures 15.34 through 15.36.

9:15 AM 12/26/05		Pete's Market-Student Name **Journal** April 2004 through April 2005						
Trans #	Type	Date	Num	Adj	Name	Account	Debit	Credit
17	Liability Check	04/15/2004	103		United States Treasury	1010 · Cash		3,043.46
					United States Treasury	2100 · Payroll Liabilities	3,043.46	
							3,043.46	3,043.46
18	Liability Check	04/30/2004	104		Mass. Dept. of Employmen...	1010 · Cash		1,363.43
					Mass. Dept. of Employmen...	2100 · Payroll Liabilities	1,363.43	
							1,363.43	1,363.43
19	Liability Check	04/30/2004	105		Massachusetts Dept. of R...	1010 · Cash		1,395.50
					Massachusetts Dept. of R...	2100 · Payroll Liabilities	1,395.50	
							1,395.50	1,395.50
20	Liability Check	04/30/2004	106		United States Treasury	1010 · Cash		168.00
					United States Treasury	2100 · Payroll Liabilities	168.00	
							168.00	168.00
TOTAL							5,970.39	5,970.39

Figure 15.34

Pete's Market-Student Name
Trial Balance
As of April 30, 2004

	Apr 30, 04	
	Debit	Credit
1010 · Cash	53,478.99	
1020 · Payroll Checking Cash	0.00	
2100 · Payroll Liabilities	0.00	
3000 · Opening Bal Equity	0.00	
3560 · Pete Reel, Capital		84,964.04
6560 · Payroll Expenses	31,485.05	
TOTAL	84,964.04	84,964.04

Figure 15.35

Pete's Market-Student Name
Payroll Liability Balances
April 30, 2004

	BALANCE
Payroll Liabilities	0.00

Figure 15.36

Processing the Quarterly Federal Tax Returns

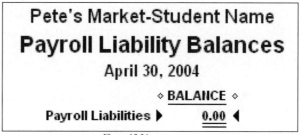

1. Click the **Process Payroll Forms** icon.

2. In the *Select Form Type* dialog box select **Federal form** and click **OK** (see Figure 15.37).

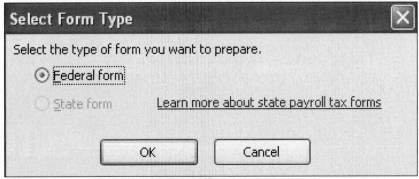

Figure 15.37

This brings up the **Select Payroll Form** dialog box, which offers a choice of three payroll reports: Form 940, Form 941, and Form W-2/W-3.

3. Select **941**, as shown in Figure 15.38, and click **OK**.

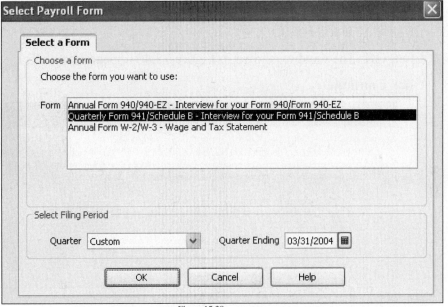

Figure 15.38

4. If prompted with the **QuickBooks Payroll Tip** dialog box (see Figure 15.39), click the radio button next to **No, and don't show me this message again**.

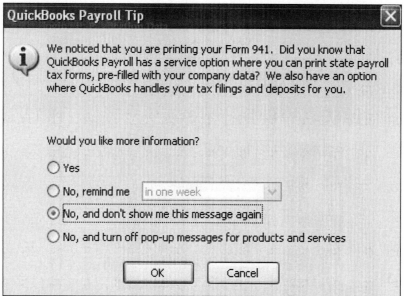

Figure 15.39

5. Click **OK**. The window shown in Figure 15.40 appears.

6. Click **Continue**.

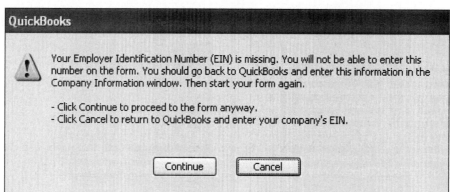

Figure 15.40

7. On the *Interview* screen check the **No** box on the first question under **Do you need a Schedule B**?

8. Enter the state code **MA** in the box shown in Figure 15.41.

9. Click **Next**.

Tax Form for EIN: _____

Interview for your Form 941/Schedule B
Employer's Quarterly Federal Tax Return

Instructions: Use this interview to help you fill out your Form 941 and Schedule B (if applicable).
* QuickBooks uses your answers to complete your Form 941.

Do you need a Schedule B?

Are you a semiweekly depositor OR a monthly depositor required to file **Schedule B**? ..... ☐ Yes ☒ No

Check this box to print **Schedule B** regardless of applicability .... ☐

To find out if you need a Schedule B, click the "Details about this form" link.

Answer the following questions for Form 941

Enter the state code for the state where you made your deposits OR select 'MU' if you made your deposits in multiple states .... MA

If you do not have to file returns in the future, check here .... ☐
and enter the date that final wages were paid ....
You would not have to file returns in the future if you went out of business or stopped paying wages this quarter, for example.

If you are a seasonal employer, check here .... ☐

Figure 15.41

10. You are presented with the window *Form 941 – Employer's Quarterly Federal Tax Return*, shown in Figure 15.42.

Form **941**	**Employer's Quarterly Federal Tax Return**	**2005**

Name (not your trade name)
Pete's Market

Employer Identification No. _____

Trade Name (if any)
Pete's Market-Student Name

Address

City	State	ZIP Code

Report for this Quarter (check one)

1	January, February, March	X
2	April, May, June	☐
3	July, August, September	☐
4	October, November, December	☐

Part 1 — Answer These Questions For This Quarter

1	Number of employees who received wages, tips, or other compensation for the pay period including March 12 (Quarter 1), June 12 (Quarter 2), September 12 (Quarter 3), December 12 (Quarter 4)	1	3
2	Wages, tips, and other compensation	2	27,825.00
3	Total income tax withheld from wages, tips, and other compensation	3	3,786.00

4	**If no wages, tips, and other compensation are subject to social security or Medicare tax**, check here and go to line 6 .... ☐				
5	**Taxable social security and Medicare wages and tips:**				
		Column 1		Column 2	
a	Taxable social security wages .	27,825.00	x .124 =	3,450.30	
b	Taxable social security tips		x .124 =		
c	Taxable Medicare wages and tips	27,825.00	x .029 =	806.93	
d	**Total social security and Medicare taxes** (Column 2, lines 5a + 5b + 5c = line 5d)			**5d**	4,257.23
6	**Total taxes before adjustments** (lines 3 + 5d = line 6)			**6**	8,043.23
7	**Tax adjustments:**				
a	**Current quarter's fractions of cents**	**7a**	0.01		
b	**Current quarter's sick pay**	**b**			
c	**Current quarter's adjustments for tips and group-term life insurance**	**c**			
d	**Current year's income tax withholding** (attach Form 941c)	**d**			
e	**Prior quarters' social security and Medicare taxes** (attach Form 941c)	**e**			
f	**Special additions to federal income tax** (reserved use)	**f**			
g	**Special additions to social security and Medicare** (reserved use)	**g**			
h	**Total adjustments** (Combine all amounts: lines 7a through 7g)			**7h**	0.01
8	**Total taxes after adjustments** (Combine lines 6 and 7h)			**8**	8,043.24

9	**Advance Earned Income Credit (EIC) payments made to employees**	**9**		
10	**Total taxes after adjustment for advance EIC** (lines 8 - 9 = line 10)	**10**	8,043.24	
11	**Total deposits for this quarter, including overpayment applied from a prior quarter**	**11**	8,043.24	
12	**Balance due** (lines 10 - 11 = line 12)	**12**		
13	**Overpayment** (If line 11 is more than line 10, enter the difference here) **13**			
	Check one: ☐ Apply to next return ☐ Send a refund			

Figure 15.42

11. Click **Print Form**.

12. If presented with the warning shown in Figure 15.43, click **Yes**.

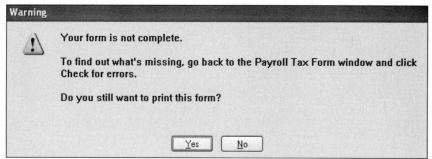

Figure 15.43

13. On the *Printing* screen select **Tax form(s) and filing instructions** (see Figure 15.44).

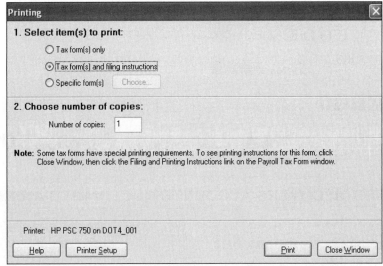

Figure 15.44

14. Click **Print**.

15. Click **Save & Close**.

Backing Up Your Company Data File

1. Click the **Backup** icon.

2. Click the **Browse** button in the **Backup Current Company** section to specify a location to keep your backup files.

3. Add **Final** to the file name. Click **Save**.

4. Click **OK**.

5. When the backup is complete, click **OK**.

   ➤ **NOTE:** For more detailed instructions on backing up files, refer to Chapter 11.

Exiting the QuickBooks Pro 2006 Program

1. Select **Close Company** from the **File** menu.

2. Select **Exit** from the **File** menu to end the current work session and return to your Windows desktop.

CHAPTER 16

Accounts Receivable and Accounts Payable—The Mars Company

THIS WORKSHOP COVERS ACCOUNTS RECEIVABLE AND ACCOUNTS PAYABLE.

Opening The Mars Company File

1. Double-click the QuickBooks icon on your desktop to open the software program.

2. Click **Open an existing company** and then locate and select **The Mars Company**.

3. Click **Open**.

    ➢ **NOTE:** Refer to Chapter 11 for more detailed instructions on opening files.

Backing Up Your Company Data File

1. Click the **Backup** icon.

2. Click the **Browse** button in the **Backup Current Company** section to specify a location to keep your backup files.

3. Add **Start** to the file name. Click **Save**.

4. Click **OK**.

5. When the backup is complete, click **OK**.

    ➢ **NOTE:** For more detailed instructions on backing up files, refer to Chapter 11.

Adding Your Name to the Company Name

1. Click the **Company** menu option and select **Company Information**. The program responds by bringing up the *Company Information* dialog box, which allows you to edit/add information about the company.

2. Click in the **Company Name** field and make sure your cursor is at the end of **The Mars Company**.

3. Add a dash and your name **(-Student's Name)**.

4. Click the **OK** button.

CUSTOMER SALES AND RECEIPTS OVERVIEW

The Customer Sales and Receipts features in QuickBooks Pro 2006 were designed to work with the Accounts Receivable and General Ledger modules in an integrated fashion. When transactions are recorded in the **Create Invoice**, **Credit Memo**, **Create Sales Receipts**, and **Receive Payments** windows, the program automatically posts to the customer's account in the Accounts Receivable subsidiary ledger, records the journal entry, and posts to all accounts affected in the General ledger.

However, the type of transactions recorded in the **Sales** and **Receipts** windows in QuickBooks Pro 2006 differ from the types of transactions recorded in the journals in a manual accounting system. An explanation of the differences appears in the following table:

Name of Computerized Entry Window	Types of Transactions Recorded in Computerized Journal
Create Invoices	Sales of merchandise on account
Credit Memo	Sales returns and allowances
Create Sales Receipts	Cash sales
Receive Payments	Payments from credit customers on account

The A/R Aging Summary Report

An A/R Aging Summary report (the computerized version of a schedule of accounts receivable) for The Mars Company appears in Figure 16.1. (Terms of 2/10, n/30 are offered to customers of The Mars Company.)

The Mars Company-Students Name
A/R Aging Summary
As of March 1, 2004

	Current	1 - 30	31 - 60	61 - 90	> 90	TOTAL
Dunbar, John	500.00	0.00	0.00	0.00	0.00	500.00
Tucker, Kevin	550.00	0.00	0.00	0.00	0.00	550.00
TOTAL	**1,050.00**	**0.00**	**0.00**	**0.00**	**0.00**	**1,050.00**

Figure 16.1

You can print the A/R Aging Summary report from the **Customer/Receivable** section in the *Report Center* window.

Recording a Sale on Account

TRANSACTION: On March 1, 2004, the company sold merchandise to Kevin Tucker on account for $800, Invoice 913, consisting of the following items:		
Stock #	**Description**	**Quantity**
001	Space Age Lamp	2
002	Solar Clock	5
005	Space Shuttle Model	1

1. Click the **Invoices**  icon in the *Home* window.

2. Using the magnifying glass next to the **Customer: Job** field, select Kevin Tucker by double-clicking his name.

3. In the **Date** field type **3/1/04** or use the calendar to the right of the field to select the date.

4. In the **Invoice** # field enter **913**.

5. In the **Item** field use the lookup icon and select the first item, **001 Space Age Lamp**, by double-clicking it.

6. In the **Quantity** field type in **2.00** and press the **Tab** key.

7. The **Description** field automatically fills in with information stored in the Inventory module. In fact, QuickBooks fills in all the remaining fields as you tab through them until you are back to the **Item** field.

8. Enter the remaining items from the table above in the same manner as for the lamp. Your screen should look like Figure 16.2.

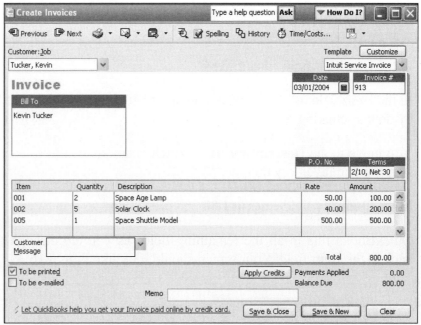

Figure 16.2

Editing a Sale Entry Prior to Posting

1. If you have made an error anywhere on the invoice, simply click in the field containing the error and correct it.

Printing Invoices

1. Click the **Print** icon.

2. Click **Print** on the *Print One Invoice* screen.

3. Click **Save & Close**.

Entering a Credit Memo

> **TRANSACTION: On March 5, 2004, the company issued credit Memorandum CM14 to Kevin Tucker for the return of one of the lamps he purchased.**

1. Click the **Refunds & Credits** icon in the Customer section of the *Home* window.

2. Using the magnifying glass next to the **Customer: Job** field, select Kevin Tucker by clicking his name.

3. In the **Date** field enter in the date **Mar 5, 2004** or use the calendar to the right of the field to select this date.

4. In the **Invoice #** field enter **CM14**.

5. In the **Item** field use the lookup icon and select the first item, **001 Space Age Lamp**, by double-clicking on it.

6. You move to the **Description** field, which is automatically filled in with information stored in the Inventory module.

7. In the **Quantity** field enter in **1.00** and press **Tab**.

8. QuickBooks fills in all the remaining fields as you tab through them until you are back to the **Item** field. Your screen should look like Figure 16.3.

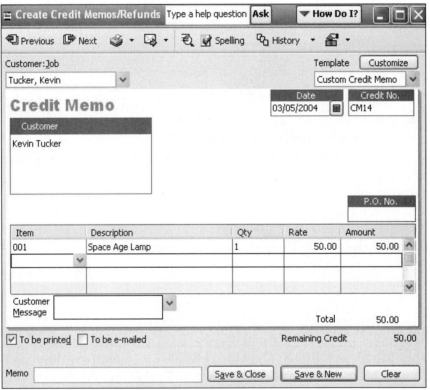

Figure 16.3

Printing the Credit Memo

1. Click the **Print** icon to print this transaction.

2. Click the **Print** button in the *Print One Credit Memo* dialog box.

3. Click the **Save & Close** button.

4. The *Available Credit* window, shown in Figure 16.4, appears. Select **Retain as an available credit** and click **OK**.

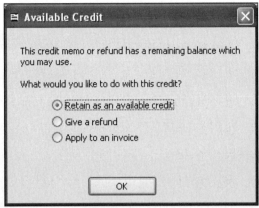

Figure 16.4

Recording a Cash Receipt from a Customer

> **TRANSACTION: On March 6, 2004, received Check 1623 from Kevin Tucker in the amount of $539 in payment of Invoice 912.**

1. Click the **Receive Payments** icon in the **Customer** section of the *Home* window.

2. In the **Customer** field use the magnifying glass to select customer Kevin Tucker. This brings up a listing of the invoices and credits currently open in his account.

3. In the **Amount** field enter **539.00**.

4. In the **Date** field enter **March 8, 2004**.

5. In the **Pmt. Method** field select **Check** from the lookup window.

6. In the **Check #** field enter Kevin's check number, **1623**.

7. Leave the **Memo** field blank.

8. QuickBooks automatically marks the first row in the column with a checkmark.

   > ➤ **NOTE:** If the company were receiving cash as the result of a cash sale or for any other reason other than a payment on account, you would use the *Create Sales Receipts* or *Record Deposits* window(s).

9. Click the **Discount & Credits** button.

10. Select the **Discount** tab, as shown in Figure 16.5.

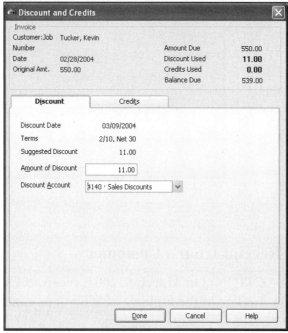

Figure 16.5

11. QuickBooks automatically suggests a discount amount and shows the discount date.

12. Enter **11.00** as the amount of discount.

13. Select **4140 – Sales Discounts** as the **discount account**.

14. Click **Done**.

15. Your screen should look like Figure 16.6.

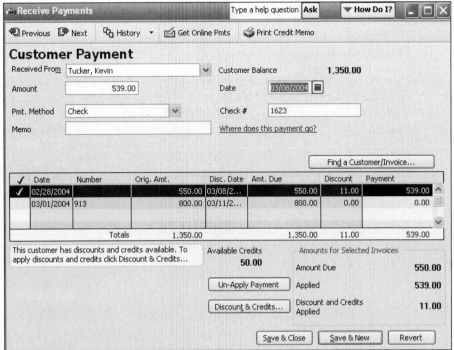

Figure 16.6

16. Click the **Save & Close** button.

Recording Additional Cash Receipts

> **TRANSACTION: On March 10, 2004, the company received Check 1634 from Kevin Tucker in the amount of $734 in payment of Invoice 913 ($800), dated March 1, less Credit Memorandum CM14 ($50), less 2% discount ($16 net sales discount).**

1. Follow the detailed instructions on page 241 to record this receipt.

2. After you click **Discounts & Credits** button, select the **Discount** tab and enter the discount.

3. Select **4140 – Sales Discounts** as the **discount account**.

4. Select the **Credits** tab and mark the CM14.

5. Click **Done**.

6. Your screen should look like Figure 16.7.

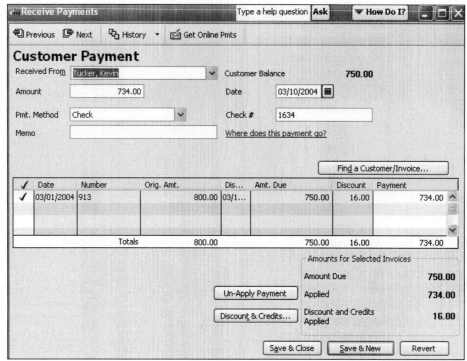

Figure 16.7

7. Click **Save & Close**.

Making a Deposit

The company has received two payments and is taking them to the bank on 3/15/04.

1. Click the **Record Deposits** icon.

2. That brings up the *Payments to Deposit* dialog box (see Figure 16.8).

3. Click the checkmark column for each payment that has been received.

4. Click **OK**. The screen shown in Figure 16.9 appears.

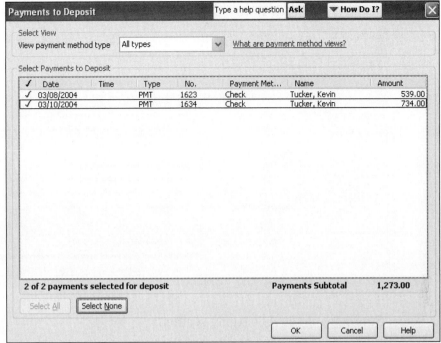

Figure 16.8

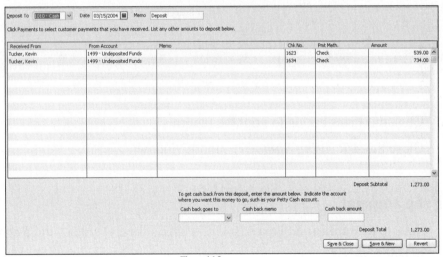

Figure 16.9

5.   Click **Save & Close**.

Displaying and Printing the A/R Aging Summary Report

1.   Click the **Report Center** Report Center icon.

2.   Select **Customers & Receivables** from the list on the left of your screen (see Figure 16.10.

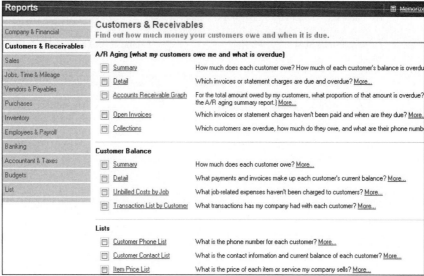

Figure 16.10

3. Select **Summary** in the A/R Aging section.

4. Change the date to **3/31/04** (see Figure 16.11).

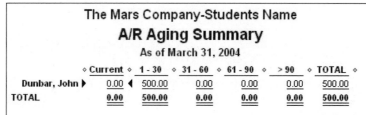

Figure 16.11

5. Click the **Print** button to print the report.

6. Close the *A/R Aging Summary* report window.

Printing the Journal

1. Select **Accountant & Taxes** from the list on the left side of the *Reports* dialog box.

2. Select **Journal**.

3. Change the dates to **3/1/04** to **3/15/04**.

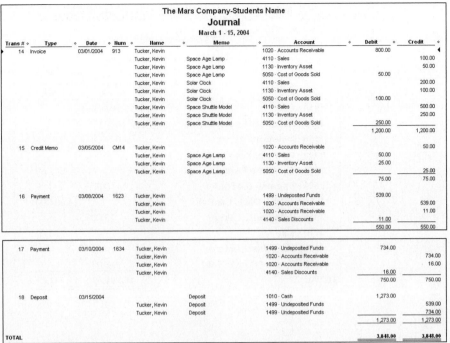

Figure 16.12

> ➤ **NOTE:** You will notice that the invoice and the credit memo post both the Sale (Sales & Accounts Receivable) and the cost of goods sold (Inventory & Cost of Goods Sold) journal entries.

4. Click the **Print** icon to print the report shown in Figure 16.12.

5. Close the *Journal* report window.

Printing the Trial Balance Report

1. Select **Accountant & Taxes** from the list on the left side of the *Reports* dialog box.

2. Select **Trial Balance**.

3. Change the dates to **3/1/04** to **3/15/04** (see Figure 16.13..

```
                The Mars Company-Students Name
                        Trial Balance
                      As of March 15, 2004

                                              Mar 15, 04
                                        ◇   Debit   ◇   Credit   ◇
        1010 · Cash                      ▶ 11,273.00 ◀
        1020 · Accounts Receivable          500.00
        1130 · Inventory Asset            4,026.00
        1499 · Undeposited Funds              0.00
        2110 · Accounts Payable                           547.00
        3000 · Opening Bal Equity             0.00
        3110 · Janice Mars, Capital                     14,904.00
        3900 · Retained Earnings              0.00
        4110 · Sales                                       750.00
        4140 · Sales Discounts              27.00
        5050 · Cost of Goods Sold          375.00
        TOTAL                            16,201.00      16,201.00
```

Figure 16.13

4. Click the **Print** icon to print the report.
5. Close the *Trial Balance* report window.
6. Close the *Reports* dialog box to return to the *Home* dialog box.

The Mars Company—Accounts Payable

Recording Purchases and Cash Payments

The Purchases and Payments features in QuickBooks Pro 2006 are designed to work with the Accounts Payable and General Ledger modules in an integrated fashion.

When transactions are recorded for bills and payments, the program automatically posts to the vendor's account in the Accounts Payable subsidiary ledger, records the journal entry, and posts to all accounts affected in the General ledger. However, the type of transactions recorded and the way the transactions are recorded differ from the types of transactions recorded in these journals in a manual accounting system. An explanation of the differences appears in the following chart:

Name of Computerized Journal	Types of Transactions Recorded in Computerized Journal
Bill	Purchases of merchandise and other items on account
Bill (Credit)	Purchase returns and allowances
Bill Payment	Payments to credit vendors
Write Checks	Cash payments to cash vendors

A/P Aging Summary Report

An A/P Aging Summary report (the computerized version of a schedule of accounts payable) for The Mars Company appears in Figure 16.14.

You can print this report from the **Vendors & Payables** section of the *Reports* dialog box.

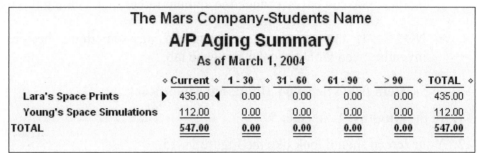

The Mars Company-Students Name

A/P Aging Summary

As of March 1, 2004

	Current	1 - 30	31 - 60	61 - 90	> 90	TOTAL
Lara's Space Prints	435.00	0.00	0.00	0.00	0.00	435.00
Young's Space Simulations	112.00	0.00	0.00	0.00	0.00	112.00
TOTAL	**547.00**	**0.00**	**0.00**	**0.00**	**0.00**	**547.00**

Figure 16.14

Purchasing and Receiving Inventory

TRANSACTION: On March 15, 2004, the company purchased merchandise from Young's Space Simulations on account, $165.50, Invoice 7960, terms 2/10, n/30, consisting of the following:

Stock #	Description	Quantity
001	Space Age Lamp	5
004	Simulated Moon Rock	9

1. Click the **Enter Bills** icon.

2. Using the magnifying glass next to the **Vendor** field, select **002 Young's Space Simulations** by clicking it.

3. In the **Date** field enter **Mar 15, 2004** or use the calendar to the right of the field to select this date.

4. In the **Reference No.** field enter **7960**.

5. Skip the **Amount** field. QuickBooks will automatically calculate the total amount.

6. Click the **Items** tab.

7. In the **Item** field click the lookup icon and select the first item, **001 Space Age Lamp,** by double-clicking it.

8. The **Description** field automatically fills in with information stored in the Inventory module.

9. In the **Quantity** field enter in **5.00**.

   ➢ **NOTE:** If your unit price is different from the one in the QuickBooks Inventory module, you can easily change the amount rather than tabbing through that field.

   ➢ **NOTE:** If the company were purchasing something besides merchandise inventory, you would use the **Expense** tab.

10. In the **Item** field select **004 Simulated Moon Rock**.

11. In the **Quantity** field enter **9**.

12. Your screen should look like the Figure 16.15.

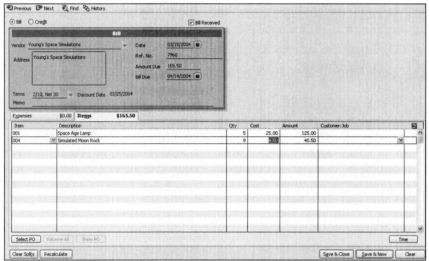

Figure 16.15

13. If you have made an error anywhere on the bill, simply click in the field containing the error and correct it.

14. Click the **Save & Close** button to post this transaction. A blank ***Enter Bills*** screen is displayed, ready for additional purchase transactions to be recorded.

Recording the Return of Merchandise Purchased (Entering a Credit Bill)

> **TRANSACTION: On March 17, 2004, the company returned two of the Space Age Lamps to Young's Space Simulations, with a value of $50. Issued Debit Memo DM27.**

1. Click the **Enter Bills** icon.

2. Select the radio button next to **Credit** at the top of the screen.

3. In the **Vendor** field click the lookup icon and select **002 Young's Space Simulations** by clicking it. Press the **Tab** key

4. In the **Date** field enter **Mar 17, 2004** or use the calendar to the right of the field to select this date.

5. In the **Ref No.** field enter **DM27**.

6. Click the **Items** tab.

7. In the **Item** field use the lookup icon and select the first item, **001 Space Age Lamp**, by double-clicking it.

8. In the **Quantity** field enter **2.00**.

9. Your screen should look like Figure 16.16.

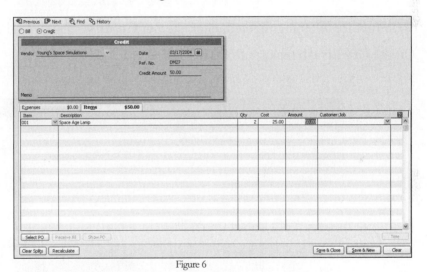

Figure 6

10. If you have made an error anywhere on the credit, simply click in the field containing the error and correct it.

11. After verifying that the entry is correct, Click the **Save & Close** button to post this transaction and return to the *Home* window.

Recording a Payment to a Vendor

> **TRANSACTION: On March 25, 2004, the company issued Check 437 to Young's Space Simulations in the amount of $224.19 in payment of Invoices 790 ($112) and 7960 ($165.50), dated March 15, less Debit Memorandum DM27 ($50), less 2% discount ($3.17 net purchases discount).**

1. Click the **Pay Bills** icon.

2. Click the **Show All** radio button.

3. Using the magnifying glass, select **Young's Space Simulations**. This brings up a listing of the invoices and credits currently open for this account.

4. Mark the check box next to both of the **Young's Space Simulations** invoices.

5. With Invoice 7960 highlighted, click the **Set Credits** [Set Credits] button.

6. On the **Credits** tab make sure **DM27** is marked.

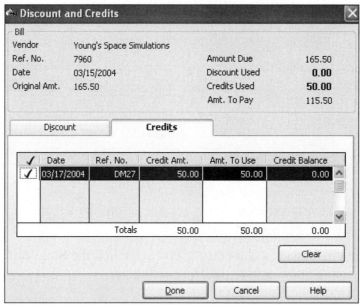

Figure 16.17

7. Click the **Discount** tab (see Figure 16.18).

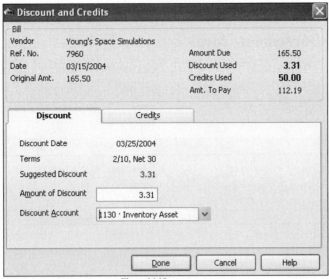

Figure 16.18

8. For **Amount of Discount** enter **3.31**.

9. For **Discount Account** select account **1130-Inventory Asset**

10. Click **Done**.

11. In the **Payment Date** field enter **March 25, 2004** or use the calendar to select this date (see Figure 16.19).

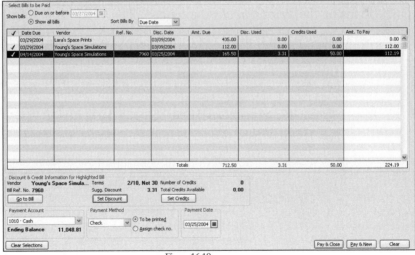

Figure 16.19

12. If you have made an error anywhere on the check, simply click in the field containing the error and correct it.

13. Click **Pay & Close**.

> ➢ **NOTE:** For something that is not already recorded in the accounts payable, you can use the **Write Checks** function. The company can write a check for any purpose, including prepaid expenses by using this feature.

Printing the Disbursement Check

1. From the **File** menu select **Print Forms** and then select **Checks**.

2. You see the ***Select Checks to Print*** dialog box (see Figure 16.20).

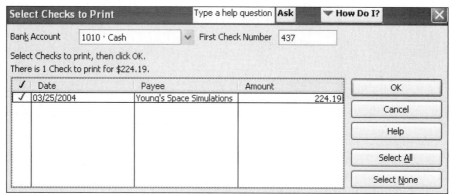

Figure 16.20

3. Set the **Bank Account** field to **1010 – Cash**.

4. Set **First Check Number** to **437**.

5. Click the **OK** button.

6. Click **Print** on the ***Print Checks*** dialog box. The check now prints.

7. You see the ***Did check(s) print OK?*** dialog box (see Figure 16.21). Click **OK.**

Figure 16.21

8. If you get the ***Set Check Reminder*** dialog box, shown in Figure 16.22, click the **Do not display this message in the future** check box.

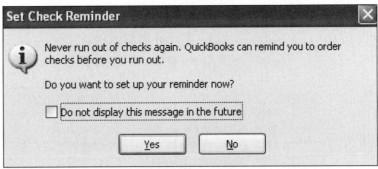

Figure 16.22

9. Click **Yes.**

Displaying and Printing a Vendor A/P Aging Summary Report

1. Click the **Report Center** 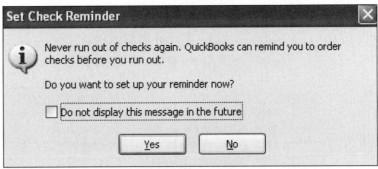 icon.

2. Select **Vendors & Payables** from the list on the left of the screen.

3. Select **Summary** from the **A/P Aging** section to bring up the schedule of payables still owed by The Mars Company.

4. Change the date to **3/31/04**.

5. Click the **Print** icon to print the report. It should look like Figure 16.23.

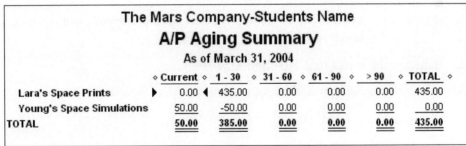

The Mars Company-Students Name
A/P Aging Summary
As of March 31, 2004

	Current	1 - 30	31 - 60	61 - 90	> 90	TOTAL
Lara's Space Prints	0.00	435.00	0.00	0.00	0.00	435.00
Young's Space Simulations	50.00	-50.00	0.00	0.00	0.00	0.00
TOTAL	50.00	385.00	0.00	0.00	0.00	435.00

Figure 16.23

6. **Close** the *A/P Aging Summary* report window.

Displaying and Printing the Trial Balance Report

1. In the *Reports* dialog box, select **Accountant & Taxes** on the left side of the screen.

2. Select **Trial Balance**.

3. Change the dates to **3/1/04** and **3/31/04** (see Figure 16.24).

```
        The Mars Company-Students Name
                 Trial Balance
               As of March 31, 2004
                                    Mar 31, 04
                              ◇  Debit   ◇   Credit   ◇
    1010 · Cash              ▶ 11,048.81 ◀
    1020 · Accounts Receivable    500.00
    1130 · Inventory Asset       4,138.19
    1499 · Undeposited Funds         0.00
    2110 · Accounts Payable                      435.00
    3000 · Opening Bal Equity        0.00
    3110 · Janice Mars, Capital               14,904.00
    3900 · Retained Earnings         0.00
    4110 · Sales                                 750.00
    4140 · Sales Discounts          27.00
    5050 · Cost of Goods Sold      375.00
    TOTAL                      16,089.00    16,089.00
```

Figure 16.24

4. Click the **Print** button.

5. Click **Print** on the *Print Reports* dialog box.

6. Close the Trial Balance report.

Displaying and Printing the Journal Report

1. From the **Accountant & Taxes** section of the *Reports* dialog box select **Journal**. The report shown in Figure 16.25 appears.

2. Change the **dates** to 3/1/04 and 3/31/04.

3. Change the column widths as necessary.

The Mars Company-Students Name
Journal
March 2004

Type	Date	Num	Name	Memo	Account	Debit	Credit
			Tucker, Kevin		1020 · Accounts Receivable		734.00
			Tucker, Kevin		1020 · Accounts Receivable		16.00
			Tucker, Kevin		4140 · Sales Discounts	16.00	
						750.00	750.00
Deposit	03/15/2004			Deposit	1010 · Cash	1,273.00	
			Tucker, Kevin	Deposit	1499 · Undeposited Funds		539.00
			Tucker, Kevin	Deposit	1499 · Undeposited Funds		734.00
						1,273.00	1,273.00
Bill	03/15/2004	7960	Young's Space Simulations		2110 · Accounts Payable		165.50
			Young's Space Simulations	Space Age Lamp	1130 · Inventory Asset	125.00	
			Young's Space Simulations	Simulated Moon Rock	1130 · Inventory Asset	40.50	
						165.50	165.50
Credit	03/17/2004	DM27	Young's Space Simulations		2110 · Accounts Payable	50.00	
			Young's Space Simulations	Space Age Lamp	1130 · Inventory Asset		50.00
						50.00	50.00
Bill Pmt -Check	03/25/2004	437	Young's Space Simulations		1010 · Cash		224.19
			Young's Space Simulations		2110 · Accounts Payable	224.19	
			Young's Space Simulations		2110 · Accounts Payable	3.31	
			Young's Space Simulations		1130 · Inventory Asset		3.31
						227.50	227.50
						4,291.00	**4,291.00**

Figure 16.25

4. Click the **Print** button.

5. Click the **Print** button on the *Print Reports* dialog box.

6. Close the Journal report.

Displaying and Printing the General Ledger Report

1. From the **Accountant & Taxes** section of the *Reports* dialog box select **General Ledger**. The report shown in Figure 16.26 appears.

2. Change the dates to **3/1/04** and **3/31/04**.

3. Adjust the column widths as necessary.

The Mars Company-Students Name
General Ledger
As of March 31, 2004

Type	Date	Num	Name	Memo	Split	Amount	Balance
1010 · Cash							**10,000.00**
Deposit	03/15/2004			Deposit	-SPLIT-	1,273.00	11,273.00
Bill Pmt -Check	03/25/2004	437	Young's Space Sim...		-SPLIT-	-224.19	11,048.81
Total 1010 · Cash						1,048.81	11,048.81
1020 · Accounts Receivable							**1,050.00**
Invoice	03/01/2004	913	Tucker, Kevin		-SPLIT-	800.00	1,850.00
Credit Memo	03/05/2004	CM14	Tucker, Kevin		4110 · Sales	-50.00	1,800.00
Payment	03/08/2004	1623	Tucker, Kevin		1499 · Undep...	-539.00	1,261.00
Discount	03/08/2004	1623	Tucker, Kevin		1499 · Undep...	-11.00	1,250.00
Payment	03/10/2004	1634	Tucker, Kevin		1499 · Undep...	-734.00	516.00
Discount	03/10/2004	1634	Tucker, Kevin		1499 · Undep...	-16.00	500.00
Total 1020 · Accounts Receivable						-550.00	500.00
1130 · Inventory Asset							**4,401.00**
Invoice	03/01/2004	913	Tucker, Kevin	Space Age ...	1020 · Accou...	-50.00	4,351.00
Invoice	03/01/2004	913	Tucker, Kevin	Solar Clock	1020 · Accou...	-100.00	4,251.00
Invoice	03/01/2004	913	Tucker, Kevin	Space Shutt...	1020 · Accou...	-250.00	4,001.00
Credit Memo	03/05/2004	CM14	Tucker, Kevin	Space Age ...	1020 · Accou...	25.00	4,026.00
Bill	03/15/2004	7960	Young's Space Sim...	Space Age ...	2110 · Accou...	125.00	4,151.00
Bill	03/15/2004	7960	Young's Space Sim...	Simulated M...	2110 · Accou...	40.50	4,191.50
Credit	03/17/2004	DM27	Young's Space Sim...	Space Age ...	2110 · Accou...	-50.00	4,141.50
Bill Pmt -Check	03/25/2004	437	Young's Space Sim...		1010 · Cash	-3.31	4,138.19
Total 1130 · Inventory Asset						-262.81	4,138.19

Figure 16.26

4. Click the **Print** icon.

5. Click **Print** on the *Print Reports* dialog box.

> ➢ **CHECK IT OUT:** You may wish to experiment with some of the other reports that are available in the various areas of the QuickBooks report area. Some examples you might want to see are Sales Journal, Purchases Journal, and Cash Receipts Journal.

6. Close the *General Ledger* report window and the *Reports* window.

Backing Up Your Company Data File

1. Click the **Backup** [Backup] icon.

2. Click the **Browse** button in the **Backup Current Company** section to specify a location to keep your backup files.

3. Add **Final** to the file name. Click **Save**.

4. Click **OK**.

5. When the backup is complete, click **OK**.

> ➢ **NOTE:** For more detailed instructions on backing up files, refer to Chapter 11.

Exiting the QuickBooks Pro 2006 Program

1. Select **Close Company** from the **File** menu.

2. Select **Exit** from the **File** menu to end the current work session and return to your Windows desktop.

Chapter 17

Abby's Toy House—Mini Practice Set

THIS WORKSHOP IS DESIGNED TO REVIEW THE CONCEPTS IN:

> ➤ **CHAPTER 12—GENERAL LEDGER TRANSACTIONS**
>
> ➤ **CHAPTER 16—ACCOUNTS RECEIVABLE AND ACCOUNTS PAYABLE TRANSACTIONS**

THIS WORKSHOP DOES NOT INCLUDE THE PAYROLL MODULE (JOURNAL ENTRIES ARE USED TO PAY SALARIES).

Opening the Abby's Toy House File

1. Double-click the **QuickBooks** icon on your desktop to open the software program.

2. Click **Open an existing company** and then locate and select **Abby's Toy House**.

3. Click **Open**.

> ➤ **NOTE:** Refer to Chapter 11 for more detailed instructions on opening files.

Backing Up Your Company Data File

1. Click the **Backup** Backup icon.

2. Click the **Browse** button in the **Backup Current Company** section to specify a location to keep your backup files.

3. Add **Start** to the file name. Click **Save**.

4. Click **OK**.

5. When the backup is complete, click **OK**.

> ➤ **NOTE:** For more detailed instructions on backing up files, refer to Chapter 11.

Adding Your Name to the Company Name

1. Click the **Company** menu option and select **Company Information**. The program responds by bringing up the *Company Information* dialog box, which allows you to edit/add information about the company.

2. Click in the **Company Name** field and make sure your cursor is at the end of **Abby's Toy House**.

3. Add a dash and your name (**-Student's Name**).

4. Click the **OK** button.

Toggling to the QuickBooks Pro 2006 Version

If you are using the QuickBooks Pro 2006 version and not the Accountant Edition 2006, you can skip this section.

If you ordered the trial version as noted in Chapter 11, you are using **QuickBooks 2006 All-in-One Trial for Accountants**. So that you see the same screenshots on your screen as are in this text, you need to toggle to **QuickBooks Pro Edition**. The following instructions walk you through the toggling process.

1. Select **Toggle to Another Edition** from the **File** menu.

2. Click the radio button next to **QuickBooks Pro** to select it.

3. Click **Next**.

4. Click the **Toggle** button.

5. It takes a few seconds for the process to complete. Your title bar then reflects (**via Accountant Edition**).

Recording the Transactions for March

Record the following transactions, using the appropriate entry windows. The entry windows used in this practice set include *Make General Journal Entries* (G), *Enter Invoices* (I), *Create Sales Receipts*(SR), *Refunds & Credits* (RC), *Receive Payments* (R), *Record Deposits* (RD), *Enter Bills* (B), *Pay Bills* (PB), and *Write Checks* (W).

Here are the transactions for March:

2004		
Mar.	1	Abby Ellen invested $8,000 in the toy store. Use Memo 1 for the entry no. (G).
	1	Paid three months' rent in advance, using an electronic funds transfer (EFT) in the amount of $3,000. Entry no. Memo 2 (G).
	3	Purchased merchandise from Earl Miller Company on account, $4,000, Invoice 410, consisting of the following: 6 Mountain Bikes, 12 Bike Carriers, 8 Deluxe Bike Seats (B).
	3	Sold merchandise to Bill Burton on account, $1,000, Invoice 1, consisting of the following: 1 Mountain Bike, 1 Bike Carrier (I).
	6	Sold merchandise to Jim Rex on account, $700, Invoice 2, consisting of the following: 3 Bike Carriers and 1 Deluxe Bike Seat (I).
	10	Purchased merchandise from Earl Miller Co. on account, $1,200, Invoice 415, terms 2/10, n/30, consisting of the following: 2 Mountain Bikes and 4 Bike Carriers (B).

	10	Sold merchandise to Bill Burton on account, $600, Invoice 3, terms 2/10, n/30, consisting of the following: 3 Bike Carriers (I).
	10	Paid cleaning service $300, using an EFT. Entry no. Memo 3 (G).
	11	Jim Rex returned merchandise for $300 to Abby's Toy House, consisting of the following: 1 Bike Carrier and 1 Deluxe Bike Seat. Abby issued Credit Memorandum 1 (CM1) to Jim Rex for $300 (RC).
	11	Purchased merchandise from Minnie Katz on account, $4,000, Invoice 311, terms 2/10, n/30, consisting of the following: 2 Doll Houses w/ Furniture, 4 Porcelain Face Dolls, 10 Yo Yo's, Designer, and 10 Magic Kits (B).
	12	Issued check 1 to Earl Miller Co. in the amount of $3,920, in payment of Invoice 410 ($4,000), dated March 2, less 2% discount ($80). If you mark the Invoice 410 check box, it automatically calculates the discount, and the net amount shows in the amount to pay column. Click radio button to assign a check number. Click Pay & Close. Enter check number 1 (PB).
	13	Sold $1,300 of toy merchandise for cash consisting of the following: 1 Doll House w/ Furniture and 1 Magic Kit. Skip the Customer Job section (SR). Record the deposit for the $1,300.00 (RD).
	13	Paid salaries, $600, using an EFT. Use Memo 4 (G).
	14	Returned merchandise to Minnie Katz in the amount of $1,000, consisting of the following: 1 Doll House w/ Furniture and 2 Porcelain Face Dolls. Abby's Toy House issued Debit Memorandum 1 (DM1). Be sure to mark the radio button next to Credit (I).
	14	Sold merchandise for $4,000 cash, consisting of the following: 3 Mountain Bikes, 3 Bike Carriers, 2 Magic Kits, and 4 Yo Yo's, Designer. Use Receipt Number 2. Skip the Customer Job and Sold to fields (SR). Record the deposit of $4,000.00 cash (RD).
	16	Received Check 9823 from Jim Rex in the amount of $392, in payment of Invoice 2 ($700), dated March 6, less Credit Memorandum 1 ($300), less 2% discount ($14 – 6 = $8 net sales discount). Be sure to select the Discount and Credits button to properly apply the discount and credit (R).
	16	Received Check 4589 from Bill Burton in the amount of $1,000, in payment of Invoice 1, dated March 2 (R). Notice that QuickBooks does not factor in the discount since it is past the discount date.
	16	Sold merchandise to Amy Rose on account, $4,000, Invoice 4, terms 2/10, n/30, consisting of the following: 1 Porcelain Face Doll, 3 Mountain Bikes, 4 Bike Carriers, and 3 Deluxe Bike Seats

		(I).
	21	Purchased delivery truck on account from Sam Katz Garage, $3,000, Invoice 111, terms 2%, 10, n/30 (B). Since this is not an inventory item, use the Expense tab and Account 1150 – Delivery Truck (B).
	22	Sold to Bill Burton merchandise on account, $900, Invoice 5, consisting of the following: 3 Magic Kits (I).
	23	Issued Check 2 to Minnie Katz in the amount of $2,970, in payment of Invoice 311 ($4,000), dated March 11, less Debit Memorandum 1 ($1,000), less 1% discount ($40 – 10 = $30 net purchases discount). You need to change the set discount amount to $30.00 (PB). (Don't forget to click Discounts & Credits).
	24	Sold toy merchandise on account to Amy Rose, $1,100, Invoice 6, consisting of the following: 1 Porcelain Face Doll, 1 Magic Kit, and 3 Yo Yo's, Designer (I).
	25	Purchased toy merchandise for cash from Woody Smith while waiting for an account to be approved, $600, Check 3, consisting of the following: 2 Marionettes, Hand Carved. Use the Write Checks window and Click the Item tab to enter the inventory purchased (W).
	27	Purchased toy merchandise from Woody Smith on account, $4,800, Invoice 211, terms 2/10, n/30, consisting of the following: 16 Marionettes, Hand Carved (PU).
	28	Received Check 4598 from Bill Burton in the amount of $882, in payment of Invoice 5 ($900), dated March 22, less 2% discount ($18). Be sure to use the Discounts & Credits button to set the discount (R).
	28	Received Check 3217 from Amy Rose in the amount of $1,078, in payment of Invoice 6, dated March 24, less 2% discount ($22). Click Discounts & Credits to set the discount (R).
	28	Abby invested an additional $5,000 in the business. Use Memo 5 (G).
	29	Purchased merchandise on account from Earl Miller Co., $1,400, Invoice 436, consisting of the following: 3 Mountain Bikes, and 2 Bike Carriers (B).
	30	Issued Check 4 to Earl Miller Co., in the amount of $1,372, in payment of Invoice 436 ($1,400), dated March 29, less 2% discount ($28) (PB).
	30	Abby took the checks received for the month to the bank. Use RD. Select the Pmt items, for a total of $3,552.00.
	30	Sold merchandise to Bonnie Flow Company on account, $3,000,

		Invoice 7, consisting of the following: 5 Marionettes, Hand Carved (I).

Printing the Reports for Abby's Toy House

1. Print the reports shown in Figures 17.1 through 17.5 from the *Reports* dialog box.

2. Change the dates to **3/1/04** to **3/31/04**.

3. Adjust the columns as necessary.

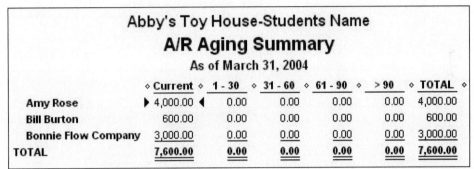

Abby's Toy House-Students Name
A/R Aging Summary
As of March 31, 2004

	Current	1 - 30	31 - 60	61 - 90	> 90	TOTAL
Amy Rose	4,000.00	0.00	0.00	0.00	0.00	4,000.00
Bill Burton	600.00	0.00	0.00	0.00	0.00	600.00
Bonnie Flow Company	3,000.00	0.00	0.00	0.00	0.00	3,000.00
TOTAL	7,600.00	0.00	0.00	0.00	0.00	7,600.00

Figure 17.1

Abby's Toy House-Students Name
A/P Aging Summary
As of March 31, 2004

	Current	1 - 30	31 - 60	61 - 90	> 90	TOTAL
Earl Miller Company	1,200.00	0.00	0.00	0.00	0.00	1,200.00
Sam Katz Garage	3,000.00	0.00	0.00	0.00	0.00	3,000.00
Woody Smith	4,800.00	0.00	0.00	0.00	0.00	4,800.00
TOTAL	9,000.00	0.00	0.00	0.00	0.00	9,000.00

Figure17.2

Abby's Toy House-Students Name

Journal

March 2004

Date	Num	Name	Memo	Account	Debit	Credit
03/01/2004	Memo 1		Owner Investment	1010 · Cash	8,000.00	
			Owner Investment	3110 · Abby Ellen, Capital		8,000.00
					8,000.00	8,000.00
03/01/2004	Memo 2		Prepaid 3 months rent	1140 · Prepaid Rent	3,000.00	
			Prepaid 3 months rent	1010 · Cash		3,000.00
					3,000.00	3,000.00
03/03/2004	410	Earl Miller Company		2110 · Accounts Payable		4,000.00
		Earl Miller Company	Mountain Bike	1130 · Inventory Asset	2,400.00	
		Earl Miller Company	Bike Carrier	1130 · Inventory Asset	1,200.00	
		Earl Miller Company	Deluxe Bike Seat	1130 · Inventory Asset	400.00	
					4,000.00	4,000.00
03/03/2004	1	Bill Burton		1020 · Accounts Receivable	1,000.00	
		Bill Burton	Mountain Bike	4110 · Sales		800.00
		Bill Burton	Mountain Bike	1130 · Inventory Asset		400.00
		Bill Burton	Mountain Bike	5050 · Cost of Goods Sold	400.00	
		Bill Burton	Bike Carrier	4110 · Sales		200.00
		Bill Burton	Bike Carrier	1130 · Inventory Asset		100.00
		Bill Burton	Bike Carrier	5050 · Cost of Goods Sold	100.00	
					1,500.00	1,500.00

Figure 17.3

Abby's Toy House-Students Name

General Ledger

As of March 31, 2004

Type	Date	Num	Name	Memo	Split	Amount	Balance
General Journal	03/01/2004	Memo 2		Prepaid 3 months rent	1140 · Prepaid Rent	-3,000.00	5,000.00
General Journal	03/10/2004	Memo 3		Paid cleaning service	5620 · Cleaning Expense	-300.00	4,700.00
Bill Pmt -Check	03/12/2004	1	Earl Miller Company		-SPLIT-	-3,920.00	780.00
General Journal	03/13/2004	Memo 4		Paid Salaries	5610 · Salaries Expense	-600.00	180.00
Deposit	03/13/2004			Deposit	1499 · Undeposited Funds	1,300.00	1,480.00
Deposit	03/14/2004			Deposit	1499 · Undeposited Funds	4,000.00	5,480.00
Bill Pmt -Check	03/23/2004	2	Minnie Katz		-SPLIT-	-2,970.00	2,510.00
Check	03/25/2004	3	Woody Smith		1130 · Inventory Asset	-600.00	1,910.00
General Journal	03/28/2004	Memo 5		Owner Investment	3110 · Abby Ellen, Capital	5,000.00	6,910.00
Bill Pmt -Check	03/30/2004	4	Earl Miller Company		-SPLIT-	-1,372.00	5,538.00
Deposit	03/30/2004			Deposit	-SPLIT-	3,352.00	8,890.00
Total 1010 · Cash						8,890.00	8,890.00
1020 · Accounts Receivable							0.00
Invoice	03/03/2004	1	Bill Burton		-SPLIT-	1,000.00	1,000.00
Invoice	03/06/2004	2	Jim Rex		-SPLIT-	700.00	1,700.00
Invoice	03/10/2004	3	Bill Burton		4110 · Sales	600.00	2,300.00
Credit Memo	03/11/2004	CM1	Jim Rex		-SPLIT-	-300.00	2,000.00
Payment	03/16/2004	9823	Jim Rex		1499 · Undeposited Funds	-392.00	1,608.00
Discount	03/16/2004	9823	Jim Rex		1499 · Undeposited Funds	-8.00	1,600.00
Payment	03/16/2004	4589	Bill Burton		1499 · Undeposited Funds	-1,000.00	600.00
Invoice	03/16/2004	4	Amy Rose		-SPLIT-	4,000.00	4,600.00
Invoice	03/22/2004	5	Bill Burton		4110 · Sales	900.00	5,500.00
Invoice	03/24/2004	6	Amy Rose		-SPLIT-	1,100.00	6,600.00
Payment	03/28/2004	4598	Bill Burton		1499 · Undeposited Funds	-882.00	5,718.00
Discount	03/28/2004	4598	Bill Burton		1499 · Undeposited Funds	-18.00	5,700.00
Payment	03/28/2004	3217	Amy Rose		1499 · Undeposited Funds	-1,078.00	4,622.00
Discount	03/28/2004	3217	Amy Rose		1499 · Undeposited Funds	-22.00	4,600.00
Invoice	03/30/2004	7	Bonnie Flow Comp...		4110 · Sales	3,000.00	7,600.00
Total 1020 · Accounts Receivable						7,600.00	7,600.00

Figure 17.4

Abby's Toy House-Students Name
Trial Balance
As of March 31, 2004

	Mar 31, 04	
	Debit	Credit
1010 · Cash	▶ 8,890.00 ◀	
1020 · Accounts Receivable	7,600.00	
1130 · Inventory Asset	6,712.00	
1140 · Prepaid Rent	3,000.00	
1499 · Undeposited Funds	0.00	
1150 · Delivery Truck	3,000.00	
2110 · Accounts Payable		9,000.00
3110 · Abby Ellen, Capital		13,000.00
4110 · Sales		16,300.00
4140 · Sales Discounts	48.00	
5050 · Cost of Goods Sold	8,150.00	
5610 · Salaries Expense	600.00	
5620 · Cleaning Expense	300.00	
TOTAL	38,300.00	38,300.00

Figure 17.5

Backing Up Your Company Data File

1. Click the **Backup** [Backup] icon.

2. Click the **Browse** button in the **Backup Current Company** section to specify a location to keep your backup files.

3. Add **Final** to the file name. Click **Save**.

4. Click **OK**.

5. When the backup is complete, click **OK**.

   ➢ **NOTE:** For more detailed instructions on backing up files, refer to Chapter 11.

Exiting the QuickBooks Pro 2006 Program

1. Select **Close Company** from the **File** menu.

2. Select **Exit** from the **File** menu to end the current work session and return to your Windows desktop.

CHAPTER 18

Accounting Cycle for a Merchandise Company—The Corner Dress Shop

THIS WORKSHOP IS A REVIEW OF ALL THE KEY CONCEPTS OF A MERCHANDISE COMPANY. IT IS RECOMMENDED THAT YOU COMPLETE THE WORKSHOPS IN THE FOLLOWING CHAPTERS PRIOR TO COMPLETING THIS WORKSHOP:

> ➤ **CHAPTER 12—GENERAL LEDGER**

> ➤ **CHAPTER 13—ADJUSTING JOURNAL ENTRIES**

> ➤ **CHAPTER 15—PAYROLL**

> ➤ **CHAPTER 16—ACCOUNTS RECEIVABLE AND ACCOUNTS PAYABLE**

Opening The Corner Dress Shop File

1. Double-click the **QuickBooks** icon on your desktop to open the software program.

2. Click **Open an existing company** and then locate and select **The Corner Dress Shop**.

3. Click **Open.**

> ➤ **NOTE:** Refer to Chapter 11 for more detailed instructions on opening files.

Backing Up Your Company Data File

1. Click the **Backup** [Backup] icon.

2. Click the **Browse** button in the **Backup Current Company** section to specify a location to keep your backup files.

3. Add **Start** to the file name. Click **Save**.

4. Click **OK**.

5. When the backup is complete, click **OK**.

> ➤ **NOTE:** For more detailed instructions on backing up files, refer to Chapter 11.

Adding Your Name to the Company Name

1. Click the **Company** menu option and select **Company Information**. The program responds by bringing up the ***Company Information*** dialog box, which allows you to edit/add information about the company.

2. Click in the **Company Name** field and make sure that your cursor is at the end of **The Corner Dress Shop**.

3. Add a dash and your name (**-Student's Name**.

4. Click the **OK** button.

Toggling to the QuickBooks Pro 2006 Version

If you are using the QuickBooks Pro 2006 version and not the Accountant Edition 2006, you can skip this section.

If you ordered the trial version, as noted in Chapter 11, you are using a **QuickBooks 2006 All-in-One Trial for Accountants**. So that you see the same screenshots as are shown in this text, you should toggle to **QuickBooks Pro Edition**. The following instructions walk you through the toggling process:

1. Select **Toggle to Another Edition** from the **File** menu.

2. Click the radio button next to **QuickBooks Pro** to select it.

3. Click **Next**.

4. Click the **Toggle** button.

5. It takes a few seconds for the process to complete. Your title bar then says (**via Accountant Edition**).

Company Information

You are the accountant for The Corner Dress Shop, and your task in this workshop is to complete the accounting cycle for March 2004.

The Corner Dress Shop, owned by Betty Loeb, is located at 1 Milgate Road, Marblehead, Massachusetts, 01945. Betty's employer identification number is 33-4158215. Federal income tax (FIT), state income tax (SIT), Social Security, Medicare, FUTA, and SUTA amounts are given in this workshop.

Employees are paid monthly. The payroll is recorded and paid on the last day of each month.

Printing the Beginning-of-the-Month Reports

1. On the ***Home*** screen Click the **Report Center** icon.

2. Select **Accountants & Taxes** from the list on the left of the screen.

3. Select **Trial Balance** from the list on the right of the screen.

4. Change the date to **3/1/04**.

5. Your screen should look like Figure 18.1.

The Corner Dress Shop-Students Name
Trial Balance
As of March 1, 2004

| | Mar 1, 04 | |
	Debit	Credit
1110 · Cash	2,502.90	
1115 · Petty Cash	35.00	
1120 · Accounts Receivable	▶ 2,200.00 ◀	
1130 · Inventory Asset	5,600.00	
1140 · Prepaid Rent	1,800.00	
1250 · Delivery Truck:1251 · Delivery Truck, Original Cost	6,000.00	
1250 · Delivery Truck:1252 · Accum. Dep-Delivery Truck		1,500.00
2110 · Accounts Payable		1,900.00
2400 · Unearned Rent		800.00
3000 · Opening Bal Equity	0.00	
3110 · Betty Loeb, Capital		13,937.90
3900 · Retained Earnings	0.00	
TOTAL	18,137.90	18,137.90

Figure 18.1

6. Click the **Print** icon to print the report.

7. Click the **Close** button to exit the report.

8. In the *Reports* dialog box select **Customers & Receivables** from the list on the left of the screen.

9. In the **A/R Aging** section select **Summary**.

10. Change the **Date** field to **3-1-04**.

11. Your screen should look like Figure 18.2.

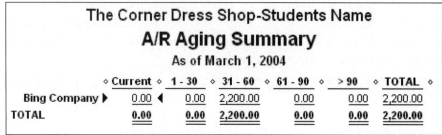

The Corner Dress Shop-Students Name
A/R Aging Summary
As of March 1, 2004

	Current	1 - 30	31 - 60	61 - 90	> 90	TOTAL
Bing Company ▶	0.00 ◀	0.00	2,200.00	0.00	0.00	2,200.00
TOTAL	0.00	0.00	2,200.00	0.00	0.00	2,200.00

Figure 18.2

12. Click the **Print** icon.

13. Click the **Close** button to close the A/R Aging Summary report and return to the *Reports* dialog box.

14. Click **Vendors & Payables** from the list on the left of your screen.

15. In the **AP Aging** section select **Summary**.

16. Change the **Date** field to **3-1-04**.

17. Your screen should look like Figure 18.3.

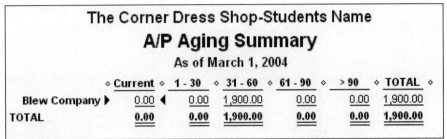

	◇ Current ◇	1 - 30 ◇	31 - 60 ◇	61 - 90 ◇	> 90 ◇	TOTAL ◇
Blew Company ▶	0.00 ◀	0.00	1,900.00	0.00	0.00	1,900.00
TOTAL	0.00	0.00	1,900.00	0.00	0.00	1,900.00

Figure 18.3

18. Click the **Print** icon.

19. Click the **Close** button to close the report.

Printing an Inventory Valuation Report

To see what inventory items The Corner Dress Shop has available, you can print a listing:

1. Click **Inventory** from the list on the left of the *Reports* dialog box.

2. Click **Summary** in the **Inventory Valuation** section.

3. In the **Date** field enter **3/1/04**.

4. Your screen should look like Figure 18.4.

The Corner Dress Shop-Students Name
Inventory Valuation Summary
As of March 1, 2004

	◇ Item Description ◇	On Hand ◇	Avg Cost ◇	Asset Value ◇	% of Tot Asset ◇	Sales Price ◇	Retail Value ◇	% of Tot Retail ◇
Inventory								
1000	▶ Dress, Style 1000	30	25.00	750.00	13.4%	50.00	1,500.00	13.4% ◀
2000	Dress, Style 2000	25	30.00	750.00	13.4%	60.00	1,500.00	13.4%
3000	Dress, Style 3000	25	35.00	875.00	15.6%	70.00	1,750.00	15.6%
4000	Dress, Style 4000	25	40.00	1,000.00	17.9%	80.00	2,000.00	17.9%
5000	Dress, Style 5000	25	45.00	1,125.00	20.1%	90.00	2,250.00	20.1%
6000	Dress, Style 6000	22	50.00	1,100.00	19.6%	100.00	2,200.00	19.6%
Total Inventory		152		5,600.00	100.0%		11,200.00	100.0%
TOTAL		152		5,600.00	100.0%		11,200.00	100.0%

Figure 18.4

5. Click the **Print** icon.

6. Click the **Close** button to exit the report.

7. Click the **Home** [Home] icon.

8. You see that the company has six items in inventory. In addition, you see the current cost of each item. Save this printed report to compare with a similar report you will print at the end of this practice set.

Maintaining Inventory Items

The QuickBooks Inventory module allows you to easily add new items or make changes to existing items, such as recording price changes. Since you will be asked to change prices later in the practice set, take a look at how that works now:

1. Click the **Items & Services** icon. That brings up the *Item List* dialog box, shown in Figure 18.5.

Figure 18.5

2. Double-click on **6000** in the **Name** column to bring up the *Edit Item* dialog box (see Figure 18.6).

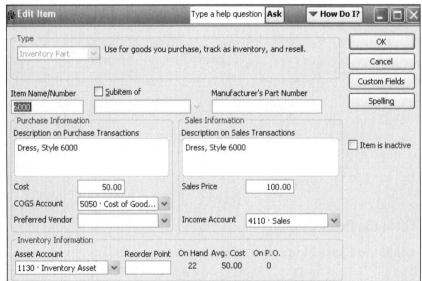

Figure 18.6

3. In the **Description on Purchase Transaction** field and the **Description on Sales Transactions** field, you see the current description of this inventory item. If a change is needed, simply place the cursor where the change needs to be made and edit as needed.

4. The program calculates the **Cost** field automatically.

5. Change the **Sales Price** field when you increase/decrease your selling price of an item.

6. QuickBooks has used default information to select the GL accounts needed for an inventory item type. If there is some need to change these, you can select any account you need. Since there is no need to change these accounts, leave them at the default settings.

7. You could establish a reorder point and have QuickBooks warn you when you fall below this level.

8. QuickBooks uses the average cost method.

9. QuickBooks uses all the information you can see in this window to work interactively with the other QuickBooks modules and report features.

Recording Transactions for March

Record the following transactions, using the appropriate entry windows. The entry windows used in this practice set include *Make General Journal Entries* (G), *Enter Invoices* (I), *Create Sales Receipts* (SR), *Refunds & Credits* (RC), *Receive Payments* (R), *Record Deposits* (RD), *Enter Bills* (B), *Pay Bills* (PB), *Write Checks* (W) and *Pay Liabilities* (PL).

Use the default forms when printing invoices, credits, and checks. Change the starting numbers as needed.

Accept the defaults for any field for which you are not given data.

Here are the transactions for March:

2004		
Mar.	1	Received Check 7634 from the Bing Co. in the amount of $2,200, in payment of Invoice 12 ($2,200), dated January 1. (R).
	3	Check 7634 received from the Bing Co. was deposited in the bank account (RD).
	3	Purchased merchandise from the Morris Co. on account, $10,000, Invoice 1210, terms 2/10, n/30, consisting of 184 Style 1000 and 180 Style 2000 dresses (B).
	3	Sold merchandise to the Ronold Co. on account, $7,000, Invoice 51, terms 2/10, n/30, consisting of 48 Style 1000, 30 Style 2000, 8 Style 3000, 9 Style 4000, 8 Style 5000, and 8 Style 6000 dresses (I).
	7	Sold merchandise to the Ronold Co. on account, $5,000, Invoice 52,

		terms 2/10, n/30, consisting of 48 Style 1000, 24 Style 2000, 5 Style 3000, 3 Style 4000, 3 Style 5000, and 3 Style 6000 dresses (I).
	10	Purchased merchandise from the Morris Co. on account, $5,000, Invoice 1286, terms 2/10, n/30, consisting of 92 Style 1000 and 90 Style 2000 dresses (B).
	10	Sold merchandise to the Ronold Co. on account $3,000, Invoice 53, terms 2/10, n/30, consisting of 20 Style 1000, 20 Style 2000, 4 Style 3000, 2 Style 4000, and 4 Style 5000 dresses (I).
	10	Paid for cleaning $300, Check 110, to Ronda's Cleaning Service (W). In the Write Checks window: ◆ Date 3/10/04. ◆ Enter Ronda Cleaning Service in the Pay to the Order of field. Select Quick Add and select Vendor. ◆ On the Expenses Tab select the correct GL account for this line (Cleaning Expense-5510) ◆ Enter the amount in the Amount column. ◆ Enter a short description in the Memo field on the Expenses tab. ◆ Print the check using Check 110.
	11	Ronold Co. returned merchandise that the company sold to it for $1,000 from Invoice 52 consisting of 4 Style 1000, 5 Style 2000, 2 Style 3000, 1 Style 4000, 2 Style 5000, and 1 Style 6000 dresses. The Corner Dress Shop issued Credit Memorandum CM 10 to the Ronald Co. for $1,000 (RC).
	11	Purchased merchandise from the Jones Co. on account, $10,000, Invoice 4639, terms 1/15, n/60, consisting of 144 Style 3000 and 124 Style 4000 dresses (B).
	12	Issued Check 111 to the Morris Co., in the amount of $9,800, in payment of Invoice 1210 ($10,000), dated March 2, less 2% discount ($200) (PB).
	13	Sold $7,000 of merchandise for cash, consisting of 24 Style 1000, 30 Style 2000, 24 Style 3000, and 29 Style 4000 dresses. Skip the Customer: Job and Sold to sections. Change the Payment Method field to Cash. Use Sale 1 (SR).
	13	The $7,000 cash was deposited in the bank (RD).
	14	Returned merchandise to the Jones Co. in the amount of $2,000, consisting of 32 Style 3000 and 22 Style 4000 dresses. Assign DM4 as the invoice number. Click the radio button next to Credit (BC).
	15	Due to increased operating costs, The Corner Dress Shop must raise its selling prices, as follows: Style 1000 $60.00 Style 2000 $70.00

		Style 3000 $80.00 Style 4000 $90.00 Style 5000 $110.00 Style 6000 $120.00 Click Items & Services to bring up the Item list. See the procedures discussed at the start of this workshop before continuing.
	15	Sold merchandise for $29,000 cash, consisting of 124 Style 1000, 144 Style 2000, 72 Style 3000, 61 Style 4000, 1 Style 5000, and 1 Style 6000 dresses. Skip the Customer: Job and Sold to sections. Use Sale 2. If you do not end up with $29,000 as your total, check to make sure you made the price changes correctly (SR).
	15	The $29,000 was taken to the bank and deposited (RD).
	15	Betty Loeb withdrew $100 for her own personal expenses, Check 112. Enter Betty Loeb in the Pay to the Order of field. Quick add her as a vendor. On the Expenses tab, be sure to code to Owner's Withdrawals (3120) (W).
	17	Received Check 5432 from the Ronold Co. in the amount of $3,920, in payment of Invoice 52 ($5,000), dated March 7, less CM10 ($1,000), less 2% discount ($100 – 20 = $80, net sales discount) (R).
	17	Received Check 5447 from the Ronold Co. in the amount of $7,000, in payment of Invoice 51, dated March 3 (R).
	17	The two checks received were taken to the bank and deposited (RD).
	17	Sold merchandise to the Bing Co. on account, $3,200, Invoice 54, terms 2/10, n/30, consisting of 12 Style 1000, 10 Style 2000, 11 Style 3000, and 10 Style 4000 dresses (I).
	21	Purchased delivery truck on account from Moe's Garage, Invoice 7113, $17,200 (B). ♦ Select Moe's Garage in the Vendor field. ♦ Enter the date and invoice number. ♦ Use the Expenses tab. ♦ Select the correct GL account for this line (Delivery Truck, original cost). ♦ Enter the amount in the Amount column. ♦ Enter a short description of the transaction in the Memo field. ♦ Save.
	22	Sold merchandise to the Ronold Co. on account $4,000, Invoice 55, consisting of 24 Style 1000, 24 Style 2000, 3 Style 3000, 2 Style 4000, 2 Style 5000, and 2 Style 6000 dresses (I).
	23	Issued Check 113 to the Jones Co. in the amount of $7,920, in payment of Invoice 4639 ($10,000), dated March 11, less DM4 ($2,000), less 1% discount ($100 – 20 = $80 net purchases discount)

		(PB).
	24	Sold merchandise to the Bing Co. on account, $2,000, Invoice 56, consisting of 1 Style 2000, 10 Style 3000, 10 Style 4000, 1 Style 5000, and 1 Style 6000 dresses (I).
	25	Purchased merchandise for $1,000 cash from the Jones Company, Check 114, consisting of 16 Style 3000 and 11 Style 4000 dresses. Use the Item tab to record the inventory purchased (W).
	27	Purchased merchandise from the Blew Co. on account, $6,000, Invoice 437, consisting of 60 Style 5000 and 66 Style 6000 dresses (I).
	28	Received Check 5562 from the Ronold Co. in the amount of $3,920, in payment of Invoice 55 ($4,000), dated March 22, less 2% discount ($80) (R).
	28	Received Check 8127 from the Bing Co. in the amount of $3,200, in payment of Invoice 54, dated March 16 (R).
	28	Made a deposit at the bank for the two checks received (RD).
	29	Purchased merchandise from the Morris Co. on account, $9,000, Invoice 1347, consisting of 150 Style 1000 and 150 Style 2000 dresses. The vendor has changed prices on these items, so instead of accepting the QuickBooks default for the unit prices, enter $28.00 and $32.00 for Style 1000 and Style 2000, respectively (B).
	30	Sold merchandise to the Bing Co. on account, $10,000, Invoice 57, terms 2/10, n/30, consisting of 6 Style 3000, 5 Style 4000, 41 Style 5000, and 38 Style 6000 dresses (I).
	30	The Auxiliary Petty Cash record for March listed the following: Postage Expense, $5; Delivery Expense, $10; Cleaning Expense, $6; Miscellaneous Expense, $10. Enter Petty Cash in the Pay to the Order of field. Quick add it as a Vendor. Issued Check 115 for $31.00 to replenish the petty cash fund (W).
	31	Issued payroll checks for March wages as follows:
		Use Pay Employees. Use 3/31/04 as the Pay End date as well as for the Check date.

Employee	March Wages	Check no.
Moore, Jackie		116
Salary	$3,325.00	
Social Security, Company	206.15	
Medicare Company	48.21	
Federal Unemployment	3.20	
MA-Unemployment Company	19.20	
Federal Withholding	348.00	
Social Security, Employee	206.15	
Medicare, Employee	48.21	

		MA Withholding	158.00	
		Net Pay	**2,564.64**	
		Holl, Jane		117
		Salary	$4,120.00	
		Social Security, Company	255.44	
		Medicare Company	59.74	
		Federal Unemployment	1.60	
		MA-Unemployment Company	9.60	
		Federal Withholding	502.00	
		Social Security, Employee	255.44	
		Medicare, Employee	59.74	
		MA Withholding	209.00	
		Net Pay	**3,093.82**	
		Case, Mel		118
		Salary	$4,760.00	
		Social Security, Company	295.12	
		Medicare Company	69.02	
		Federal Unemployment	4.80	
		MA-Unemployment Company	28.80	
		Federal Withholding	728.00	
		Social Security, Employee	295.12	
		Medicare, Employee	69.02	
		MA Withholding	269.00	
		Net Pay	**3,398.86**	

Printing the Reports

1. Print the reports shown in Figures 18.7 through 18.13.

2. Change the dates to **3/1/04** and **3/31/04**.

3. Adjust the column widths as necessary.

The Corner Dress Shop-Students Name
Trial Balance
As of March 31, 2004

	Mar 31, 04	
	Debit	Credit
1110 · Cash	30,534.58	
1115 · Petty Cash	35.00	
1120 · Accounts Receivable	15,000.00	
1130 · Inventory Asset	13,235.00	
1140 · Prepaid Rent	1,800.00	
1499 · Undeposited Funds	0.00	
1250 · Delivery Truck:1251 · Delivery Truck, Original Cost	23,200.00	
1250 · Delivery Truck:1252 · Accum. Dep-Delivery Truck		1,500.00
2110 · Accounts Payable		39,100.00
2100 · Payroll Liabilities		4,148.56
2400 · Unearned Rent		800.00
3000 · Opening Bal Equity	0.00	
3110 · Betty Loeb, Capital		13,937.90
3120 · Betty Loeb, Withdrawals	100.00	
3900 · Retained Earnings	0.00	
4110 · Sales		69,200.00
4140 · Sales Discounts	160.00	
5050 · Cost of Goods Sold	31,085.00	
5100 · Delivery Expense	10.00	
5500 · Postage Expense	5.00	
5510 · Cleaning Expense	306.00	
5560 · Miscellaneous Exense	10.00	
6560 · Payroll Expenses	13,205.88	
TOTAL	128,686.46	128,686.46

Figure 18.7

The Corner Dress Shop-Students Name
Journal
March 2004

Trans #	Type	Date	Num	Name	Memo	Account	Debit	Credit
19	Payment	03/01/2004	7634	Bing Company		1499 · Undeposited Funds	2,200.00	
				Bing Company		1120 · Accounts Receivable		2,200.00
							2,200.00	2,200.00
20	Deposit	03/03/2004			Deposit	1110 · Cash	2,200.00	
				Bing Company	Deposit	1499 · Undeposited Funds		2,200.00
							2,200.00	2,200.00
21	Bill	03/03/2004	1210	Morris Company		2110 · Accounts Payable		10,000.00
				Morris Company	Dress, Style 1000	1130 · Inventory Asset	4,600.00	
				Morris Company	Dress, Style 2000	1130 · Inventory Asset	5,400.00	
							10,000.00	10,000.00
22	Invoice	03/03/2004	51	Ronold Company		1120 · Accounts Receivable	7,000.00	
				Ronold Company	Dress, Style 1000	4110 · Sales		2,400.00
				Ronold Company	Dress, Style 1000	1130 · Inventory Asset		1,200.00
				Ronold Company	Dress, Style 1000	5050 · Cost of Goods Sold	1,200.00	
				Ronold Company	Dress, Style 2000	4110 · Sales		1,800.00
				Ronold Company	Dress, Style 2000	1130 · Inventory Asset		900.00
				Ronold Company	Dress, Style 2000	5050 · Cost of Goods Sold	900.00	
				Ronold Company	Dress, Style 3000	4110 · Sales		560.00
				Ronold Company	Dress, Style 3000	1130 · Inventory Asset		280.00
				Ronold Company	Dress, Style 3000	5050 · Cost of Goods Sold	280.00	
				Ronold Company	Dress, Style 4000	4110 · Sales		720.00
				Ronold Company	Dress, Style 4000	1130 · Inventory Asset		360.00
				Ronold Company	Dress, Style 4000	5050 · Cost of Goods Sold	360.00	
				Ronold Company	Dress, Style 5000	4110 · Sales		720.00
				Ronold Company	Dress, Style 5000	1130 · Inventory Asset		360.00
				Ronold Company	Dress, Style 5000	5050 · Cost of Goods Sold	360.00	
				Ronold Company	Dress, Style 6000	4110 · Sales		800.00

Figure 18.8

The Corner Dress Shop-Students Name
A/R Aging Summary
As of March 31, 2004

	Current	1 - 30	31 - 60	61 - 90	> 90	TOTAL
Bing Company	12,000.00	0.00	0.00	0.00	0.00	12,000.00
Ronold Company	3,000.00	0.00	0.00	0.00	0.00	3,000.00
TOTAL	15,000.00	0.00	0.00	0.00	0.00	15,000.00

Figure 18.9

The Corner Dress Shop-Students Name
Inventory Valuation Summary
As of March 31, 2004

	Item Description	On Hand	Avg Cost	Asset Value	% of Tot Asset	Sales Price	Retail Value	% of Tot Retail
Inventory								
1000	Dress, Style 1000	160	27.81	4,450.00	32.9%	60.00	9,600.00	31.7%
2000	Dress, Style 2000	167	31.80	5,310.00	39.3%	70.00	11,690.00	38.6%
3000	Dress, Style 3000	12	35.00	420.00	3.1%	80.00	960.00	3.2%
4000	Dress, Style 4000	8	40.00	320.00	2.4%	90.00	720.00	2.4%
5000	Dress, Style 5000	27	45.00	1,215.00	9.0%	110.00	2,970.00	9.8%
6000	Dress, Style 6000	36	50.00	1,800.00	13.3%	120.00	4,320.00	14.3%
Total Inventory		410		13,515.00	100.0%		30,260.00	100.0%
TOTAL		410		13,515.00	100.0%		30,260.00	100.0%

Figure 18.10

The Corner Dress Shop-Students Name
A/P Aging Summary
As of March 31, 2004

	Current	1 - 30	31 - 60	61 - 90	> 90	TOTAL
Blew Company	6,000.00	0.00	0.00	1,900.00	0.00	7,900.00
Moe's Garage	17,200.00	0.00	0.00	0.00	0.00	17,200.00
Morris Company	14,000.00	0.00	0.00	0.00	0.00	14,000.00
TOTAL	37,200.00	0.00	0.00	1,900.00	0.00	39,100.00

Figure 18.11

The Corner Dress Shop-Students Name
Payroll Liability Balances
March 2004

	BALANCE
Payroll Liabilities	
Federal Withholding	1,578.00
Medicare Employee	176.97
Social Security Employee	756.71
Federal Unemployment	9.60
Medicare Company	176.97
Social Security Company	756.71
MA - Withholding	636.00
MA - Unemployment Company	57.60
Total Payroll Liabilities	**4,148.56**

Figure 18.12

The Corner Dress Shop-Students Name
Payroll Summary
March 2004

	Jackie Moore			Jane Holl			Mel Case			TOTAL		
	Hours	Rate	Mar 04	Hours	Rate	Mar 04	Hours	Rate	Mar 04	Hours	Rate	Mar 04
Employee Wages, Taxes and Adjustments												
Gross Pay												
Salary			3,325.00			4,120.00			4,760.00			12,205.00
Total Gross Pay			3,325.00			4,120.00			4,760.00			12,205.00
Adjusted Gross Pay			3,325.00			4,120.00			4,760.00			12,205.00
Taxes Withheld												
Federal Withholding			-348.00			-502.00			-728.00			-1,578.00
Medicare Employee			-48.21			-59.74			-69.02			-176.97
Social Security Employee			-206.15			-255.44			-295.12			-756.71
MA - Withholding			-158.00			-209.00			-269.00			-636.00
Total Taxes Withheld			-760.36			-1,026.18			-1,361.14			-3,147.68
Net Pay			**2,564.64**			**3,093.82**			**3,398.86**			**9,057.32**
Employer Taxes and Contributions												
Federal Unemployment			3.20			1.60			4.80			9.60
Medicare Company			48.21			59.74			69.02			176.97
Social Security Company			206.15			255.44			295.12			756.71
MA - Unemployment Company			19.20			9.60			28.80			57.60
Total Employer Taxes and Contributions			276.76			326.38			397.74			1,000.88

Figure 18.13

Adjusting Journal Entries

Record the following adjustments:

1. Open the *Make General Journal Entries* window from the **Company** menu

2. In the **Date** field enter **3/31/04**.

3. In the **Entry No.** field enter **ADJ**.

4. Enter all the adjustments in the same entry window (see Figure 18.14):

    a. During March, rent expired, $600.

    b. Truck depreciated $150.

    c. Rental income earned, $200 (debit to unearned rent).

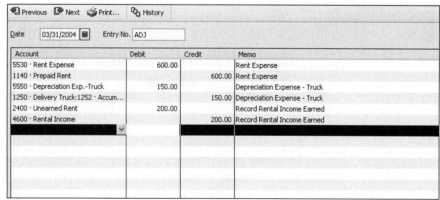

Figure 18.14

5. Review your entry before continuing. Make any corrections if necessary.

6. Click **Save & Close** button to post the journal entry

Displaying and Printing Reports

1. Print the reports shown in Figures 18.15 and 18.16.

2. Change the dates to **3/1/04** and **3/31/04**.

3. Adjust the columns as necessary.

Trans #	Type	Date	Num	Name	Memo	Account	Debit	Credit
				Jane Holl		6560 · Payroll Expenses	9.60	
				Jane Holl		2100 · Payroll Liabilities		9.60
							4,446.38	4,446.38
54	Paycheck	03/31/2004	118	Mel Case		1110 · Cash		3,398.86
				Mel Case		6560 · Payroll Expenses	4,760.00	
				Mel Case		2100 · Payroll Liabilities		728.00
				Mel Case		6560 · Payroll Expenses	295.12	
				Mel Case		2100 · Payroll Liabilities		295.12
				Mel Case		2100 · Payroll Liabilities		295.12
				Mel Case		6560 · Payroll Expenses	69.02	
				Mel Case		2100 · Payroll Liabilities		69.02
				Mel Case		2100 · Payroll Liabilities		69.02
				Mel Case		6560 · Payroll Expenses	4.80	
				Mel Case		2100 · Payroll Liabilities		4.80
				Mel Case		2100 · Payroll Liabilities		269.00
				Mel Case		6560 · Payroll Expenses	28.80	
				Mel Case		2100 · Payroll Liabilities		28.80
							5,157.74	5,157.74
55	General ...	03/31/2004	ADJ	Rent Expense		5530 · Rent Expense	600.00	
				Rent Expense		1140 · Prepaid Rent		600.00
				Depreciation Expense - Truck		5550 · Depreciation Exp.-Truck	150.00	
				Depreciation Expense - Truck		1252 · Accum. Dep-Delivery Truck		150.00
				Record Rental Income Earned		2400 · Unearned Rent	200.00	
				Record Rental Income Earned		4600 · Rental Income		200.00
							950.00	950.00
TOTAL							272,711.88	272,711.88

The Corner Dress Shop-Students Name
Journal
March 2004

Figure 18.15

The Corner Dress Shop-Students Name
Trial Balance
As of March 31, 2004

	Mar 31, 04	
	Debit	Credit
1110 · Cash	30,534.58	
1115 · Petty Cash	35.00	
1120 · Accounts Receivable	15,000.00	
1130 · Inventory Asset	13,235.00	
1140 · Prepaid Rent	1,200.00	
1499 · Undeposited Funds	0.00	
1250 · Delivery Truck:1251 · Delivery Truck, Original Cost	23,200.00	
1250 · Delivery Truck:1252 · Accum. Dep-Delivery Truck		1,650.00
2110 · Accounts Payable		39,100.00
2100 · Payroll Liabilities		4,148.56
2400 · Unearned Rent		600.00
3000 · Opening Bal Equity	0.00	
3110 · Betty Loeb, Capital		13,937.90
3120 · Betty Loeb, Withdrawals	100.00	
3900 · Retained Earnings	0.00	
4110 · Sales		69,200.00
4140 · Sales Discounts	160.00	
4600 · Rental Income		200.00
5050 · Cost of Goods Sold	31,085.00	
5100 · Delivery Expense	10.00	
5500 · Postage Expense	5.00	
5510 · Cleaning Expense	306.00	
5530 · Rent Expense	600.00	
5550 · Depreciation Exp.-Truck	150.00	
5560 · Miscellaneous Exsense	10.00	
6560 · Payroll Expenses	13,205.88	
TOTAL	**128,836.46**	**128,836.46**

Figure 18.16

Printing the General Ledger Report

1. Display the General ledger report on your screen.

2. Change the Dates to **3/1/04** and **3/31/04**

3. Click **Modify Report** to bring up the *Modify Report: General Ledger* dialog box. See Figure 18.17.

4. In the **Columns** section, scroll down the list and click next to **Debit** and **Credit** to select them. Unselect **Amount.**

5. Click **OK**. The report shown in Figure 18.18 appears.

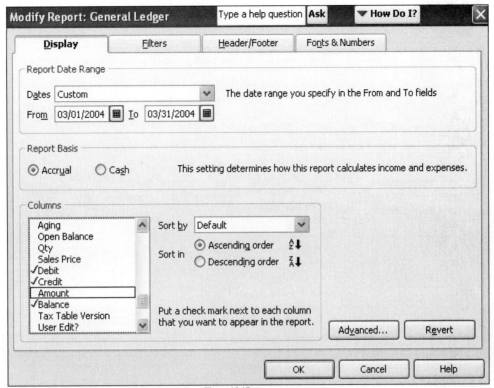

Figure 18.17

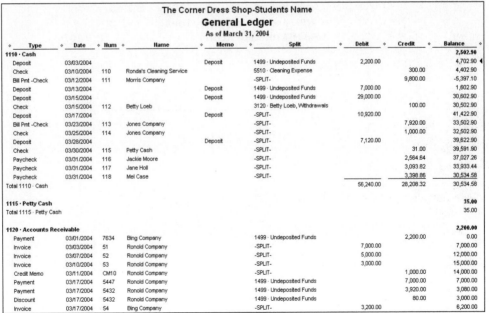

Figure 18.18

Printing the Financial Statements

1. Print the reports shown in Figures 18.19 and 18.20.

2. Change the dates to **3/1/04** and **3/31/04**.

3. Adjust the columns as necessary.

The Corner Dress Shop-Students Name
Balance Sheet
As of March 31, 2004

	Mar 31, 04
ASSETS	
Current Assets	
Checking/Savings	
1110 · Cash	30,534.58
1115 · Petty Cash	35.00
Total Checking/Savings	30,569.58
Accounts Receivable	
1120 · Accounts Receivable	15,000.00
Total Accounts Receivable	15,000.00
Other Current Assets	
1130 · Inventory Asset	13,235.00
1140 · Prepaid Rent	1,200.00
Total Other Current Assets	14,435.00
Total Current Assets	60,004.58
Fixed Assets	
1250 · Delivery Truck	
1251 · Delivery Truck, Original Cost	23,200.00
1252 · Accum. Dep-Delivery Truck	-1,650.00
Total 1250 · Delivery Truck	21,550.00
Total Fixed Assets	21,550.00
TOTAL ASSETS	**81,554.58**

```
LIABILITIES & EQUITY
   Liabilities
      Current Liabilities
         Accounts Payable
            2110 · Accounts Payable              39,100.00
         Total Accounts Payable                  39,100.00

         Other Current Liabilities
            2100 · Payroll Liabilities            4,148.56
            2400 · Unearned Rent                    600.00
         Total Other Current Liabilities          4,748.56

      Total Current Liabilities                  43,848.56

   Total Liabilities                             43,848.56

   Equity
      3110 · Betty Loeb, Capital                 13,937.90
      3120 · Betty Loeb, Withdrawals              -100.00
      Net Income                                 23,868.12
   Total Equity                                  37,706.02

TOTAL LIABILITIES & EQUITY                       81,554.58
```

Figure 18.19

The Corner Dress Shop-Students Name
Profit & Loss
March 2004

	Mar 04
Income	
4110 · Sales	▶ 69,200.00 ◀
4140 · Sales Discounts	-160.00
4600 · Rental Income	200.00
Total Income	69,240.00
Cost of Goods Sold	
5050 · Cost of Goods Sold	31,085.00
Total COGS	31,085.00
Gross Profit	38,155.00
Expense	
5100 · Delivery Expense	10.00
5500 · Postage Expense	5.00
5510 · Cleaning Expense	306.00
5530 · Rent Expense	600.00
5550 · Depreciation Exp.-Truck	150.00
5560 · Miscellaneous Exense	10.00
6560 · Payroll Expenses	13,205.88
Total Expense	14,286.88
Net Income	**23,868.12**

Figure 18.20

Weighted-Average Inventory Cost

Compare the Inventory Valuation report you just printed (refer to Figure 18.10) with the one created at the start of this workshop. Note that the first two items, the ones whose cost price changed when the company last purchased them, have neither the original prices of $25.00 and $30.00 nor the new prices of $28.00 and $32.00, respectively. QuickBooks has created a weighted-average for these items.

Backing Up Your Company Data File

1. Click the **Backup** `Backup` icon.

2. Click the **Browse** button in the **Backup Current Company** section to specify a location to keep your backup files.

3. Add **EndMar** to the file name. Click **Save**.

4. Click **OK**.

5. When the backup is complete, click **OK**.

   ➤ **NOTE:** For more detailed instructions on backing up files, refer to Chapter 11.

Advancing the Accounting Period to April

You must now advance the period to prepare QuickBooks for the April transactions:

1. Select **Set up users** from the **Company** menu.

2. Click the **Closing Date** button.

3. In the **Closing Date** section enter **3/31/04**.

4. Click the **OK** button.

5. Click the **Close** button to exit the *User List* dialog box.

Backing Up Your Company Data File

1. Click the **Backup** [Backup] icon.

2. Click the **Browse** button in the **Backup Current Company** section to specify a location to keep your backup files.

3. Add **Final** to the file name. Click **Save**.

4. Click **OK**.

5. When the backup is complete, click **OK**.

   ➢ **NOTE:** For more detailed instructions on backing up files, refer to Chapter 11.

Exiting the QuickBooks Pro 2006 Program

1. Select **Close Company** from the **File** menu.

2. Select **Exit** from the **File** menu to end the current work session and return to your Windows desktop.

CHAPTER 19

Perpetual Inventory System—The Paint Place

THIS WORKSHOP INCLUDES MAINTAINING PERPETUAL INVENTORY RECORDS AND ITEMS, ACCOUNTS RECEIVABLE, AND ACCOUNTS PAYABLE.

IT IS RECOMMENDED THAT YOU COMPLETE THE WORKSHOP IN CHAPTER 16 BEFORE DOING THIS WORKSHOP.

THIS WORKSHOP DOES NOT COVER PAYROLL, GENERAL JOURNAL ENTRIES, OR ADJUSTING JOURNAL ENTRIES.

Opening The Paint Place File

1. Double-click the **QuickBooks** icon on your desktop to open the software program.

2. Click **Open an existing company** and then locate and select **The Paint Place**.

3. Click **Open**.

> ➢ **NOTE:** Refer to Chapter 11 for more detailed instructions on opening files.

Backing Up Your Company Data File

1. Click the **Backup** Backup icon.

2. Click the **Browse** button in the **Backup Current Company** section to specify a location to keep your backup files.

3. Add **Start** to the file name. Click **Save**.

4. Click **OK**.

5. When the backup is complete, click **OK**.

> ➢ **NOTE:** For more detailed instructions on backing up files, refer to Chapter 11.

Adding Your Name to the Company Name

5. Click the **Company** menu option and select **Company Information**. The program responds by bringing up the ***Company Information*** dialog box, which allows you to edit/add information about the company.

6. Click in the **Company Name** field and make sure that your cursor is at the end of **The Paint Place**.

7. Add a dash and your name (**-Student's Name**.

8. Click the **OK** button.

Toggling to the QuickBooks Pro 2006 Version

If you are using the QuickBooks Pro 2006 version and not the Accountant Edition 2006, you can skip this section.

If you ordered the trial version, as noted in Chapter 11, you are using a **QuickBooks 2006 All-in-One Trial for Accountants**. So that you see the same screenshots as are shown in this text, you should toggle to **QuickBooks Pro Edition**. The following instructions walk you through the toggling process:

6. Select **Toggle to Another Edition** from the **File** menu.

7. Click the radio button next to **QuickBooks Pro** to select it.

8. Click **Next**.

9. Click the **Toggle** button.

10. It takes a few seconds for the process to complete. Your title bar then says **(via Accountant Edition)**.

Overview of Perpetual Inventory

One of the most powerful features of a computerized accounting system is its ability to maintain perpetual inventory records easily and accurately. Earlier chapters demonstrate this feature was by having you record purchases and sales of inventory. QuickBooks Pro 2006 has the ability to maintain perpetual inventory records through its Inventory module. QuickBooks Pro 2006 uses the weighted-average method as its inventory cost flow assumption.

In this Chapter you work with the data files for a company called The Paint Place. The Paint Place uses the Invoices, Receive Payments, Record Deposits, Enter Bills, Pay Bills, and Inventory modules of QuickBooks Pro 2006 to maintain its accounting and perpetual inventory records.

The Paint Place extends terms of 2/10, n/30 to all its credit customers.

Printing the Beginning Balance Reports

1. Print the following reports shown in Figures 19.1 through 19.4.

   ➢ **NOTE:** For more detail instructions on printing reports, refer to Chapter 12.

2. Change the date to **3/1/04**.

3. Adjust the column widths as necessary.

The Paint Place
Trial Balance
As of March 1, 2004

	Mar 1, 04	
	Debit	Credit
1110 · Cash	23,872.94	
1120 · Accounts Receivable	8,259.95	
1121 · Inventory Asset	28,928.67	
1140 · Prepaid Rent	2,200.00	
1150 · Store Supplies	1,622.30	
1250 · Office Equipment:1251 · Office Equipment Original Cost	12,800.00	
1250 · Office Equipment:1252 · Accum. Dep.- Office Equipment		1,469.44
1350 · Store Equipment:1351 · Store Equipment Original Cost	13,500.00	
1350 · Store Equipment:1352 · Accum. Dep.-Store Equipment		1,916.67
2110 · Accounts Payable		4,142.12
3000 · Opening Bal Equity	▶ 0.00 ◀	
3110 · Mike Poole, Capital		94,655.63
3120 · Mike Poole, Withdrawals	11,000.00	
3900 · Retained Earnings	0.00	
TOTAL	102,183.86	102,183.86

Figure 19.1

The Paint Place-Student Name
A/R Aging Summary
As of March 1, 2004

	Current	1 - 30	31 - 60	61 - 90	> 90	TOTAL
Anderson, Elaine ▶	0.00 ◀	0.00	2,293.05	0.00	0.00	2,293.05
Kerns, Jake	0.00	0.00	2,675.95	0.00	0.00	2,675.95
Young, Wes	0.00	0.00	3,290.95	0.00	0.00	3,290.95
TOTAL	0.00	0.00	8,259.95	0.00	0.00	8,259.95

Figure 19.2

The Paint Place-Student Name
Inventory Valuation Summary
As of March 1, 2004

	Item Description	On Hand	Avg Cost	Asset Value	% of Tot Asset	Sales Price	Retail Value	% of Tot Retail
Inventory								
001	▶ Latex Flat	642	7.47	4,795.74	16.6%	16.95	10,881.90	17.4% ◀
002	Latex Semi-Gloss	1,066	7.47	7,963.02	27.5%	16.95	18,068.70	28.9%
003	Latex High-Gloss	600	7.47	4,482.00	15.5%	16.95	10,170.00	16.3%
004	Oil High-Gloss	801	8.97	7,184.97	24.8%	17.95	14,377.95	23.0%
005	Oil Semi-Gloss	502	8.97	4,502.94	15.6%	17.95	9,010.90	14.4%
Total Inventory		3,611		28,928.67	100.0%		62,509.45	100.0%
TOTAL		3,611		28,928.67	100.0%		62,509.45	100.0%

Figure 19.3

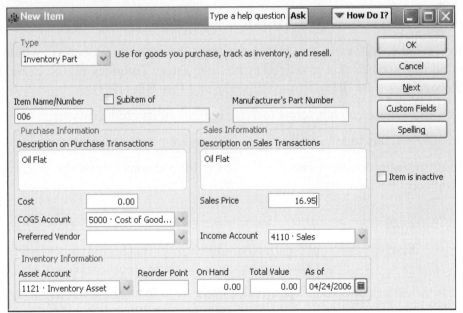

The Paint Place-Student Name
A/P Aging Summary
As of March 1, 2004

	Current	1 - 30	31 - 60	61 - 90	> 90	TOTAL
Painter's Supply ▶	0.00 ◀	0.00	975.34	0.00	0.00	975.34
Vantage Tints	0.00	0.00	1,116.33	0.00	0.00	1,116.33
Wholesale Paints	0.00	0.00	2,050.45	0.00	0.00	2,050.45
TOTAL	0.00	0.00	4,142.12	0.00	0.00	4,142.12

Figure 19.4

4. Compare the A/R Aging Summary, Inventory Valuation Summary, and A/P Aging Summary reports to the balances on the Trial Balance report. They should match.

Adding Inventory Items

QuickBooks Pro 2006 allows you to quickly and easily add new inventory items or edit information about items currently in the inventory.

To add a new product to the **The Paint Place** inventory, follow these steps:

1. Click the **Items & Services** icon in the *Home* window.

2. Click the **Item** button and select **New Item**. The dialog box shown in Figure 19.5 appears.

Figure 19.5

3. In the **Type** field select **Inventory Part** from the lookup window.

4. In the **Item Name/Number** field type **006**.

5. In the **Purchases Information** section type **Oil Flat** in the **Description on Purchase Transactions** field.

6. Leave the **Cost** field empty.

7. Tab to the **Sales Information** section. Notice that the description you entered in the **Description on Purchase Transactions** field is automatically copied to **Description on Sales Transactions**.

8. In the **Sales Price** field enter **16.95**. This is the normal selling price for this item.

9. In the **Income Account** field, select **4110 – Sales**.

10. Accept the QuickBooks default information on the rest of the fields in this window.

11. Click **OK** to save this new inventory item.

Editing Inventory Items

1. With the *Item List* dialog box open, follow these steps to edit inventory items as necessary:

2. Double-click any item to display it on your screen.

3. Click any field and change the information as needed.

4. Click the **OK** button to save any changes you have made.

5. Click the **Close** button to exit the *Item List* dialog box.

Recording Transactions for March

Record the following transactions, using the appropriate entry windows. The entry windows used in this practice set include **Enter Invoices** (I), **Receive Payments** (R), **Record Deposits** (RD), **Enter Bills** (B), and **Pay Bills** (PB).

The Paint Place extends terms of 2/10, n/30 to all its credit customers.

Accept defaults for any fields for which you are not given information.

Insert the appropriate number given in the transactions during the printing process for all print activities.

2004		
Mar.	1	Sold 5 gallons of Oil High-gloss (Item 4) at $17.95 per gallon to Elaine Anderson on account, Invoice 5469, for $89.75 (I).
	3	Received Invoice 6892 from Wholesale Paints, in the amount of $1,504, for the purchase of 200 gallons of Latex High-gloss (Item 3) at $7.52 per gallon Don't forget to change the unit price. You are prompted with the question Do you want to update the item with the new cost? Select Yes (B).

	3	Received Invoice CC675 from Painter's Supply in the amount of $906, for the purchase of 100 gallons of Oil High-gloss (Item 4) at 9.06 per gallon. Don't forget to change the unit price and update the new cost (B).
	4	Sold 5 gallons of Oil High-gloss paint (Item 4) at $17.95 per gallon to Jake Kerns on account, Invoice 5470 for $89.75 (I).
	6	Received Check 8723 from Wes Young in the amount of $3,290.95, in payment of invoice no. 5401, dated December 31 (R).
	6	Deposited Check 8723 for $3,290.95 in the bank (RD).
	7	Issued Check 2345 to Vantage Tints, in the amount of $1,116.33, in payment of Invoice 2300, dated December 31 (PB).
	8	Received Check 5476 from Elaine Anderson, in the amount of $2293.05, for Invoice 5402, dated December 31 (R).
	8	Received Check 202 from Jake Kerns, in the amount of $2,675.95 for the Invoice 5403, dated December 31 (R).
	9	Deposited in the bank the two checks received on 3/8/04. Total deposit of $4,969.00 (RD).
	14	Sold 10 gallons of Latex Semi-gloss (Item 2) at $16.95 per gallon to Elaine Anderson on account, $169.50, invoice 5471 (I).
	15	Issued check 2346 to Painters Supply for $975.34, in payment of invoice CC671, dated December 31 (PB).
	17	Received Invoice 6943 from Wholesale Paints in the amount of $1,134, for the purchase of 150 gallons of Latex Semi-gloss (Item 2) at 7.56 per gallon. Don't forget to change the unit price and update the new cost (B).
	19	Received Invoice CC691 from Painter's Supply in the amount of $1,618.75, for the purchase of 175 gallons of Oil Semi-gloss (Item 5) at 9.25 per gallon. Don't forget to change the unit price and update the new cost (B).
	19	Issued Check 2347 to Wholesale Paints for $2,050.45, in payment of Invoice 6753, dated December 31 (PB).
	21	Sold 10 gallons of Latex Semi-gloss (Item 2) at $16.95 per gallon to Jake Kerns on account, $169.50, Invoice 5472 (I).
	24	Sold 25 gallons of Oil Semi-gloss paint (Item 5) at $17.95 per gallon to Elaine Anderson on account, $448.75, Invoice 5473 (I).
	25	Received Invoice CC787 from Painter's Supply, in the amount of $465, for the purchase of 50 gallons of Oil Semi-gloss (Item 5) at $9.30 per gallon. Don't forget to change the unit price and

		update the new cost (B).
	31	Sold 25 gallons of Oil Semi-gloss (Item 5) at $17.95 per gallon to Jake Kerns on account, $448.75, Invoice 5474 (I).

Displaying and Printing the Inventory Valuation Detail

You may wish to see how active the items in your inventory have been. For such situations, QuickBooks has two Inventory Valuation reports that summarize the units bought and sold for any selected period.

1. Select **Inventory** from the list on the left side of the **Reports** dialog box.

2. Select **Inventory Valuation Detail** from the **Inventory Valuation** section.

3. Change the dates to **1/1/04** and **3/31/04** (January through March).

4. Adjust the column widths as necessary.

5. Your screen will look like Figure 19.6.

The Paint Place-Student Name
Inventory Valuation Detail
January through March 2004

Type	Date	Name	Num	Qty	Cost	On Hand	Avg Cost	Asset Value
002								
Inventory Adjust	02/28/2004			1,066		1,066	7.47	7,963.02
Invoice	03/14/2004	Anderson...	5471	-10		1,056	7.47	7,888.32
Bill	03/17/2004	Wholesale...	6943	150	1,134.00	1,206	7.48	9,022.32
Invoice	03/21/2004	Kerns, Jake	5472	-10		1,196	7.48	8,947.51
Total 002						1,196		8,947.51
003								
Inventory Adjust	02/28/2004			600		600	7.47	4,482.00
Bill	03/03/2004	Wholesale...	6892	200	1,504.00	800	7.48	5,986.00
Total 003						800		5,986.00
004								
Inventory Adjust	02/28/2004			801		801	8.97	7,184.97
Invoice	03/01/2004	Anderson...	5469	-5		796	8.97	7,140.12
Bill	03/03/2004	Painter's S...	CC675	100	906.00	896	8.98	8,046.12
Invoice	03/04/2004	Kerns, Jake	5470	-5		891	8.98	8,001.22
Total 004						891		8,001.22
005								
Inventory Adjust	02/28/2004			502		502	8.97	4,502.94
Bill	03/19/2004	Painter's S...	CC691	175	1,618.75	677	9.04	6,121.69
Invoice	03/24/2004	Anderson...	5473	-25		652	9.04	5,895.63
Bill	03/25/2004	Painter's S...	CC787	50	465.00	702	9.06	6,360.63
Invoice	03/31/2004	Kerns, Jake	5474	-25		677	9.06	6,134.11
Total 005						677		6,134.11
Total Inventory						4,206		33,864.58

Figure 19.6

6. Click the **Print** icon.

7. Click the **Close** button to exit the report.

Displaying and Printing the Inventory Valuation Summary

The Inventory Valuation Summary report is one of the most valuable reports for inventory management.

1. In the *Reports* window select **Summary** from the **Inventory Valuation** section.

2. Change the date to **3/31/04**.

3. Adjust the column widths as necessary.

4. Your screen will look like Figure 19.7.

The Paint Place-Student Name
Inventory Valuation Summary
As of March 31, 2004

Item Description	On Hand	Avg Cost	Asset Value	% of Tot Asset	Sales Price	Retail Value	% of Tot Retail
Inventory							
001 ▶ Latex Flat	642	7.47	4,795.74	14.2%	16.95	10,881.90	14.9% ◀
002 Latex Semi-Gloss	1,196	7.48	8,947.51	26.4%	16.95	20,272.20	27.8%
003 Latex High-Gloss	800	7.48	5,986.00	17.7%	16.95	13,560.00	18.6%
004 Oil High-Gloss	891	8.98	8,001.22	23.6%	17.95	15,993.45	22.0%
005 Oil Semi-Gloss	677	9.06	6,134.11	18.1%	17.95	12,152.15	16.7%
006 Oil Flat	0	0.00	0.00	0.0%	16.95	0.00	0.0%
Total Inventory	4,206		33,864.58	100.0%		72,859.70	100.0%
TOTAL	**4,206**		**33,864.58**	**100.0%**		**72,859.70**	**100.0%**

Figure 19.7

5. Click the **Print** icon.

6. Click the **Close** button to exit the report.

Printing the Reports for March

1. Print the additional reports shown in Figures 19.8 through 19.14.

2. Change the dates to **3/1/04** to **3/31/04**.

3. Adjust the column widths as necessary.

The Paint Place-Student Name
Trial Balance
As of March 31, 2004

	Mar 31, 04	
	Debit	Credit
1110 · Cash	27,990.77	
1120 · Accounts Receivable	1,416.00	
1121 · Inventory Asset	33,864.58	
1140 · Prepaid Rent	2,200.00	
1150 · Store Supplies	1,622.30	
1499 · Undeposited Funds	0.00	
1250 · Office Equipment:1251 · Office Equipment Original Cost	12,800.00	
1250 · Office Equipment:1252 · Accum. Dep.- Office Equipment		1,469.44
1350 · Store Equipment:1351 · Store Equipment Original Cost	13,500.00	
1350 · Store Equipment:1352 · Accum. Dep.-Store Equipment		1,916.67
2110 · Accounts Payable		5,627.75
3000 · Opening Bal Equity	0.00	
3110 · Mike Poole, Capital		94,655.63
3120 · Mike Poole, Withdrawals	11,000.00	
3900 · Retained Earnings	0.00	
4110 · Sales		1,416.00
5000 · Cost of Goods Sold	691.84	
TOTAL	105,085.49	105,085.49

Figure 19.8

The Paint Place-Student Name
Journal
March 2004

Trans #	Type	Date	Num	Adj	Name	Memo	Account	Debit	Credit
24	Invoice	03/01/2004	5469		Anderson, Elaine		1120 · Accounts Receivable	89.75	
					Anderson, Elaine	Oil High-Gloss	4110 · Sales		89.75
					Anderson, Elaine	Oil High-Gloss	1121 · Inventory Asset		44.85
					Anderson, Elaine	Oil High-Gloss	5000 · Cost of Goods Sold	44.85	
								134.60	134.60
25	Bill	03/03/2004	6892		Wholesale Paints		2110 · Accounts Payable		1,504.00
					Wholesale Paints	Latex High-Gloss	1121 · Inventory Asset	1,504.00	
								1,504.00	1,504.00
26	Bill	03/03/2004	CC675		Painter's Supply		2110 · Accounts Payable		906.00
					Painter's Supply	Oil High-Gloss	1121 · Inventory Asset	906.00	
								906.00	906.00
27	Invoice	03/04/2004	5470		Kerns, Jake		1120 · Accounts Receivable	89.75	
					Kerns, Jake	Oil High-Gloss	4110 · Sales		89.75
					Kerns, Jake	Oil High-Gloss	1121 · Inventory Asset		44.90
					Kerns, Jake	Oil High-Gloss	5000 · Cost of Goods Sold	44.90	
								134.65	134.65
28	Payment	03/06/2004	8723		Young, Wes		1499 · Undeposited Funds	3,290.95	
					Young, Wes		1120 · Accounts Receivable		3,290.95
								3,290.95	3,290.95
29	Deposit	03/06/2004				Deposit	1110 · Cash	3,290.95	
					Young, Wes	Deposit	1499 · Undeposited Funds		3,290.95
								3,290.95	3,290.95

Figure 19.9

The Paint Place-Student Name
A/R Aging Summary
As of March 31, 2004

	Current	1 - 30	31 - 60	61 - 90	> 90	TOTAL
Anderson, Elaine	708.00	0.00	0.00	0.00	0.00	708.00
Kerns, Jake	708.00	0.00	0.00	0.00	0.00	708.00
TOTAL	1,416.00	0.00	0.00	0.00	0.00	1,416.00

Figure 19.10

The Paint Place-Student Name
A/P Aging Summary
As of March 31, 2004

	Current	1 - 30	31 - 60	61 - 90	> 90	TOTAL
Painter's Supply	2,989.75	0.00	0.00	0.00	0.00	2,989.75
Wholesale Paints	2,638.00	0.00	0.00	0.00	0.00	2,638.00
TOTAL	5,627.75	0.00	0.00	0.00	0.00	5,627.75

Figure 19.11

The Paint Place-Student Name
Profit & Loss
March 2004

	Mar 04
Income	
4110 · Sales	1,416.00
Total Income	1,416.00
Cost of Goods Sold	
5000 · Cost of Goods Sold	691.84
Total COGS	691.84
Gross Profit	724.16
Expense	0.00
Net Income	724.16

Figure 19.12

The Paint Place-Student Name

Profit & Loss Detail

March 2004

Type	Date	Num	Name	Memo	Split	Debit	Credit	Balance
4110 · Sales								
Invoice	03/01/2004	5469	Anderson, Elaine	Oil High-Gloss	1120 · Accounts Receivable		89.75	89.75
Invoice	03/04/2004	5470	Kerns, Jake	Oil High-Gloss	1120 · Accounts Receivable		89.75	179.50
Invoice	03/14/2004	5471	Anderson, Elaine	Latex Semi-Gloss	1120 · Accounts Receivable		169.50	349.00
Invoice	03/21/2004	5472	Kerns, Jake	Latex Semi-Gloss	1120 · Accounts Receivable		169.50	518.50
Invoice	03/24/2004	5473	Anderson, Elaine	Oil Semi-Gloss	1120 · Accounts Receivable		448.75	967.25
Invoice	03/31/2004	5474	Kerns, Jake	Oil Semi-Gloss	1120 · Accounts Receivable		448.75	1,416.00
Total 4110 · Sales						0.00	1,416.00	1,416.00
Total Income						0.00	1,416.00	1,416.00
Cost of Goods Sold								
5000 · Cost of Goods Sold								
Invoice	03/01/2004	5469	Anderson, Elaine	Oil High-Gloss	1120 · Accounts Receivable	44.85		44.85
Invoice	03/04/2004	5470	Kerns, Jake	Oil High-Gloss	1120 · Accounts Receivable	44.90		89.75
Invoice	03/14/2004	5471	Anderson, Elaine	Latex Semi-Gloss	1120 · Accounts Receivable	74.70		164.45
Invoice	03/21/2004	5472	Kerns, Jake	Latex Semi-Gloss	1120 · Accounts Receivable	74.81		239.26
Invoice	03/24/2004	5473	Anderson, Elaine	Oil Semi-Gloss	1120 · Accounts Receivable	226.06		465.32
Invoice	03/31/2004	5474	Kerns, Jake	Oil Semi-Gloss	1120 · Accounts Receivable	226.52		691.84
Total 5000 · Cost of Goods Sold						691.84	0.00	691.84
Total COGS						691.84	0.00	691.84
Gross Profit						691.84	1,416.00	724.16
Expense								0.00
Net Income						**691.84**	**1,416.00**	**724.16**

Figure 19.13

The Paint Place-Student Name
Balance Sheet
As of March 31, 2004

	Mar 31, 04
ASSETS	
Current Assets	
Checking/Savings	
1110 · Cash	27,990.77
Total Checking/Savings	27,990.77
Accounts Receivable	
1120 · Accounts Receivable	1,416.00
Total Accounts Receivable	1,416.00
Other Current Assets	
1121 · Inventory Asset	33,864.58
1140 · Prepaid Rent	2,200.00
1150 · Store Supplies	1,622.30
Total Other Current Assets	37,686.88
Total Current Assets	67,093.65
Fixed Assets	
1250 · Office Equipment	
1251 · Office Equipment Original Cost	12,800.00
1252 · Accum. Dep.- Office Equipment	-1,469.44
Total 1250 · Office Equipment	11,330.56
1350 · Store Equipment	
1351 · Store Equipment Original Cost	13,500.00
1352 · Accum. Dep.-Store Equipment	-1,916.67
Total 1350 · Store Equipment	11,583.33

Total Fixed Assets	22,913.89
TOTAL ASSETS	**90,007.54**
LIABILITIES & EQUITY	
Liabilities	
Current Liabilities	
Accounts Payable	
2110 · Accounts Payable	5,627.75
Total Accounts Payable	5,627.75
Total Current Liabilities	5,627.75
Total Liabilities	5,627.75
Equity	
3110 · Mike Poole, Capital	94,655.63
3120 · Mike Poole, Withdrawals	-11,000.00
Net Income	724.16
Total Equity	84,379.79
TOTAL LIABILITIES & EQUITY	**90,007.54**

Figure 19.14

Backing Up Your Company Data File

1. Click the **Backup** [Backup] icon.

2. Click the **Browse** button in the **Backup Current Company** section to specify a location to keep your backup files.

3. Add **Final** to the file name. Click **Save**.

4. Click **OK**.

5. When the backup is complete, click **OK**.

> ➢ **NOTE:** For more detailed instructions on backing up files, refer to Chapter 11.

Exiting the QuickBooks Pro 2006 Program

1. Select **Close Company** from the **File** menu.

2. Select **Exit** from the **File** menu to end the current work session and return to your Windows desktop.

CHAPTER 20

Notes Receivable and Notes Payable—Lundquist Custom Woodworking

THIS WORKSHOP COVERS SHORT-TERM NOTES RECEIVABLE AND NOTES PAYABLES THAT ORIGINATE FROM ACCOUNTS RECEIVABLE AND ACCOUNTS PAYABLE BALANCES.

QuickBooks does not have a specific provision for the recording of promissory notes from either the buyer's or the seller's prospective. QuickBooks does, however, have a Loan Manager feature for tracking Long-Term Notes Payables. This workshop does not cover the use of the Loan Manager because it is beyond the scope of this book. Generally speaking, promissory note entries that do not involve accounts receivable or accounts payable, such as cash loans, can be entered through the *General Journal Entry* window.

Entries that involve accounts receivable and/or accounts payable must be entered through a window that can also perform a posting to the appropriate Subsidiary ledger using either the *Receive Payments* window or *Bill (Credits)* window. Using these entry windows allows you to maintain the balance between the Subsidiary ledgers, and their controlling accounts in the General ledger.

QuickBooks does *not* automatically calculate interest, so you are required to calculate interest manually.

Opening the Lundquist Custom Woodworking File

1. Double-click the **QuickBooks** icon on your desktop to open the software program.

2. Click **Open an existing company** and then locate and select **Lundquist Custom Woodworking**.

3. Click **Open**.

   ➢ **NOTE:** Refer to Chapter 11 for more detailed instructions on opening files.

Backing Up Your Company Data File

1. Click the **Backup**  icon.

2. Click the **Browse** button in the **Backup Current Company** section to specify a location to keep your backup files.

3. Add **Start** to the file name. Click **Save**.

4. Click **OK**.

5. When the backup is complete, click **OK**.

> **NOTE:** For more detailed instructions on backing up files, refer to Chapter 11.

Adding Your Name to the Company Name

1. Click the **Company** menu option and select **Company Information**. The program responds by bringing up the *Company Information* dialog box, which allows you to edit/add information about the company.

2. Click in the **Company Name** field and make sure that your cursor is at the end of **Lundquist Custom Woodworking**.

3. Add a dash and your name **(-Student's Name**.

4. Click the **OK** button**.**

Toggling to the QuickBooks Pro 2006 Version

If you are using the QuickBooks Pro 2006 version and not the Accountant Edition 2006, you can skip this section.

If you ordered the trial version, as noted in Chapter 11, you are using a **QuickBooks 2006 All-in-One Trial for Accountants**. So that you see the same screenshots as are shown in this text, you should toggle to **QuickBooks Pro Edition**. The following instructions walk you through the toggling process:

1. Select **Toggle to Another Edition** from the **File** menu.

2. Click the radio button next to **QuickBooks Pro** to select it.

3. Click **Next**.

4. Click the **Toggle** button.

5. It takes a few seconds for the process to complete. Your title bar then says **(via Accountant Edition)**.

Printing the Beginning-of-the-Month Reports

Print the Trial Balance report from the **General Ledger** section of the *Reports* dialog box:

1. Click the **Report Center** icon.

2. Select **Accountant & Taxes** from the list on the left.

3. Select **Trial Balance**.

4. Change the date to **8/1/04**.

5. Click the **Print** button to print the report which is shown in Figure 20.1.

Lundquist Custom Woodworking
Trial Balance
As of August 1, 2004

	Aug 1, 04	
	Debit	Credit
1110 · Cash	30,000.00	
1120 · Accounts Receivable	52,000.00	
1130 · Notes Receivable	5,000.00	
1150 · Shop Supplies	5,800.00	
1210 · Shop Equipment	156,000.00	
1221 · Accum Depr - Shop Equipment		34,000.00
1230 · Automobile	16,000.00	
1241 · Accum Depr - Automobile		4,000.00
2110 · Accounts Payable		2,000.00
2130 · Notes Payable		3,000.00
3000 · Opening Bal Equity	0.00	
3110 · Vernon Lundquist, Capital		10,000.00
3130 · Retained Earnings		211,800.00
TOTAL	**264,800.00**	**264,800.00**

Figure 20.1

6. Click the **Close** button to close the Trial Balance report.

   Print the A/R Aging Summary report from the **Customers & Receivable** section of the *Reports* dialog box:

7. Click the **Customers & Receivable** button from the list on the left of the *Reports* dialog box.

8. Click on **Summary** in the **A/R Aging** section of the list on the right.

9. Change the date to **8/1/04**.

10. Click the **Print** button.

11. Click **Print** to print the report, which is shown in Figure 20.2.

Lundquist Custom Woodworking
A/R Aging Summary
As of August 1, 2004

	Current	1 - 30	31 - 60	61 - 90	> 90	TOTAL
Betty's Botique	4,000.00	0.00	0.00	0.00	0.00	4,000.00
Carl's Accounting Service	6,000.00	0.00	0.00	0.00	0.00	6,000.00
Salina School District	42,000.00	0.00	0.00	0.00	0.00	42,000.00
TOTAL	**52,000.00**	**0.00**	**0.00**	**0.00**	**0.00**	**52,000.00**

Figure 20.2

12. Click the **Close** button to exit the A/R Aging Summary report.

Print the A/P Aging Summary report from the **Vendors & Payables** section of the *Reports* dialog box:

13. Select **Vendors & Payables** from the list on the left of the *Reports* screen.

14. Select **Summary** from the **A/P Aging** section of the list on the right.

15. Change the date to **8/1/04**.

16. Click the **Print** button to print the report, which is shown in Figure 20.3.

Lundquist Custom Woodworking
A/P Aging Summary
As of August 1, 2004

	Current	1 - 30	31 - 60	61 - 90	> 90	TOTAL
Elmer Lumber Supply	800.00	0.00	0.00	0.00	0.00	800.00
Orchard Supply Hardware	1,200.00	0.00	0.00	0.00	0.00	1,200.00
TOTAL	2,000.00	0.00	0.00	0.00	0.00	2,000.00

Figure 20.3

17. Click the **Close** button to exit the A/P Aging Summary report.

18. Click the **Close** button to close the *Reports* dialog box.

Recording a Note Receivable in Settlement of an Accounts Receivable Balance

A common reason for issuing a promissory note is to extend the amount of time for settlement of an account receivable. To illustrate how easily notes can be added, you can add a new note receivable to Lundquist Custom Woodworking.

The amount owed to the company will be transferred from one Asset account (Accounts Receivable) to another Asset account (Notes Receivable). While you could accomplish this in QuickBooks quickly and easily with a General Journal entry, the balance owed to the company would continue to show in the Subsidiary Accounts Receivable ledger. Instead of using the General Journal entry window, you will use the *Receive Payments* window, changing the debit to Cash into a debit to Notes Receivable.

> **TRANSACTION: On August 15, 2004, Betty's Boutique, a customer of Lundquist Custom Woodworking, will settle her accounts receivable balance of $4,000.00 by issuing a 12% 60-day note.**

1. Click the **Receive Payments** icon. The window shown in Figure 20.4 appears.

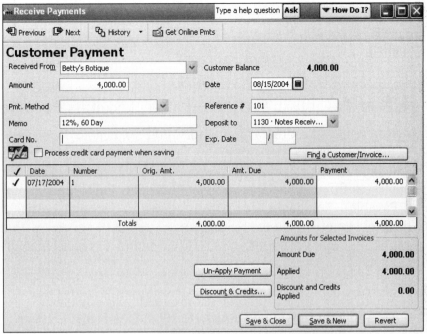

Figure 20.4

2. Using the lookup icon, select **Betty's Boutique** in the **Received From** field.

3. Leave the **Amount** field blank.

4. In the **Date** field enter or select **8/15/04** and press **Tab**.

5. Leave the **Pmt. Method** field blank.

6. In the **Reference No.** field enter **101**.

7. In the **Memo** field type **12%, 60 Day**.

8. In the **Deposit To** field select **1130 Notes Receivable**. This forces the debit to Account 1130 instead of to Cash Account 1110.

> **IMPORTANT WARNING: By changing the Cash account to 1130, you cause QuickBooks to use this account number again in the next transaction entered through the *Receive Payments* window. Be sure to change the Deposit To account back to 1110 the next time this window is used.**

9. Click the Check Mark column next to the $4,000 invoice to select it.

10. Click on **Save & Close** to post the transaction.

To view the impact of your transaction on the Subsidiary Accounts Receivable Ledger, you can look at an A/R Aging Summary report dated 8/31/04 from the **Customers & Receivable** report area of the *Reports* dialog box. Note that the invoice is no longer listed on this report. To view the impact on the General ledger, you can look at the Trial

Balance report dated 8/31/04 from the **Accountant & Taxes** report area of the ***Reports*** dialog box. You can view these reports on your screen or print them for later examination.

Recording a Note Payable in Settlement of an Accounts Payable Balance

When one business records a promissory note as a note receivable, another business records the same note as a note payable. The second company, known as the *maker* of the note, extends the time it has for payment of debt. You need to move the amount a company owes from one liability account (Accounts Payable) to another liability account (Notes Payable). You could accomplish this with a General journal entry, but then you have the problem of having the Subsidiary ledger out of balance with the General ledger. To prevent this, you can use the ***Enter Bills*** window to record a credit bill and then ***Pay Bills*** to apply the credit to the original bill.

> **TRANSACTION: On August 18, 2004, Lundquist Custom Woodworking extended the time for payment of the balance due to Elmer Lumber Supply. Lundquist Custom Woodworking will settle its accounts payable by issuing an $800.00 12% 60-day note.**

1. Click the **Enter Bills** Enter Bills icon.

2. Select the radio button next to **Credit**. The window shown in Figure 20.5 appears.

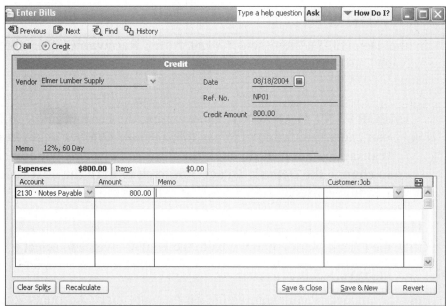

Figure 20.5

3. Select **Elmer Lumber Supply** in the **Vendor ID** field.

4. Enter or select **8/18/04** as the date and press **Tab**.

5. In the **Ref. No.** field enter **NP01**.

6. In the **Memo** field enter **12%, 60 Day**.

7. Click the **Expense** tab

8. In the **Account** field select **2130 Notes Payable**. This forces the credit to Account 2130.

9. In the **Credit Amount** field enter **$800.00**.

10. Click the **Save & Close** button to post the transaction.

11. Click the **Pay Bills** icon.

12. Click the checkmark column next to the bill for Elmer Lumber Company.

13. Your screen should look like Figure 20.6.

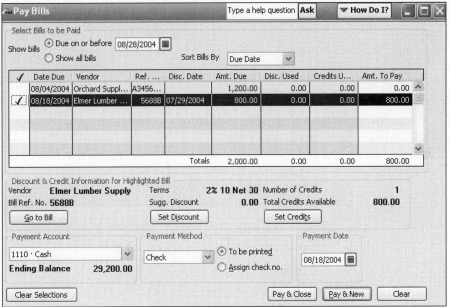

Figure 20.6

14. Notice that in the **Discount & Credit Information for Highlighted Bill** section there is one credit for $800.00 available.

15. Click the **Set Credits** button.

16. The ***Discounts & Credits*** dialog box appears with the credit already selected and the total amount to pay at zero (see Figure 20.7).

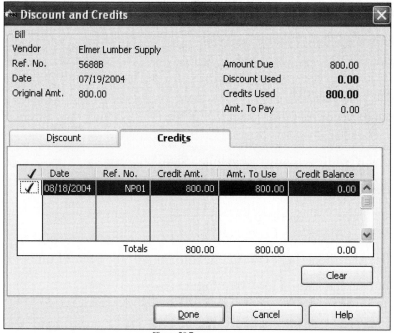

Figure 20.7

17. Click the **Done** button.

18. Click **Pay & Close** to post the transaction.

19. You see the ***Bills Paid By Credits*** screen, as shown in Figure 20.8. Click **OK**. Because the vendor already knows about the note payable, you do not need to print the transaction history report.

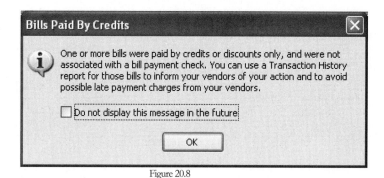

Figure 20.8

To view the impact of your transaction on the Subsidiary Accounts Payable ledger, you can look at an A/P Aging Summary report from the Vendor & Payables menu. Note that the invoice is no longer listed on this report. To view the impact on the General ledger, you can look at the Trial Balance report either on your screen or after you print it.

Recording the Receipt of a Note Receivable Payment

Once recorded, a promissory note no longer has an impact on the Subsidiary ledgers. You could record the receipt of the note in the General journal; however, cash receipts collected for the notes receivables are best entered through the *Make Deposits* window. QuickBooks does not calculate the interest for you. You calculate the interest in the same manner as you would in a manual accounting system, by using this formula:

$$I = P \times R \times T$$

> **TRANSACTION: On August 15, 2004, the company received check number 1501 from Erin's Design for the existing note receivable principal of $5,000.00 plus $100.00 interest (I = $5,000.00 X 12% X 60/360 = $100.00). The company accepted a 12% 60-day note on June 15, 2004. It is now 60 days later, and payment in full has been received.**

1. Click the **Record Deposits** icon on the *Home* screen and the screen shown in Figure 20.9 appears.

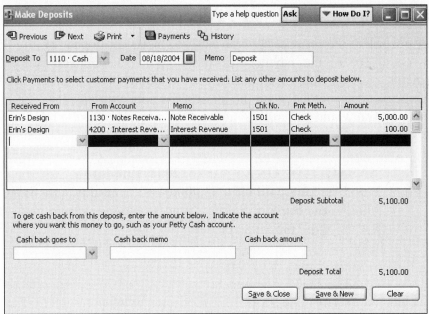

Figure 20.9

2. In the **Deposit To** field make sure that account **1110 Cash** is selected.

3. Enter or select **8/15/04** as the date.

4. In the **Memo** field leave the description as **Deposit**.

5. In the **Received From** field select **Erin's Design**.

6. In the **From Account** field use the lookup icon and select **1130 Notes Receivable** since you are applying this cash receipt in part to the Notes Receivable account.

7. In the **Memo** column enter **Note Receivable**.

8. In the **Chk No.** field enter **1501**.

9. In the **Payment Meth.** field select **Check**.

10. Enter **5000.00** in the **Amount** column; this was the original amount of the note.

11. On the second row in the **Received From** field select **Erin's Design**.

12. In the **From Account** field use the lookup icon and select **4200 Interest Revenue**.

13. In the **Memo** column enter **Interest Revenue**.

14. In the **Chk No.** field enter **1501**.

15. In the **Payment Meth.** field select **Check**.

16. Enter **100.00** in the **Amount** column. This is the amount of interest revenue calculated using the interest formula (5,000.00 X 12% X 60/360).

17. Click the **Save & Close** button to post the deposit.

Recording the Payment of a Note Payable

Once recorded, the promissory note no longer has an impact on the Subsidiary ledgers. You could record the payment of the note in the General journal. However, cash payments paid on notes payables are best made through the *Write Checks* window. QuickBooks does not calculate the interest for you. You calculate the interest in the same manner as you would in a manual accounting system, by using this formula:

$$I = P \: X \: R \: X \: T$$

> **TRANSACTION: On August 18, 2004, Lundquist Custom Woodworking paid off a \$3,000.00 12% 60-day note dated June 18, 2004, to the Bank of Salina. Interest expense would be I = \$3,000.00 X 12% X 60/360 = \$60.00.**

1. Click the **Write Checks** icon on the *Home* screen. The screen shown in Figure 20.10 appears.

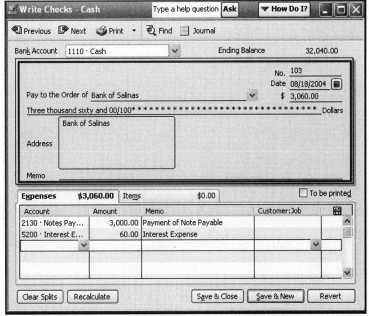

Figure 20.10

2. Make sure the **Bank Account** field contains **1110 Cash**.

3. Enter or select **8/18/04** as the date.

4. In the **Pay to the Order of** field enter **Bank of Salinas**.

5. Click the **Expenses** tab.

6. In the **Account** field use the lookup icon and select **2130 Notes Payable** since you are applying this payment in part to the Notes Payable account.

7. Enter **3000.00** in the **Amount** column; this was the original amount of the note.

8. In the **Memo** column of the first row type **Payment of note payable**.

9. In the account field on the second row, use the lookup icon and select **5200 Interest Expense**.

10. Enter **60.00** in the **Amount** column. This is the amount calculated using the interest formula.

11. Type **Interest expense** in the **Memo** column.

12. Click the **Print** icon.

13. Enter **103** as the check number. Click **OK**.

14. Click **Print** to print the check.

15. Click the **Save & Close** button.

Printing the August Reports

Print the reports shown in Figures 20.11 through 20.14, dated 8/1/04 to 8/31/04, accepting all defaults.

➢ **NOTE:** Refer to Chapter 12 for more detailed instructions on printing reports.

Lundquist Custom Woodworking
Trial Balance
As of August 31, 2004

	Aug 31, 04	
	Debit	Credit
1110 · Cash	32,040.00	
1120 · Accounts Receivable	48,000.00	
1130 · Notes Receivable	4,000.00	
1150 · Shop Supplies	5,800.00	
1210 · Shop Equipment	156,000.00	
1221 · Accum Depr - Shop Equipment		34,000.00
1230 · Automobile	16,000.00	
1241 · Accum Depr - Automobile		4,000.00
2110 · Accounts Payable		1,200.00
2130 · Notes Payable		800.00
3000 · Opening Bal Equity	0.00	
3110 · Vernon Lundquist, Capital		10,000.00
3130 · Retained Earnings		211,800.00
4200 · Interest Revenue		100.00
5200 · Interest Expense	60.00	
TOTAL	**261,900.00**	**261,900.00**

Figure 20.11

Lundquist Custom Woodworking
Journal
August 2004

Trans #	Type	Date	Num	Name	Memo	Account	Debit	Credit
16	Payment	08/15/2004	101	Betty's Botique	12%, 60 Day	1130 · Notes Receivable	4,000.00	
				Betty's Botique	12%, 60 Day	1120 · Accounts Receiv...		4,000.00
							4,000.00	4,000.00
17	Credit	08/18/2004	NP01	Elmer Lumber Sup...	12%, 60 Day	2110 · Accounts Payable	800.00	
				Elmer Lumber Sup...	12%, 60 Day	2130 · Notes Payable		800.00
							800.00	800.00
18	Deposit	08/18/2004			Deposit	1110 · Cash	5,100.00	
				Erin's Design	Note Receivable	1130 · Notes Receivable		5,000.00
				Erin's Design	Interest Revenue	4200 · Interest Revenue		100.00
							5,100.00	5,100.00
19	Check	08/18/2004	103	Bank of Salinas		1110 · Cash		3,060.00
				Bank of Salinas	Payment of Note Payable	2130 · Notes Payable	3,000.00	
				Bank of Salinas	Interest Expense	5200 · Interest Expense	60.00	
							3,060.00	3,060.00
TOTAL							**12,960.00**	**12,960.00**

Figure 20.12

Lundquist Custom Woodworking
A/R Aging Summary
As of August 31, 2004

	Current	1 - 30	31 - 60	61 - 90	> 90	TOTAL
Carl's Accounting Service ▶	0.00	◀ 6,000.00	0.00	0.00	0.00	6,000.00
Salina School District	0.00	42,000.00	0.00	0.00	0.00	42,000.00
TOTAL	0.00	48,000.00	0.00	0.00	0.00	48,000.00

Figure 20.13

Lundquist Custom Woodworking
A/P Aging Summary
As of August 31, 2004

	Current	1 - 30	31 - 60	61 - 90	> 90	TOTAL
Orchard Supply Hardware ▶	0.00	◀ 1,200.00	0.00	0.00	0.00	1,200.00
TOTAL	0.00	1,200.00	0.00	0.00	0.00	1,200.00

Figure 20.14

Backing Up Your Company Data File

1. Click the **Backup** [Backup] icon.

2. Click the **Browse** button in the **Backup Current Company** section to specify a location to keep your backup files.

3. Add **Jan04** to the file name. Click **Save**.

4. Click **OK**.

5. When the backup is complete, click **OK**.

   ➤ **NOTE:** For more detailed instructions on backing up files, refer to Chapter 11.

Exiting the QuickBooks Pro 2006 Program

1. Select **Close Company** from the **File** menu.

2. Select **Exit** from the **File** menu to end the current work session and return to your Windows desktop.

Appendix A

AN INTRODUCTION TO ACCOUNTING SOFTWARE

Accounting procedures are essentially the same whether they are performed manually or on a computer. The following is a list of the account cycle steps in a manual accounting system as compared to the steps in a computerized accounting system:

STEPS IN THE ACCOUNTING CYCLE

Manual Accounting System	Computerized Accounting System
1. Business transactions occur and generate source documents.	1. Business transactions occur and generate source documents.
2. Analyze and record business transactions in a manual journal.	2. Analyze and enter business transactions in a computerized journal.
3. Post or transfer information from journal to ledger.	3. Computer automatically posts information from journal to ledger.
4. Prepare a trial balance.	4. Trial balance is prepared automatically.
5. Prepare a worksheet.	5. Adjusting entries are entered directly into the software.
6. Prepare financial statements.	6. Financial statements are prepared automatically.
7. Journalize and post adjusting entries.	7. Journal entries are completed prior to preparation of financial statements.
8. Journalize and post closing entries.	8. Closing procedures are completed automatically.
9. Prepare a post closing trial balance.	9. Trial balance is automatically prepared.

This accounting cycle comparison shows that the accountant's task of initially analyzing business transactions in terms of debits and credits (both routine business transactions and adjusting entries) is required in both manual and computerized accounting systems. However, in a computerized accounting system, the drudge work of posting transactions, creating and completing worksheets and financial statements, and performing the closing procedures is all handled automatically by the computerized accounting system.

In addition, computerized accounting systems can perform accounting procedures at greater speeds and with greater accuracy than can be achieved in a manual accounting system. It is important to recognize, however, that the computer is only a *tool* that can accept and process information supplied by the accountant. Each business transaction and adjusting entry must first be analyzed and recorded in a computerized journal correctly. Otherwise, the financial statements generated by the computerized accounting system will contain errors and will not be useful to the business.

APPLICATIONS SOFTWARE

Applications software refers to programs designed for a specific use. The five most common types of business applications software are as follows:

> **Spreadsheet** software allows the manipulation of data and has the ability to project answers to "what if" questions.

> **Word processing** software enables the user to write and print letters, memos, and other documents.

> **Graphics** software displays data visually, in the form of graphic images.

> **Communications** software allows a computer to "talk" to other computers.

> Most computerized accounting systems are designed as **database management** software. Accounting information is data that must be organized and stored in a common base of data. This allows the entry of data and the retrieval of information in an organized and systematic way.

Accounting Applications Software

Most computerized accounting software is organized into modules. Each module is designed to process a particular type of accounting data, such as accounts receivable, accounts payable, or payroll. Each module is also designed to work in conjunction with the other modules. When modules are designed to work together in this manner, they are referred to as *integrated software*. In an integrated accounting system, each module handles a different function but also communicates with the other modules. For example, to record a sale on account, you would make an entry into the accounts receivable module. The integration feature automatically records this entry in the sales journal, updates the customer's account in the accounts receivable subsidiary ledger, and posts all accounts affected in the general ledger. Thus in an integrated accounting system, transaction data are entered only once. All the other accounting procedures required to bring the accounting records up-to-date are performed automatically through the integration function.

Peachtree and QuickBooks Applications Software

The 2006 versions of Peachtree Complete Accounting and QuickBooks Pro have been selected for use in this text to demonstrate and help you learn how to use a computerized accounting system. They are easy to use, fully integrated, and also available in versions that work with several different operating systems. The software programs can be used to maintain the accounting data for a sole proprietorship, a partnership, or a corporation. They accommodate service, merchandising, and manufacturing businesses. The workshops contained in this text are designed to illustrate how manual accounting concepts are handled by a computerized accounting system; they are not intended to provide a comprehensive course of study for a computerized accounting system.

WORKING WITH PEACHTREE COMPLETE ACCOUNTING

Before you begin to work with Peachtree Complete Accounting 2006, you need to be familiar with the software.

The Peachtree Applications Window

In Peachtree Complete Accounting 2006, the **main menu** window (see Figure A.1) is where all activities begin. The name of the application (Peachtree Accounting) and the application's **menu bar** appear at the top of the application window.

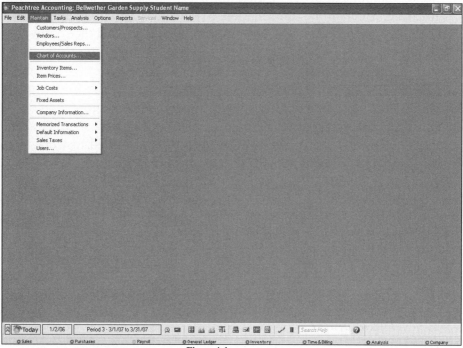

Figure A.1

The items located on the **main menu** window are described below:

◆ **Title bar:** The title bar, shown in Figure A.2, displays the name of the application.

Figure A.2

◆ **Main menu bar:** Main menu bar, as shown in Figure A.3, lists the available menus (commands) for the software program.

Figure A.3

◆ **Drop-down menu:** As shown in Figure A.4, this type of menu shows the options available under each menu option.

Figure A.4

◆ **Highlighted (selected) item:** The active selection in a drop-down menu is highlighted. For example the highlighted item in Figure A.4 is the **Chart of Accounts**.

◆ **Minimize button** **:** Clicking this button minimizes the window and displays it as a task button on the taskbar. It is located on the right side of title bar.

◆ **Maximize button** **:** Clicking this button enlarges the window so that it fills the entire desktop. It is located on the right side of the title bar.

◆ **Close button** **:** Clicking on this button closes the window. It is located on the right side of the title bar.

◆ **Status bar:** The status bar, as shown in Figure A.5, is a line of text at the bottom of many windows that gives more information about a field. If you are unsure of what to enter in a field, select it with your mouse and read the status bar.

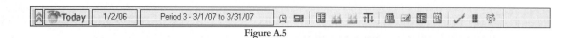

Figure A.5

Navigation Aids toolbar: This toolbar, shown in Figure A.6, is specific to Peachtree and is a shortcut to view the navigation aids by module. If your Navigation Aids toolbar is not showing, click **Options** and then select **View Navigation Aids**.

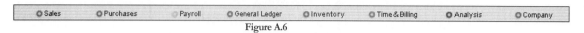

Figure A.6

Peachtree Dialog Boxes

A dialog box appears when additional information is needed to execute a command. There are different ways to supply that information; consequently, there are different types of dialog boxes. Most dialog boxes are for specific functions and tasks that require you to supply the data for those tasks. After you supply the needed information, you can click a command button to carry out a command, such as **Save**, **Post** or **Print**.

You can get to the dialog box shown in Figure A.7 by clicking the **Tasks** menu and selecting **Sales/Invoicing**. The *Sales/Invoicing* dialog box is then displayed on your screen.

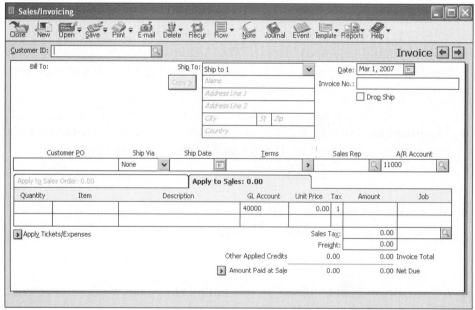

Figure A.7

♦ **Folder tabs:** Some dialog boxes have multiple pages of entry fields available to them. Figure A.8 shows an example. These tabs allow you to switch between available screens.

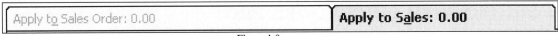

Figure A.8

♦ **Arrow button:** A button with an arrow (see Figure A.9) generally brings up a pull-down menu of options for that field.

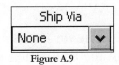

Figure A.9

♦ **Text box:** When you move to an empty text box, an insertion point appears at the far left side of the box (see Figure A.10). The text you type starts at the insertion point. If the box you move to already contains text, that text is selected (highlighted), and any text you type replaces it. You can delete the selected text by pressing the **Delete** or **Backspace** key.

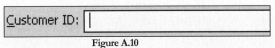

Figure A.10

♦ **Command icons:** You click on a command icon to initiate an immediate action, such as carrying out or canceling a command. The **Close**, **Print** and **Save** icons are common command icons. The command icons are located on the Icon toolbar, shown in Figure A.11.

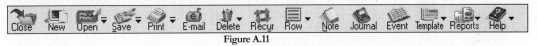

Figure A.11

♦ **Magnifying glass button:** You click this button, shown in Figure A.12, to pull-down a list of choices. Some fields do not show the magnifying glass until the field has been selected.

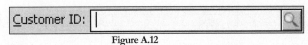

Figure A.12

♦ **Calendar button:** You click this button, shown in Figure A.13, to bring up a calendar in order to select the date to be inserted in the field next to the button.

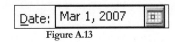

Figure A.13

Other dialog boxes require that choices be made, request additional information, provide warnings, and give messages indicating why a requested task cannot be accomplished.

WORKING WITH QUICKBOOKS PRO

Before you begin to work with QuickBooks Pro 2006, you need to be familiar with the software's windows and terminology.

The QuickBooks Applications Window

In QuickBooks Pro 2006, the **main menu** window (see Figure A.14) is where all activities begin. The name of the application (QuickBooks) and the application's **menu bar** appear at the top of the application window.

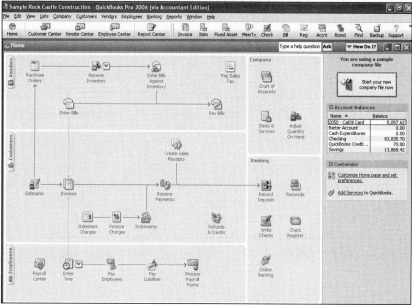

Figure A.14

♦ **Title bar:** The title bar, shown in Figure A.15, displays the name of the application.

Figure A.15

♦ **Main menu bar:** The main menu bar, as shown in Figure A.16, lists the available menus (commands) for the software program.

Figure A.16

♦ **Drop-down menu:** As shown in Figure A.17, shows the options available under each menu option.

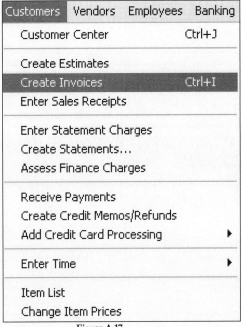

Figure A.17

♦ **Highlighted (selected) item:** The active selection in a drop-down menu is highlighted. For example, in Figure A.17 the highlighted item is **Create Invoices**.

♦ **Minimize button** : Clicking this button minimizes the window and displays it as a task button on the taskbar. It is located on the right side of title bar.

♦ **Maximize button** : Clicking this button enlarges the window so that it fills the entire desktop. It is located on the right side of the title bar.

♦ **Close button** : Clicking on this button closes the window. It is located on the right side of the title bar.

QuickBooks Dialog Boxes

A dialog box appears when additional information is needed to execute a command. There are different ways to supply that information; consequently, there are different types of dialog boxes. Most dialog boxes are for specific functions and tasks that require you to supply the data for those tasks. After you supply the needed information, you can click a command button to carry out a command, such as **Save**, **Post** or **Print**.

You can get to the dialog box, shown in Figure A.18 by clicking the **Customer** menu and selecting **Create Invoices**. The *Create Invoices* dialog box is then displayed on your screen.

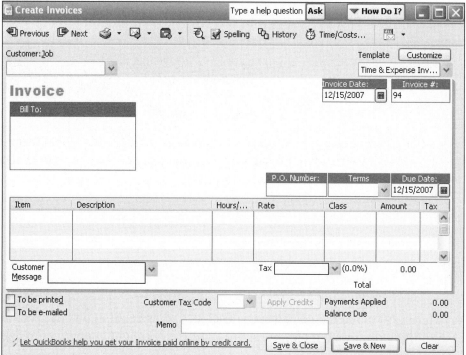

Figure A.18

♦ **Arrow button:** A button with an arrow (see Figure A.19) generally brings up a pull-down menu of options for that field.

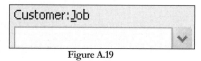

Figure A.19

♦ **Text box:** When you move to an empty text box, an insertion point appears at the far left side of the box. The text you type starts at the insertion point. If the box you move to already contains text, that text is selected (highlighted), and any text you type replaces it. You can also the selected text by pressing the **Delete** or **Backspace** key.

♦ **Command icons:** You click a command icon to initiate an immediate action, such as carrying out or canceling a command. The **Previous**, **Next** and **Print** icons are common command icons. The command icons are located on the Icon toolbar, as shown in Figure A.20.

Figure A.20

♦ **Magnifying glass button** 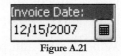**:** Click this button to pull-down a list of choices. Some fields do not show the magnifying glass until the field is selected.

♦ **Calendar button:** You click this button, shown in Figure A.21, to bring up a calendar in order to select the date to be inserted in the field next to the button.

Invoice Date:
12/15/2007
Figure A.21

Other dialog boxes require that choices be made, request additional information, provide warnings, and give messages indicating why a requested task cannot be accomplished.

Appendix B

Print and Display Settings

When you install the Peachtree Complete and QuickBooks software, the programs automatically select the printer established as the default Windows printer as the default printer for the software. If you have not yet installed a default printer in Windows, you need to do so prior to attempting to print any reports from the software programs. Refer to your Windows manual for information on installing a printer.

The installation process for the Windows default printer does not ensure that the default printer and display settings within Peachtree and QuickBooks will work to your satisfaction; consequently, you must test, and if necessary, adjust your printer and display settings before you complete any of the assignments in the text. Once the print and display settings are adjusted, they will become the default printer and display settings and it will be applied to all of the company data files. You need only make these adjustments once in each software program.

Peachtree Printing Options

If you need to change the font sizes or typefaces on your reports, you can do so from within Peachtree. Each report that you select has an **Options** button, as illustrated in Figure B.1.

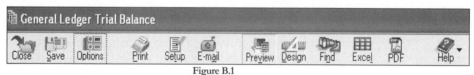

Figure B.1

Clicking **Options** brings up a dialog box with multiple tabs containing various parameters that can be changed for the report (see Figure B.2). One of these tabs is **Fonts** from which you can change the font for each item on a report.

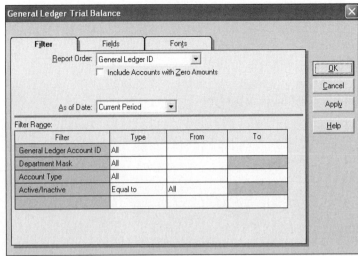

Figure B.2

QuickBooks Printing Options

If you need to change the font sizes or typefaces on your reports, you can do so from within QuickBooks. Each report that you select has a **Modify Report** button, as illustrated in Figure B.3.

Figure B.3

Clicking **Modify Report** brings up a dialog box with multiple tabs containing various parameters that can be changed for the report (see Figure B.4). One of these tabs is **Fonts & Numbers**, which you can use to change the font for each item on a report.

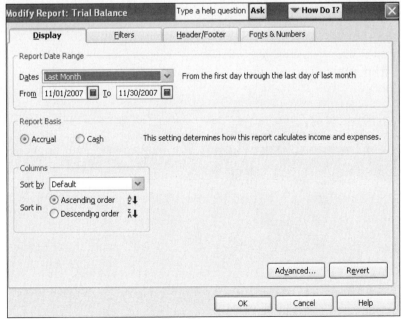

Figure B.4